Conversations Between Economists and Anthropologists

Conversations Between
Economists
and
Anthropologists

Methodological Issues in Measuring Economic Change in Rural India

edited by

PRANAB BARDHAN

DELHI
OXFORD UNIVERSITY PRESS
OXFORD NEW YORK
1989

Oxford University Press, Walton Street, Oxford OX2 6DP

NEW YORK TORONTO
DELHI BOMBAY CALCUTTA MADRAS KARACHI
PETALING JAYA SINGAPORE HONG KONG TOKYO
NAIROBI DAR ES SALAAM
MELBOURNE AUCKLAND
and associates in
BERLIN IBADAN

Phototypeset at Taj Services Ltd., Noida. U.P. 201301
printed at Rekha Printers Pvt. Ltd., New Delhi 110020
and published by S. K. Mookerjee, Oxford University Press
YMCA Library Building, Jai Singh Road, New Delhi 110001

Contents

Contents

Preface

The world of scholars studying rural social and economic life has its own caste system, with different disciplinary groups zealously observing their internal codes of conduct, status symbols, rituals and taboos. The methodological gulf is particularly wide between economists and anthropologists. I have often observed between the two groups an attitude of mutual indifference (and worse), and on those rare occasions when they meet they usually talk past each other. The image of economists is that of 'mimic physicists', crackling with the static of electronic data crunching, while anthropologists smell of the outdoors and manure. The purpose of this book is to blur these respective images a bit and gently nudge scholars towards some meaningful conversation, focusing for the sake of coherence on the narrowly defined issue of measuring economic change in rural India.

India has a long history of reasonably efficient statistical surveys of rural areas and a rich array of ethnographic accounts of village life, and as such provides an ample factual background for starting such a methodological dialogue. In spite of that the difficulties and pitfalls of such a venture are partly reflected in the thematically loose nature, and in places the patchwork-quilt quality, of the collection of essays in this book. Yet I for one have found this exploratory exercise amply rewarding, and this is in large measure due to the spirit of co-operation and empathy among the particular group of economists and social anthropologists put together in this volume. We are also the beneficiaries of critical comments from Clive Bell and Ronald Herring, who reviewed an earlier version of the manuscript on behalf of the Social Science Research Council, New York. Michael Kevane provided able assistance in preparing the index.

Finally, I would like to dedicate this book to the memory of Daniel Thorner, who, nearly twenty years ago, engaged me in a lively private discussion of the problems of large-scale sample survey data (of which I was an enthusiastic user) and planted in me the seeds of the idea of this book.

March 1989   Pranab Bardhan

Contributors

PRANAB BARDHAN, University of California, Berkeley.

A. VAIDYANATHAN, Madras Institute of Development Studies, Madras.

N. BHATTACHARYA and M. CHATTOPADHYAY, Indian Statistical Institute, Calcutta.

SUSAN S. WADLEY and BRUCE W. DERR, Syracuse University, Syracuse.

JAN BREMAN, Centre for Asian Studies, Amsterdam.

JOHN HARRISS, University of East Anglia, Norwich.

N. S. JODHA, International Centre for Integrated Mountain Development, Kathmandu.

SURESH D. TENDULKAR, Delhi School of Economics, Delhi.

ASHOK RUDRA, Visva Bharati University, Santiniketan.

T. N. SRINIVASAN, Yale University, New Haven.

ARJUN APPADURAI, University of Pennsylvania, Philadelphia.

Chapter 1: Introduction

PRANAB BARDHAN

For quite some time now economic change in the villages of South Asia has been studied in different ways by social observers and analysts within different disciplines, occasionally with different results. Economists and statisticians have often used for this purpose large data systems generated by the Census, or sample surveys of many thousands of households (such as the National Sample Survey in India), often aggregated over regions, states or the country as a whole. Others, mainly social anthropologists but also some economists, have carried out or relied upon re-studies or re-surveys of individual villages or a group of villages. Here also, methods of investigation have varied between the close participant-observation of resident ethnographers and the one-shot or periodic interviews of villagers by visiting social scientists or their agents. The tension between these alternative methods, when they yielded contrasting results, became particularly relevant in academic debates that raged in India in the 1970s on the question of the measurement of rural poverty. The National Sample Survey (NSS) data that were available *then*, on consumer expenditure in different classes of households and on real wages of rural labourers, often showed a stark and even worsening picture of poverty in rural India.[1] Among economists and statisticians this led to an intensive examination of the statistical techniques used in the estimates of poverty.[2] A more sceptical note, which went

[1] There are signs of declining poverty in the more recent NSS data on consumer expenditure, though the picture is not always clear from the data on per capita consumption of foodgrains or real wages.

[2] For an early discussion on these issues, see the collection of articles in Srinivasan and Bardhan (1974).

beyond the technicalities of sampling designs, appropriate index numbers, etc., was struck by some observers at the micro level. They blámed, like Srinivas (1979), the economist's habit of armchair crunching data collected by subordinates; some, like Thorner (1980) and Etienne (1982), narrated individual accounts of general improvement in village India. Some of these accounts were, however, based on casual empiricism or at best impressionistic surveys from quick tours, as economists and statisticians on the opposite side were ready to point out. There have been very few careful and detailed ethnographic re-studies focusing on the question of measurement of economic change.

Nor have disputes necessarily pointed to a systematic underestimation or overestimation on the part of opposing groups. If in connection with the poverty debate the macro data users in the early seventies were, by and large, showing a more gloomy picture than were micro observers, one can provide examples of other cases of measurement where the bias seemed to be working the opposite way. Take the case in more recent years of the evaluations of a major ambitious poverty alleviation programme in India, the Integrated Rural Development Programme (IRDP). Several of these evaluations, based on large-scale household surveys, have come out with a rather rosy picture of the achievements of IRDP: for example, the first round of the Concurrent Evaluation of IRDP (undertaken by the Government of India, Department of Rural Development, with the active participation of a large number of independent research institutions) came out in 1987 with the finding that as many as 78 per cent of the households involved in IRDP were initially below the 'poverty line', and that 52 per cent of these turned out to have 'crossed the poverty line' three years later. These findings are in sharp contrast to those of the detailed field studies of the programme by several micro observers who report a much more negative picture and a serious failure of the programme to reach out to the very poor.[3]

It is with this background of conflicting methods and results that in August 1985 the Social Science Research Council, New York, in collaboration with the Indian Statistical Institute,

---

[3] For a discussion of the reasons for this discrepancy of results, as well as the relevant references, see Dreze (1988).

sponsored a workshop at Bangalore on 'Rural Economic Change in South Asia: Differences in Approach and in Results between Large-Scale Surveys and Intensive Micro Studies.' The main purpose of the workshop was to bring together some members of different groups of social observers, primarily anthropologists, economists and statisticians working on rural South Asia, to thrash out their essential methodological differences in an atmosphere of scholarly give-and-take, and to explore ways of learning from one another's kit of tools, conceptual categories and methods of inquiry. I think the workshop, among the first of its kind in South Asia, was in a limited way successful in changing somewhat the existing state of non-communication and mutual incomprehension between these groups of social scientists. With regard to the measurement of rural change, the seminar helped increase their awareness of the limitations that the standard methods of their respective disciplines often imposed. As a continuation of the process started in that workshop, this volume puts together a selection of papers by anthropologists and economists on different aspects of the measurement issues that are involved.

At some levels of discourse the disputes between anthropologists and economists are, of course, insoluble: cultural anthropologists like Geertz (1973, 1983), look upon their task as essentially interpretive and apply the metaphor of a text to social phenomena, clearly allowing for different readings of the same text. Their essentially hermeneutic approach contrasts sharply with that of measurement in social science followed even by the relatively rare non-positivist economists. Whether description can be sharply distinguished from evaluation and shapes of knowledge separated from their instruments and encasements are old disputes in social theory. In this book the discussion is conducted at a lower epistemological level and with a much narrower focus. We concentrate largely on economic change *measurable* in some well-defined sense and discuss the strengths and weaknesses of alternative methods of measurement.

Even with measurement there is some question with regard to the level of abstraction at which we pose our issues. T. N. Srinivasan is obviously right when he states in chapter 10 that 'there is nothing inherent in the survey method that precludes it from generating the same information as a village study based

on participant-observation.'. Given infinite resources, highly
trained and motivated investigators, very carefully designed and
pre-tested schedules of enquiry, etc., large-scale sample surveys
can in principle replicate the richness, the intensity and the
comprehensiveness of micro studies. But at usual levels of prac-
ticality even our best sample surveys clearly miss many important features of economic change and yield, in some respects,
systematically biased results. Many of the problems arise not
from the survey method as such, but from the bureaucratic
organization of large-scale data collection systems; this has its
impact on the implementation of the method in the form of
numerous compromises that have to be adopted at each level.
For such large operations definitions have necessarily to be
standardized, concepts homogenized, and information com-
pressed into easily codified categories. In a country like
India—with its bewildering variety of terms, categories and
local perceptions of similar-sounding questions even from one
village to the next (not to speak of its vast territories and ethnic
and cultural heterogeneities)—this approach leads at best to
lowest-common-denominator information-gathering, and to
certain sorts of systematic distortions at worst. As in any
centralized operation, where feedback is costly and time-
consuming and where what economists call the 'agency
problem'[4] is rampant, there is persistent loss of information,
particularly where there are inevitable ambiguities in interpretations of terms, categories with overlapping boundaries, and
multidimensionality within particular concepts. There are also
systematic differences between what respondents say in the
context of a óne-shot interview by an outsider and what they
say in private or trusted company.[5] Resident ethnographers are
in these circumstances often able to crosscheck data from one
context to another in a way which the salaried itinerant field
investigator may have neither the time nor the motivation to

[4] The 'agents'—in this case field investigators—have an incentive
structure not always consistent with the original intentions of the
'principal'.

[5] Such an interview is often a public event in the village, where crowds
of onlookers include informers for people with whom the respondent may
be in conflict, for instance his landlord, or employer or social superiors or
rivals.

carry out. There is also a tendency in remote-control bureaucratic investigations to underestimate phenomena unanticipated in highly structured pre-coded schedules, or to straitjacket them into pre-existing boxes to be tick-marked. This is a particularly important problem in measurement of change. A micro study is more flexible in reshaping its investigative strategy midstream and probing an unanticipated or new phenomenon in depth.

How important these problems of macro surveys actually are depends, of course, on what is being measured. There are some aspects of economic change where measurement is a reasonably straightforward matter and where problems in regard to ambiguities, contextuality and the degree of rapport with respondent are not, relatively speaking, very serious issues. This is true, for instance, in measuring changes in crop yields (except when changes in interplanting are involved), the adoption of high-yielding varieties of seeds, the use of pumps, the availability of electricity, roads and other infrastructural facilities,[6] fertility and mortality, ownership of livestock, housing and so on. The problems are much more serious in measuring 'sensitive' or multidimensional economic or demographic variables, as in the following cases: (a) indebtedness; (b) the ownership of financial assets; (c) land and security of land tenure (particularly in view of land legislation); (d) income (where the capacity to aggregate or even to comprehend what economists mean by income is absent, particularly in small-family enterprises); (e) unemployment (where questions about availability for work are often interpreted as availability for wage employment, or where discouraged drop-outs from the labour force are often counted as domestic workers to whom the questions about unemployment are not even asked); (f) morbidity (where perceptions often depend on access to medical facilities); (g) family planning; (h) the age composition of members of the household (particularly in the case of women); (i) the occupational classification of households when they carry out a multiplicity of economic activities (as John Harriss emphasizes in chapter 6); (j) the cost of access to public subsidies (when

---

[6] Except when the investigator is seen as connected with government, when there may be a systematic bias in the respondents' answers, made with a view to influencing the supply of these public facilities.

payment of bribes to officials are involved), etc. Of course, even
where there is systematic over- or underestimation, one may
make meaningful measurements of economic trends over time if
there are no reasons to believe that the extent of bias itself has
changed significantly over the period. In chapter 3 N. Bhattacharya and M. Chattopadhyay put together the NSS evidence
on trends in living standard (certainly a multidimensional
variable) in rural India over more than two decades, and
comment on the inadequacy and problems of the comparability
of the data. In chapter 4 Susan Wadley and Bruce Derr give us
an account of changes in the economic status (another multidimensional concept) of different socio-economic groups in an
Uttar Pradesh village over sixty years, and analyse the strengths
and weaknesses of village re-studies to capture these changes.
These two chapters usefully illustrate the results of two
alternative modes of measurement of long-run economic
change in different contexts.

The macro surveys are particularly weak in capturing what in
the Bangalore workshop came to be described as 'dynamics,
processes and relations'. In studying changes over time on the
basis of the NSS data, for example, we essentially compare the
results of surveys of independently selected sets of households at
two or more points in time, not the results of re-interviewing
the same set of households, as in the panel method. But even in
the rare large-scale longitudinal surveys all we compare are
outcomes at different points in time, without much information
on the dynamic processes of change; in the economist's jargon,
the method is one of comparative statics, not of disequilibrium
dynamics or adjustment paths. For these one needs more
intensive case studies, with a detailed probing of the mechanism
of, and individual responses to, change and the social and
economic mobility matrix of different rural households. Such
case studies can also focus, more than large-scale sample
surveys, on telltale straws in the wind in fluid transitional
situations: changes that are still marginal and statistically
insignificant but in the larger dynamic context serve, to the
perceptive observer, as significant pointers towards substantial
changes on the horizon.

The large-scale surveys give us estimates of the distribution of
goods, expenditure or wealth among different groups, or their

work, occupation or earning structure. But they do not capture the nature of on-going or changing relationships among people. The Land Holdings Surveys by the NSS, for example, give us aggregative estimates on the distribution of ownership and operational holdings, or on the proportion of area that is leased in. But we learn from them very little about the nature of lease contracts (formal or, more often, informal) between landlords and tenants, not to speak of the linkages of land-ownership or land-lease patterns with wage labour or credit transactions. The Rural Labour Enquiries of the Labour Bureau give us information on wages, unemployment, indebtedness and living standards of rural labour households. They tell us very little about forms of segmentation in the labour market, or labour recruitment and the job rationing process, not to speak of the interrelationship between indebtedness and various forms of labour-tying with the employer. The Census and NSS data are used to prepare migration totals, but we do not get any clue from them about the network of 'connections' and migration linkages, or about the working of labour intermediaries and contract systems. The irrigation statistics give us copious information on the irrigated acreage and major sources of irrigation, but nothing on the network of local community participation and relations in water management and conflict resolution. The Rural Credit (or Debt and Investment) Surveys of the Reserve Bank of India give us estimates of borrowings of different rural groups by source and purpose of borrowing, but they do not indicate how the terms of borrowing interact with terms with regard to land, labour and output sales transactions.

These relational attributes social processes are often too delicate to be handled by the blunt instruments at the disposal of the statistical bureaucracy. Small-scale fine-comb field studies can handle them better, although many anthropological accounts of village 're-studies' or the village surveys carried out by the Agro-Economic Research Centres in different parts of India leave them out of their focus of enquiry. Intensive field surveys not merely give us insights into the process of economic change, they also make us aware, as N. S. Jodha in chapter 7 points out (as also Wadley and Derr in chapter 4), how important the relational dimensions are in the respondent's own perception of economic change. While the economic statistician

may count calories or assets or wages to decipher possible
improvements in the lot of the poor, the poor themselves may
give at least as much importance to the relational aspects of their
lives: i.e. to questions such as are they less dependent now on
the landlord than before; have their insecurities arising from
relationships with others declined; is there a perceived sense of
prosperity in their lives *vis-à-vis* other comparison groups in the
village, etc. Of course, to go by the respondent's expressed
attitudes and perceptions can sometimes be tricky on questions
of social measurement. Articulate protestations by villagers can
sometimes be a form of strategic behaviour under certain
social constraints. Cultural materialists like Harris (1979) have
cited many examples of this and made, for this reason, an
important distinction between what they call 'emic' and 'etic'
structures of knowledge. There are also cases of impoverished
groups trying to handle 'cognitive dissonance' by adjusting their
beliefs to their circumstances, internalizing their constraints.

But the major problem with even the best designed and
executed intensive field studies is the fact that they are far too
fragmentary and minuscule to capture the distribution and
variations of features across any sizeable population. The
intensity of gaze at localized particularities can be a hindrance
for breadth of vision. The lack of standardization in the concepts
and categories used in different studies makes comparability
across areas and time particularly difficult. There is also a
tendency in ethnographic accounts to give undue attention to
dramatic events or changes, to the 'outliers' rather than to the
central tendency. As Geertz (1973), an ethnographic practitioner
himself, comments:

The problem of how to get from a collection of ethnographic
miniatures . . . —an assortment of remarks and anecdotes—to wall-
sized culturescapes of the nation . . . is not easily passed over with
vague allusions to the virtues of concreteness and the down-to-earth
mind. For a science born in [American] Indian tribes, Pacific islands,
and African lineages and subsequently seized with grander ambitions,
this has come to be a major methodological problem, and for the most
part, a badly handled one.

It is not just that anthropologists and other small-scale field
workers should use more explicit sampling procedures for their

selection of communities and informants, and thus increase the efficiency of their method of measurements in terms of cost per unit of information. Neither is it just a matter of reproducing village re-studies on a much wider scale in different parts of the country, with more standardized concepts and categories to improve cross-community comparability of results. Rather, it is imperative to devise and improve hitherto largely unexplored ways of sampling economic processes and relations that are amenable to aggregation and generalization without losing their essential properties. In a series of papers (referred to in Ashok Rudra, chapter 9) he and I have reported results of some intermediate-type (neither as large-scale as NSS nor as small as single-village studies) surveys of production relations in agriculture that we have carried out. These comprise randomly chosen villages but purposively chosen respondents within each village, to capture a generalizable picture of some agrarian relations for a whole state, e.g. West Bengal. Similar (and improved) sample surveys in other states and agro-climatic regions in India would be highly desirable. Rudra, in chapter 9, offers a number of constructive suggestions for simplifying procedures and workloads in such surveys. It is, of course, more difficult to sample processes than their relational outcomes. Even here there is considerable scope for experimenting with sampling events as they take place—what Arjun Appadurai calls 'entitlement events' in chapter 11, e.g. the operation of delivery systems of public facilities, or disfranchisement or dispossession of weaker groups in the course of some identifiable typologies of economic growth.

Both Jan Breman in chapter 5 and Arjun Appadurai in chapter 11 have pointed to the difficulties of taking the village as the unit of analysis in fieldwork in certain contexts, such as with villages that experience substantial migration or possess commercialization links with the larger regional economy. Here also there is need for trans-local intermediate-type surveys (now intermediate in the sense of territoriality of the unit of analysis). As an example, let me cite a study of rural labour market segmentation, within Bardhan and Rudra (1986), where quantitative results on the basis of 'clusters' of adjacent villages as the unit of analysis are reported.

Apart from trying to reduce these methodological gaps

between large-scale and small-scale surveys, one should not lose sight of the less difficult but no less important task of improving complementarities between them (as emphasized by Suresh Tendulkar and A. Vaidyanathan in chapters 8 and 2 respectively), even when the economist's and the anthropologist's universes of discourse do not overlap in many key respects. Small-scale field studies can very productively feed into the operation of large-scale surveys by providing guidelines for pilot studies or pre-tests that usually precede large surveys; sifting relevant items in the questionnaire; suggesting hypotheses and identifying critical indicators; warning against ambiguous terms and overlapping categories; and interpreting answers and putting them in context (Tendulkar shows in his chapter how a macro-statistical survey pinpoints findings that require micro studies to explain). Similarly, the estimates of large-scale surveys can·give some general idea of the representativeness of particular micro-level observations, point to their problems of comparability across communities, and help in flagging atypical findings—however attention-grabbing these may seem to the individual ethnographer immersed in the local social milieu. Given the usual resource constraint, it may be worthwhile, as Stone and Campbell (1984) suggest, for large survey organizations to have their data crosschecked for systematic non-sampling errors with a randomly selected sub-sample of respondents by fieldworkers more used to small-scale intensive investigation. Given the scarcity of longitudinal surveys in India, selected sub-samples may also be used for panel data in estimating economic change over time. (Bhattacharya and Chattopadhyay, in chapter 3, report some useful results on changes in levels of living from their own re-survey of NSS villages and rural households in three districts in West Bengal). There are thus many possibilities for innovation in methodology and in avenues of co-operation between economists and anthropologists. Purists on both sides may raise their eyebrows, but, even apart from helping the practical cause of better social measurement, any step away from intellectual provincialization is surely one in the right direction.

It would be unwise, and possibly unfair to the authors of the subsequent chapters in this volume to conclude in a falsely ecumenical spirit. While there seems considerable scope for recognizing and building on the specific complementarities of their methods, there is no way of ignoring fundamental differences in the concerns and perspectives of economists and anthropologists; such differences transcend their distinct methods of collecting information. Further, they involve not merely the larger epistemological issues of what constitute 'scientific objectivity' and (what Appadurai calls) the 'ideology of measurement', but even, at a lower level, as Vaidyanathan has emphasized, how the observational techniques of one discipline may be ill suited to the nature of the primary questions asked in another. But most of us agree that starting a dialogue which both highlights unsuspected areas of potential agreement and co-ordination, as well as exposes legitimate rock-bottom differences, will help us all in our rethinking.

REFERENCES

Bardhan, P. and Rudra, A., 'Labour Mobility and the Boundaries of the Village Moral Economy', *Journal of Peasant Studies*, April 1986.

Dreze, J., 'Social Insecurity in India: A Case Study', London School of Economics, 1988, unpublished.

Etienne, G., *India's Changing Rural Scene*, New Delhi: Oxford University Press, 1982.

Greetz, C., 'Thick Description: Toward an Interpretive Theory of Culture,' in *The Interpretation of Cultures: Selected Essays*, New York: Basic Books, 1973.

Geertz, C., 'Introduction,' in *Local Knowledge: Further Essays in Interpretive Anthropology*, New York: Rasic Books, 1983.

Harris, M., *Cultural Materialism: The Struggle for a Science of Culture*, New York: Random House, 1979.

Srinivas, M. N., 'Village Studies, Participant Observation and Social Science Research in India', *Economic and Political Weekly*, special no., August 1979.

Srinivasan, T. N. and P. Bardhan , *Poverty and Income Distribution in India*, Calcutta: Statistical Publishing Society, 1974.

Stone, L. and Campbell, J. G., 'The Use and Misuse of Surveys in International Development: An Experiment from Nepal,' *Human Organization*, Spring 1984.

Thorner, D., *The Shaping of Modern India*, Bombay: Allied Publishers, 1980.

Chapter 2: Macro and Micro Approaches to Studying Rural Economic Change: Some Pointers from Indian Experience*

A. VAIDYANATHAN

INTRODUCTION

It is useful to begin by clarifying what we mean by 'studying economic change' and by 'macro' and 'micro' approaches. The study of economic change has two aspects: one has to do with mapping the direction and rates of change in terms of certain well-defined indicators of economic performance/conditions in the country as a whole, its constituent regions and population groups. The other is the more difficult task of unravelling factors and processes underlying these changes and the relations among them.

The macro approach is generally seen to consist of large-scale surveys designed to get information on selected characteristics for the entire population (as in the case of the censuses) or from a representative cross-section thereof (sample surveys). The micro approach, by contrast, refers to detailed investigations of particular localities or groups. Anthropologists, who are ardent advocates of this approach, also emphasize the importance of participant observation unhindered by presuppositions of what is important, as well as the importance of comprehending far

* This is a substantially revised version of the paper presented at the Bangalore seminar. In making these revisions I have benefited from discussions at the seminar, and by suggestions from Pranab Bardhan and S. Guhan.

more facets of socio-economic process and evolution than one usually comes across in macro-economic surveys. But the question of the scope and method of studying socio-economic life must be kept distinct from the scope and method of observations relevant to studying particular questions at hand.

Part of the differences between economists and anthropologists lies in their perspectives and concerns. Economists tend to focus on the allocation of productive resources between different activities, the disposition of output between different end-uses, the mechanisms by and terms on which goods and services are exchanged, the way wealth and income are distributed among various classes, the living standards of people, and so on. They have evolved a conceptual apparatus and operational techniques to gather quantitative data on most of these subjects. Social anthropologists, on the other hand, are much more concerned with questions such as the place of individuals in society, the structure and functioning of different kinds of social groups, and the interrelations among them. These are inherently more difficult to capture with the sorts of observational techniques adopted by economists. The anthropologists' predilection for the detailed and direct observation of society and its constituent units as they function *in fact* is therefore understandable.

However, the anthropologist's distrust of quantitative observations through structured surveys, and the claim that participant observation is the only way to get a true picture of society and its workings, represent an untenable position. Equally untenable, in our view, is the position that all aspects of socio-economic life are in principle measurable and that what cannot be measured is not 'scientific'. The fact that many socio-economic phenomena are amenable to quantitative observation through structured surveys does not mean that socio-economic life as a whole can be so 'measured'. Nor are structured surveys necessarily or always reliable. It is also apparent that a proper understanding of forces determining the nature, direction and pace of socio-economic change and its ramifications takes us well beyond the domain of economists into an exploration of underlying social structures and processes for which, at present at any rate, macro survey techniques seem inadequate. Here, techniques of micro study developed by sociologists and social anthropologists seem much more promising. A combination of both macro and micro approaches is thus indicated. In what follows we discuss their respective roles and limitations, illustrating from the Indian experience, and indicate the ways in which they can be combined to expand and deepen our understanding of socio-economic change in rural areas.

MACRO SURVEYS IN INDIA

One of the major preoccupations of macro surveys is with mapping structure and change. The emphasis is generally on getting, at periodic intervals, data on the level and structure of production, incomes and consumption; prices; skilled education; the composition of the work force; sectoral patterns of employment; wage rates; savings and capital formation; living standards, etc. In all these cases the emphasis is on collecting information on well-defined quantifiable indices which have to be standardized so that they can be aggregated and/or compared across individuals, groups or regions, as the case may be. Moreover, statements about the behaviour of selected indices in any given population necessarily require that we get either complete information on that indicator for all relevant members of that population, or for a representative sample thereof. Substantial resources are spent on macro surveys of this type in India.

The scale and diversity of this effort has increased greatly in the past four decades. At the time of Independence, macro data were largely confined to the decennial population censuses and quinquennial livestock censuses; estimates of land use, cropwise area sown, yield and production on an annual basis, and the compilation of data on public finance, foreign trade and social services occurred largely as by-products of administration. By the early 1950s the systematic survey of major segments of organised industry had barely started.

The creation of the National Sample Survey (NSS) marked a major step forward in applying techniques of large-scale sample surveys to collect data on almost all aspects of socio-economic life, and giving estimates upto state and occasionally sub-state levels. Over the years the NSS has collected data on vital rates and morbidity; migration; private and social consumption; landholdings, wealth and indebtedness; employment, unemployment and wages; land use; area under and yields of major crops; animal husbandry; industry (including small-scale and unorganized industry), transport, trade and services. In several cases these inquiries are repeated at periodic intervals, thereby providing, in principle, an independent basis for assessing changes over time.

Nationwide or regional sample surveys have also come to be widely used in other agencies, including the Registrar General's office (to monitor trends in vital rates and in the adoption of family planning); the ministry of food and agriculture (to assess crop yields and to monitor costs of cultivation of the major crops); and the Planning Commission (among other things for ex post-evaluation of selected projects to get a better idea of the structure of urban economy and society). Practically all the state governments participate in the NSS enquiries and conduct special sample surveys of their own.

These surveys have been valuable in highlighting the range and pattern of variation across states, and occasionally across sub-regions of states, in respect of important socio-economic indices. Also since, typically, they collect information on several other characteristics of the sample units, the data make it possible to explore several aspects of structure and structural relationships, and to test hypotheses concerning them. The availability of these data has stimulated and facilitated systematic enquiry into important aspects of India's economy and society, including, to mention but the more striking examples— the pattern of private consumption and its responsiveness to changes in income and prices; the structure and working of rural labour markets; inequality in incomes, wealth and consumption across regions and classes; the incidence of poverty and characteristics of the poor; savings and investment behaviour; and size-productivity relations in agriculture. The utility of these studies lies not only in their analysis of substantive questions but also in their contribution to changing and refining the concepts and categories in terms of which data are collected.

Increasingly, macro surveys are also used to explore specific aspects of the economy in depth. The National Council of Applied Economic Research (NCAER) surveys of household savings; the NSS and the NCAER surveys of diffusion and intensity of fertiliser use; the NSS surveys of irrigated farms, livestock sector, physically handicapped, and social consumption; the Textile Commissioner's survey of cloth purchases; and the Reserve Bank of India's surveys of corporate finance and foreign enterprises—all are illustrations of this.[1] The surveys of the structure and working of input and output markets in rural areas by Rudra and Bardhan, and more recently by Srinivasan, also belong in this category. Being more sharply focused and often concerned with exploring concrete theoretical hypotheses, this kind of survey needs to be given much greater importance.

PROBLEMS WITH MACRO SURVEYS

Serious lacunae, however, remain.[2] In the first place, there are significant gaps in the coverage of these surveys, and even more in the extent to which they provide comparable information at different points of time. While a nationwide system of crop cutting experiments to determine per hectare yields of major crops season by season, and year after year, has been built up, none exists for the livestock sector. It is only within the last decade that the NSS has conducted a comprehensive survey of this sector. Though the NSS has at one time or another surveyed small-scale and household industry, construction, and trade and services, the tabulations are far less detailed when compared to consumption or employment, and are not usable for assessing changes over time.

Second, there are problems of an organizational nature. Despite expert committees appointed to advise on the design of the surveys and the scope and content of tabulations, and despite the fact that representatives of users (including both officials and academic researchers) serve on these committees, the interaction between users and those who collect and process data is not as close as it should be. Part of the reason is clearly the attitude of

[1] The growing use of macro survey techniques for studies of political behaviour, social attitudes and public opinion is also noteworthy.

[2] These problems have been widely discussed among economists and statisticians in India. See for example the three volumes on the Data Base of the Indian Economy brought out by the Indian Econometric Society. Rao ed. (1972); Dandekar and Venkataramiah (1975); Bose, ed. (1978).

policy makers and administrators to data: they neither make much demand on data and data-based analysis for making or evaluating their decisions, nor are they particularly keen that others use the data which are available. Outside researchers have to rely mostly on published tabulations which use but a fraction of the information originally collected. The primary data are rarely stored in a retrievable form—though the situation is beginning to change notably in the NSS—and even where they are, access to outsiders interested in deeper analysis from a different perspective is, in general, quite difficult. This is despite the experience that the intensive use of data gives rise to suggestions for significant modifications in concepts and tabulations in order to make the data more meaningful. Difficulty of access to original data is one reason why there is avoidable duplication in data-gathering efforts.

The third, and perhaps most important problem, in the context of the present discussion, lies in getting reliable and comparable data from large-scale surveys. The quality of the macro surveys—in terms of design and fieldwork—varies a great deal. There are problems even when, as in the case of NSS, a high level of professional expertise goes into the construction of the questionnaire and sampling design, and the schedules are canvassed by a relatively stable, well-trained cadre of field staff. Part of the problem is that the information sought is often wide-ranging and detailed, and touches on sensitive subjects. When a survey is designed to serve several purposes—or cover several subjects at the same time—the difficulty is compounded. Comprehensive, multi-purpose surveys have the merit, in principle, of enabling the investigator to verify the accuracy of data by built-in internal consistency checks. But they also make the schedules so long and complicated that the likelihood of both investigator fatigue and respondent resistance increases. The recent shift to focusing on one or two subjects in each year has mitigated these problems but not eliminated them.

In principle, the given stock of field staff could be used to canvass a smaller number of sample households at several sittings instead of at one or two. The reduction of sample size need not affect the precision of estimates, provided the design is modified and greater attention given to appropriate methods of stratifying the population for sampling. But what kinds of stratification would be appropriate, as well as whether these would substantially reduce the overall sample size and still give reasonably precise estimates at the desired level of regional/ class disaggregation, are issues that do not seem to have been seriously investigated. The desirable level of precision/ disaggregation is again an open question. To expect, as is being done in some regions, a national or even a state-level sample survey to provide accurate estimates of output of major crops at the level of a community development block (with an average population of perhaps 200,000) would put an unmanageably large burden on a centralized survey organization. Even if it were feasible otherwise, the cost would be excessive.

The function of an efficient sampling design is to provide unbiased estimates of the value of one or more characteristics in a given population with minimal sampling error for a given amount of resources spent on the survey. But it cannot take care of non-sampling errors arising from ambiguities/inconsistencies in questions, non-response, incorrect response, biases in the way questions are asked, and/or answers given by respondents. These are often far more important than sampling errors. For instance, the NSS consumption enquiries seek to get at the quantum of food consumed by each sample household in the form of homecooked meals for some dozen or more categories of cereals, purchases of cooked food from outside, meals provided to guests, and meals eaten at employer's household. There are ambiguities in how all this information is elicited by investigators. In any case, the level of detail and the complexity of the information to be recalled by the respondent are likely to tax even those who maintain some sort of a record of their consumption. There is also good reason to believe that meals for workers may be getting double-counted in the consumption of both the employee and the employer households. (On this see Chatterjee and Bhattacharya, 1975, and Vaidyanathan, 1986.)

Non-response rates in the NSS are generally reported to be quite small,[3] but little is known about the characteristics of non-responding households. This is important because if the non-response is concentrated in the upper end of the income

[3] Not much is known about non-response or degree of co-operativeness of informants in other surveys, including the censuses.

scale, the survey estimate of both the mean and the distribution around it will be biased. Apart from non-response, the extent to which respondents co-operate with the interviewer and are willing to give accurate information affect the quality of the data. While there is little direct evidence to sustain the claim that upper income households tend to understate their consumption to a greater degree than poor households, the field staff generally report the former to be less co-operative in answering questions. These sources of bias are possibly stronger when it comes to enquiries on landholding and wealth, especially when concealment of the true state of affairs in order to avoid land and taxation laws is widespread.

The existence of these errors naturally affects the reliability of sample survey estimates of various characteristics as measures of their 'true' value. Even in the case of census-type enquiries, reporting errors and biases can be quite important. There is no easy way to assess their magnitude. Independent verification— of the kind done in connection with the censuses of population and livestock—provides a broad check on the veracity of data.[4] However, systematic biases in reporting by respondents or on the part of investigators cannot really be captured by this means.

That survey estimates are liable to error does not, of course, wholly vitiate their usefulness. Often, one is not interested so much in the absolute value of a characteristic in a particular region or at a given point of time as in the relative position of that region *vis-à-vis* other regions, or *vis-à-vis* other points in time. So long as sampling errors are reasonable and there is no systematic regional or time pattern to the incidence of non-sampling errors, the data are useful for studying inter-regional or temporal variations. This at any rate is the underlying assumption on which macro survey data are being used—and used quite extensively—to study differences across space and time in the levels of living, relative inequalities of consumption and wealth, employment and wages, and the like.

[4] Note that in the case of the censuses, the sample verification gives a good idea of the margins of error of estimates at a relatively high level of aggregation—e.g. state-level estimates and estimates for broad categories in the population—but not at the level of villages/towns or even districts. There is reason to believe that census data for particular villages/towns are liable to larger error than regional or higher level units.

While this seems defensible in respect of regional variations, the use of macro survey data for studying changes over time is more problematic. For one thing, comparability over time is often vitiated by changes in the coverage, scope and design of the schedules, and the way schedules are canvassed.[5] Thus though the decennial census of population collects a great many details regarding the industry and occupation of individual workers, changes in the definition of 'worker' seriously limit the value of this data for assessing changes in labour force participation, sectoral distribution of workers, and unemployment. In some cases, e.g. with the statistics of land use and cropping and of livestock, there is reason to believe that with the decline in the importance of the land tax as a source of revenue and with the village officials who collect the primary data becoming increasingly burdened with a variety of other functions, the quality of reporting may have deteriorated. In some areas the recent trend towards replacing the traditional system of appointing local people as village officials with a cadre selected from a wider area (these being often transferred) is contributing to further deterioration.

Similar problems exist in the case of sample surveys as well. For instance, a detailed review of the NSS consumption inquiries,[6] which have been used extensively to study the trends in inequality and poverty, has revealed that there have been significant variations across years in the number of items specified in the schedules: the definition of 'consumption' in respect of some items, notably clothing and durables; the treatment of gifts and second-hand purchases; the manner in which foodgrain consumption of the respondent household is estimated; the treatment of cooked food given to/received from outsiders on ceremonial occasions and/or for work done.

[5] Similar problems exist in most other surveys, including the censuses of population and livestock. In the latter, apart from changes in concepts/categories, the tabulations at the sub-state levels sometimes cannot be compared because of changes in territorial boundaries.

[6] See Vaidyanathan (1986). Similar problems seem likely in respect of other aspects as well, but these have not been investigated in detail. The significant exceptions to all this are the employment surveys which, thanks to careful work done in the 1960s, have led to conceptual improvements and a high degree of comparability, especially since 1972.

Moreover, while upto the early 1960s the consumption schedules were administered to a distinct set of sample households
selected for the purpose, the consumption enquiry was made
part of an integrated household survey from 1964–5 to 1970–1.
Thereafter sample households are being administered two
schedules: one relating to consumption and the other to
employment and unemployment. The sample size varies.

All this, together with the fact that the rate of change in per
capita consumption has been relatively low compared to the
magnitude of the sampling error in the estimates, makes it
difficult to rely on the NSS for measuring the magnitude and
even the direction of changes in mean per capita total
consumption—and much more so in the consumption of
particular commodity groups, classes or regions. The wide
divergences between the time pattern of change shown by the
NSS and by other independent estimates—as has been found in
the case of crop production and of private consumption—
compounds the problem. Altogether, a close scrutiny of macro
survey experience suggests abundant caution in using such data
to assess change.

DIRECTIONS OF IMPROVEMENT

Clearly, there is much that can and needs to be done in order to
improve the quality and comparability of macro survey data.
First, the sources and magnitudes of error in data need to be
examined more closely. The practice of publishing sub-sample
estimates, which is being followed by the NSS, gives an
indication of sampling errors, but none of non-sampling errors.
A critical study of non-response and of the characteristics of
non-co-operative sample units would be useful.

Second, the design of the schedules, the clarity of concepts/
categories in terms of which information is sought, the way the
investigators frame their questions to elicit the information,
ways of checking their veracity, and similar other aspects of
survey methodology need to be the focus of sustained critical
review and experiment.

A third, related, aspect concerns the sampling design and the
scope of the enquiries. More careful stratification with a view to
reducing sample size and allowing more time to be spent on

each sample unit could improve the quality of data. So might a shift of emphasis from multi-purpose to single-purpose surveys, and, further, to narrowing down the scope of single-purpose surveys. For instance, if one were interested in the pattern of cloth consumption, the sampling design and strategy of enquiry would be very different from that currently adopted by the NSS. There has to be, at least, a substantial increase in the number of more narrowly focused, intensive inquiries into particular aspects of resource use, production, consumption, and the like to complement the comprehensive inquiries currently in vogue.

Fourth, changes in design, concepts, etc. need to be kept to the minimum, and at any rate must be relatively infrequent. Where changes are found, on the basis of careful study or in response to evolving policy needs, to be necessary, they must be introduced only after proper preparation. This must include field testing, and be done in such a manner that the nature, direction and magnitude of difference which they make to the estimates, compared to earlier methods/designs, can be calibrated. Without these, the comparability of estimates is vitiated and their usefulness as the basis for studying change seriously compromised.

There is also room for trying out panel sampling techniques. The NCAER adopted this approach to assess changes in incomes and consumption patterns for the same set of households at different points in time. The results, however, highlight some major problems. For example, a rather high percentage of the original sample could not be located even in rural areas in the repeat survey conducted after an interval of ten years. There is also the difficulty that the set of households selected to be representative of the population at one point of time may not remain representative at another time. Consequently, panel data by themselves cannot give a reliable picture of changes in the characteristics of the population as a whole. This would require the panel survey to be somehow integrated with a sampling procedure, to obtain a representative picture of the entire population at each point of time. This is a promising area for innovative approaches.

Among the essential preconditions for effecting these improvements are greater clarity on the part of users of data as to what is being measured and why; encouragement of detailed analysis, by policy makers and researchers, of data already collected, and a closer interaction between them and those who are responsible for the collection of data. The situation in this respect leaves a great deal of room for improvement.

ROLE OF THE MICRO APPROACH

Affirming the utility and necessity of the macro approach to studying social and economic change does not in any way imply a rejection of the value of micro enquiries. The latter obviously have a very important role for planning at the local level.[7] They are also important in that intensive studies of particular communities can give a degree of detail, depth and perspective which large-scale surveys cannot. The latter are mostly designed by economists/statisticians who have a predilection for quantifiable information and a tendency to underplay, if not ignore, non-economic factors which affect economic activity. Even when their role is recognized—and there is some indication that awareness on this is increasing—they are difficult to incorporate in macro surveys.

Part of the reason is that far too little is known of the nature and role of non-economic factors in relation to socio-economic change; the theoretical work on this interface is as yet rudimentary. Moreover, non-economic factors are not always readily amenable to measurement in terms of standardized categories, but require collection of more or less qualitative information with a sensitivity to nuances which differentiate one situation from another. This is specially true in studying the process of change. Even when quantification is possible, there are difficulties in getting accurate information within one or two sittings, on several important aspects (extent of landholding and other assets, indebtedness, tenancy, the interlinking of markets). There is no question that detailed indepth studies in fewer localities spread over a period of time and after establishing a good rapport with the informants would provide a much better

---

[7] Note, however, that even here the necessity for gathering information according to well-defined categories for the entire population, or a representative cross-section thereof, remains.

and wider range of information than is possible with large-scale macro surveys. One does not have to accept the anthropologist's view of the nature of social enquiry in order to appreciate this important point.

Numerous examples can be cited from Indian experience to show that micro studies can provide much richer and more detailed information on rural economy than any macro enquiry. Take for instance rural wage labour: several macro surveys[8] give data on the incidence of wage labour, the relative importance of attached and casual labour, operation-wise employment, and earnings by sex. But the village-level studies[9] show a great variety of contractual arrangements in terms of duration, basis of payment (time *vs.* piece), and modes of payment (cash and kind, share and fixed, with and without the allotment of small plots on a sharecropping basis) which are not fully captured in macro surveys. The surveys by Rudra and Bardhan,[10] as well as the more recent one by Srinivasan,[11] explore among other things the extent to which the labourer and the employer are involved simultaneously in transactions in the labour, commodity and credit markets.

Village studies have a fairly long history in India. Among economists, Gilbert Slater pioneered them in the early part of this century (Slater, 1981). Innumerable other economic surveys of particular villages from different parts of the country have since been made.[12] These studies generally tend to be descriptive accounts of the village population and its composition, pattern of landholdings, land use of cropping, yield land labour use,

[8] Notably the Agricultural Labour Enquiries of 1950–1 and 1956–7, the two Rural Labour Enquiries of 1963–4 and 1974–5, and the quinquennial NSS surveys of employment and unemployment since 1972–3.

[9] See for instance the collection of papers published in the *Indian Journal of Agricultural Economics*, 1948, and the village studies conducted at the time of the first Agricultural Labour Enquiry.

[10] Rudra and Bardhan (1978, 1980).

[11] As part of a World Bank research project, forthcoming.

[12] Reports of several of these have been published in the *Indian Journal of Agricultural Economics*, especially during the twenties and thirties. The early phases of the planning era saw a mushrooming of such surveys; this has, however, slackened since the 1960s. For a listing of village studies conducted during 1950–75, see Lambert, ed. (1976).

and the like. But they differ widely in terms of scope and details, methods of compilation, and in the concepts and categories in terms of which data are provided. The use of structured surveys to elicit information according to well-defined categories for the village as a whole and for its residents has increased over the years, but this is not always reflected in published reports—partly because many of the surveys have not been written up at all, or written only partially. These data have been used to explore particular aspects of rural economy (e.g. size-productivity relation, employment and wage rates), but rarely to present a comprehensive analysis of the functioning of village economic structure. A significant exception—though not the only one—is the study of Palanpur by Bliss and Stern (Bliss and Stern, 1982) which serves to highlight both the potential of the village survey and also how demanding it is.

Social anthropologists have also carried out numerous micro studies. While a few deal with the broad relation between economic and social structure (eg. Beteille, 1965; Mencher, 1977; Srinivas, 1976), or the impact of new technology on rural society (e.g. Epstein, 1962, Farmer, ed., 1977), their studies more often tend to focus on particular aspects of rural society—e.g. caste and kinship; ritual; the *jajmani* system; lineage and family; the relation between caste, economic position and political power, and processes of change therein. [13]

Comprehensive micro studies of change in village economy and society are even rarer. Some notable recent efforts include the Kessinger study of a century of change in a north Indian village (Kessinger, 1979); the re-survey of some of the Slater villages in the 1960s and again in the early 1980s (Guhan and Mencher, 1982; Guhan and Bharathan, 1984; Athreya, 1984); agrarian change in a Tanjavur village (Gough, 1977); and in a Mysore village (Epstein; 1962); the study of socio-cultural change in selected villages in Trichy district of Tamil Nadu over the past century;[14] and sample surveys to map change in

[13] The following is an indicative list of such studies: Srinivas, ed. (1955), Mandelbaum, ed. (1972), Beidleman (1959), Wiser (1936), Breman (1985).

[14] This study was done in the seventies by a team of Japanese scholars in collaboration with Indian scholars, under the auspices of the Institute for the Study of Oriental Languages and Culture of Asia and Africa, in Tokyo. A few monographs giving the results are available.

Matar taluka over a period of fifty years/(Shah & Shah, 1974). Again, these vary a great deal in scope and quality. In general, thanks to information available from revenue department records, they usually give a broad picture of changes in land holding, land use, irrigation, livestock and cropping patterns. A few attempt to reconstruct, through a combination of official records, they usually give a broad picture of changes in land-control. In some cases they also give an idea of change in caste composition, the socio-economic position of different castes, inter-caste relations, and the forms of wage labour and wage rates. But these are, in general, rather sketchy and less reliable, inasmuch as different people conducted the surveys at different times without any attempt at ensuring comparability in concept, coverage or methods of getting data. Moreover, hardly any of the surveys—and this applies particularly to the earlier surveys—provide a representative picture of the situation in the village at different points of time. And with observations for hardly two or three points in time, spanning several decades, it is difficult, even if the surveys were otherwise carefully done, to draw inferences about secular change in all their aspects (unless the years when the surveys were done happen to have more or less the same weather conditions).

Moreover, such intensive studies require a degree of direct involvement in data gathering on the part of the researcher which is so time consuming that an individual researcher can hope to cover only a limited number of villages. In principle, different researchers working within a broadly similar framework and focusing on a common set of questions could generate a sufficient number of micro studies of diverse situations to permit reasonably confident inferences about macro patterns as well as generalizations on underlying forces. This seems to have been the idea behind the establishment of the Agro-Economic Research Centres under the auspices of the ministry of food and agriculture. These centres were expected to conduct continuing studies of all major facets of social and economic change in selected villages all over the country. But the experiment did not prove successful and has been abandoned. This does not mean that the approach is not workable, only that the conditions of success are demanding. Continuous or even periodic village surveys cannot be viewed as merely a mechanical collection of data, but should be seen as an integral part of a well-focused and sustained research programme. At a minimum, many more studies of the type attempted in the Trichy villages, and careful preservation of primary data from these and other village surveys—which can be drawn upon by future researchers interested in studying change—would help.

While the idea of continuous and detailed study of change in a sufficiently large number of villages to secure representativeness seems impractical, the idea of keeping track of changes in selected important socio-economic indicators through regularly repeated surveys of a reasonably large panel of villages seems more feasible and deserves to be pursued seriously. The panel could be so selected as to at least capture different types of situations by region, if not to get a truly representative sample. And by confining the scope of the surveys to monitoring well-defined village-level indicators which do not involve sensitive or detailed probing into activities and relations of individual households, it is possible to envisage a programme of data collection through a network of local colleges spread throughout each region. This could then provide the basis and even the frame for more detailed village studies of the type necessary for a full understanding of the processes of change in rural economy and society.[15]

Another, and somewhat more modest, approach within the reach of individual researchers is to combine micro survey techniques to examine concrete macro issues. A recent instance of this is the work of Rudra and Bardhan exploring the nature and extent of the inter-linking of rural markets. For this purpose they first selected a number of villages typical of different agro-climatic conditions and agrarian structures prevailing in east India. The number of villages selected was much smaller than in the usual NSS-type inquiry, but contained a sufficient variety of situations to examine whether interlinking was at all widespread, what kinds of interlinking were prevalent, and

[15] Surveys to monitor development indicators (some at the village level and some relating to households) in a few selected villages are being tried out in Kerala under the auspices of UNRISD (Scott and Mathew, 1985). This could provide a useful starting point to examine how to select the villages, how many of them, and what the appropriate scope and design for the household survey should be.

under what conditions. They used a structured questionnaire but also provided for a deeper qualitative exploration of the nature of exchange relations in which each sample household was involved. The survey depended on field investigators, who had to be selected and trained with more-than-usual care, and who had an intimate knowledge of the area. While it may not satisfy the anthropologist's ideal, the survey demonstrated that quite a wealth of detailed and qualitative information on selected aspects of rural economy can be gathered by this method. Srinivasan's survey has further refined this approach.

Another example is a recent study of caste–class interactions in rural India (Sundari, 1984). The study, though confined to part of a district, showed that there exists a great deal of variation in caste composition, in the relative importance of wage labour, as well as in demographic pressure and agricultural productivity among villages within even this small area. By suitably classifying the villages, the researcher was able to select a manageable number typical of different configurations of these features, and to examine the differences in the nature of labour contracts and wage rates across categories as well as in the historical pattern of evolution. The study suggests that caste–class configurations do matter in determining forms of wage labour and wage rates, and also that present caste–class configurations are shaped in an important degree by configurations in the past.

CONCLUSION

In sum, it is neither valid nor, at any rate, helpful to view micro and macro approaches to study socio-economic change in rural India as mutually exclusive and in some sense antithetic. There is enough experience to show that they are better viewed as complementary, and that there is much scope for an imaginative combination of the two approaches.

REFERENCES

Athreya, V. B., *Vadamalaipuram: A Resurvey* (MIDS, Working Paper 50, 1984).

30 *Studying Rural Economic Change*

Beidleman, T. O., *A Comparative Analysis of the Jajmani System* (New York, *JJ*. August 1959).

Beteille, A., *Caste, class and power* (Berkeley, University of California Press. 1965).

Bliss, C. J., and Stern, N. H., *Palanpur: The Economy of an Indian Village* (OUP, Delhi. 1982).

Bose, A., ed. *Data Base of Indian Economy:* Vol. III (Calcutta Statistical Publ. Society. 1978).

Breman, J., *Patronage and Exploitation: Changing Agrarian Relations in Gujarat*. University of California Press, Berkeley, (1974).

Breman, J., *Of Peasants, Migrants and Paupers: Rural Labour Circulation and Capitalist Production in West India* (OUP, Delhi. 1985).

Chatterjee, G. S. and Bhattacharya, N., 'Some Observations on NSS Household Budget data', in Dandekar, V. M., and Venkaramiah, P., eds. (1975).

Dandekar, V. M. and Venkataramiah, P., eds. *Data Base of the Indian Economy: Role of Sample Surveys*, Vol. II (Calcutta, Statistical Publ. Society. 1975).

Epstein, S., *Economic Development and Social Change in South India* (Manchester, Manchester University Press. 1962).

Farmer, B. H., ed. *Green Revolution?* (London, Macmillan. 1977).

Gough, K., *Agrarian Change in Tanjavur*, in K. S. Krishnaswamy *et al.*, eds., *Society and Change: Essays in Honour of Sachin Chandhuri* (OUP, Bombay. 1977).

Guhan, S. and Mencher, J., *Iruvelipattu Revisited* (MIDS Working Paper 42. 1982).

Guhan, S. and Bharathan, K., *Dusi: A Resurvey* (MIDS Working Paper 52. 1984).

Kessinger, T., *Vilayatpur 1841–1968: Social and Economic Change in a North Indian Village* (Young Asia Publications, New Delhi. 1979).

Lambert, Claire M., *Village Studies: Data Analysis and Bibliography*, vol. I, *India 1950–75* (IDS, Sussex. 1976).

Mandelbaum, D. G., ed. *Society in India*, 2 vols (University of California Press, Berkeley. 1972).

Mencher, Joan, *Agriculture and Social Structure in Tamil Nadu* (Bombay, Allied. 1977).

Rao, C. R., ed., *Data Base of Indian Economy: Review and Appraisal,* vol. I (Calcutta, Statistical Publ. Society. 1972).

Rudra, A., & Bardhan, P. K., 'Interlinking of Land, Labour and Credit Relations: An Analysis of Village Survey Data in East India', *EPW.* 1978.

———— 'Types of Labour Attachment in Agriculture; Results of a Survey in West Bengal' (*EPW.* August 1980).

Slater, G., ed. *Some South Indian Villages* (OUP, Oxford. 1980).

Shah, Vimal & Shah, C. H., *Resurvey of Matar Taluka* (Bombay University. 1974).

Scott, W. and Mathew, N. T., *A development monitoring service on the local level: monitoring of change in Kerala: the first five years* (Geneva, UNRISD. 1985).

Srinivas, M. N., ed., *India's Villages* (Calcutta, Govt. of West Bengal. 1955).

Srinivas, M. N., *The Remembered Village* (OUP, Delhi. 1976).

Sundari, T. K., 'Caste and the Agrarian Structures: A Study of Chingleput District' (Unpublished Ph.D thesis, Centre for Development Studies Trivandrum. 1984).

Vaidyanathan, A., 'On the Validity of NSS Consumption Data', *EPW.* 1986.

Wiser, W. H., and Wiser, C. V., *Behind Mud Walls* (Berkeley, University of California Press. 1936).

Chapter 3: Time Trends in the Level of Living in Rural India: A Critical Study of the Evidence from Large-Scale Surveys*

N. BHATTACHARYA and
M. CHATTOPADHYAY

1. INTRODUCTION

Studies on the level of living in rural India have been conducted by numerous researchers and institutions ever since Independence. These studies have been based on two main approaches.

* A preliminary version of this essay (*vide* Bhattacharya *et al.* 1985) was presented to a workshop on Rural Economic Change in South Asia: Difference in Approach and in Results between Large-Scale and Intensive Micro Studies, organized by the Social Science Research Council, New York, at Bangalore, during 5–8 August 1985. The authors are indebted to the organizers of this workshop, especially Professor Pranab Bardhan, for their efforts towards bringing together economic statisticians and anthropologists at this workshop. The present paper is an outcome of that stimulating experience. Professor Bardhan also offered many useful suggestions for improving the original version of this essay. Professor Ashok Rudra has been collaborating with the authors on the re-survey project briefly reported in section 4; the authors also benefited from his comments on earlier versions of this essay. The authors have to thank the authorities of the NSSO for supplying them original lists of households, and enquiry schedules needed for the resurvey of NSS villages/households reported in section 4. Dr Prafulla Chakrabarti of ISI and N. C. Das, S. Sengupta K. Sankaranayana and A. Chatterjee of NSSO helped on many technical points.

Large-scale sample surveys have been carried out by economic statisticians covering nation- or regionwide random samples of households. The National Sample Survey (NSS) enquiries on consumer expenditure, housing conditions, etc., are the most well-known among the surveys following this 'macro approach'. There has been little emphasis so far, in this approach, on revisiting the same households after a suitable interval of time; thus, the samples of households for different 'rounds' (i.e. years, roughly speaking), of the NSS have, in general, been independently selected. Anthropologists and sociologists, on the other hand, have conducted a number of intensive village-level or micro studies covering a few purposively selected villages, revisiting the same village(s) after a number of years. An essential feature of the latter approach is the amount of time spent by the social scientists themselves to collect the data. The sample-survey approach relies largely on a team of insufficiently motivated investigators who spend only a few hours to interview each sample household and fill up the schedule or questionnaire, whereas the anthropological approach uses the participant-observation method as well as others likely to give a more comprehensive and accurate picture of reality.

A controversy over the relative merits and flaws of the two approaches is only to be expected (Leach, 1967; Etienne, 1982; Srinivas *et al.*, 1979). So far as changes over time in living standards in rural India are concerned, the findings of the two approaches have sometimes been reported as considerably divergent. Sample surveys conducted by the NSS and other agencies have reportedly indicated relative stagnation over time in the level of living in rural India. Anthropologists, on the other hand, seem to have observed significant improvements over time in the villages/regions covered in their intensive studies (*vide* Appadurai, this volume).

The first aim of the present essay is to present the evidence on time trends in living standards in rural India emanating from the NSS. A further aim is to indicate how the macro or sample-survey approach can be improved in the light of the criticisms and suggestions made by anthropologists following the micro approach. In particular, we present some preliminary results of a sample survey carried out in rural areas of West Bengal which show that the sample-survey approach can easily detect changes in level of living if a moderate-sized sample of villages and households is revisited after a lapse of, say, ten years.

Level of living is a multidimensional concept and covers a number of aspects, e.g. domestic consumption, housing conditions, stocks of consumer durables, consumption of public goods, mortality and morbidity, terms and conditions of work, security, leisure and recreation. Many, though not all, of these aspects have been covered in large-scale sample surveys conducted in India, especially by the NSS. Section 2 presents the main results on inter-temporal changes in level of living in rural India obtained through the NSS and other enquiries. It is divided into a number of sub-sections: sub-section 2.1 is devoted to domestic consumption, 2.2 to housing conditions, 2.3 to availability of public goods, and 2.4 to rates of mortality. In each sub-section we briefly comment on the quality and inter-temporal comparability of the available data. Section 3 deals with observations on the comparative findings of the two approaches and on the strengths and weaknesses of large-scale surveys such as the NSS *vis-à-vis* anthropological studies. Section 4 presents some provisional results of a resurvey of NSS villages and households, carried out in rural areas of three districts in West Bengal, after an interval of twelve or thirteen years, broadly speaking.[1] The aim of this resurvey is to explore the problems and potentialities of such resurveys for the purpose of measuring changes in living standards within the Indian rural population. The results seem to be quite encouraging and in tune with those based on the NSS and other large-scale surveys. Section 5 presents a summary of findings and makes some observations of a concluding nature.

2. CRITICAL EXAMINATION OF LARGE-SCALE SURVEY DATA

In this section we mainly examine time-series data available from the NSS on different aspects of the level of living in rural India. To be precise, we consider only the results obtained from the Central Sample of the NSS and make no attempt to compile

[1] Professor Ashok Rudra has been collaborating with the authors in this survey project.

the fragmentary evidence from the corresponding State Sample material. We also utilize data from other important large-scale surveys to fill up gaps in the picture drawn from the NSS data.

2.1 *Changes in domestic consumption standards*

As is well known, the NSS conducted enquiries on household consumption covering nationwide samples of households almost continuously from 1950 to 1973–4. Since then such enquiries are being conducted at intervals of four or five years. The latest available results relate to the thirty-second round (July 1977–8) and the thirty-eighth round (January–December 1983).

The data thrown up by these enquiries have been most extensively used for national planning and policy-making in India, for studies on the incidence of poverty, on intra- and inter-regional disparities in level of living, and for statistical demand analyses (*vide* references under 'A'). The results of various studies have, on the whole, pointed to a fair amount of validity of the data. Aggregate household consumption estimated from NSS data compares favourably with private consumption expenditure estimated from national accounts statistics (*vide* references under 'A'). The composition of the two aggregates, however, differ appreciably. Thus, the NSS data show a larger share of foodgrains and a smaller share of other food items. It is quite possible that the NSS estimates for foodgrains consumption are overestimates for the richer sections of the rural population and for all sections taken together (Mukherjee, 1986; Vaidyanathan, 1986; Chatterjee and Bhattacharya, 1974a).

As regards inter-temporal comparability of NSS household-budget data, it may be noted that although the concepts, definitions and procedures were uniform to a considerable extent over time, some important changes had been made from time to time which vitiated the comparability of the data. The following points may be mentioned:

(a) Consumption out of home-grown produce was imputed at local retail prices upto the eighth round (July 1954–March 1955), but at ex-farm or ex-factory prices from the ninth round (May–November 1955) onwards.

(b) The data were collected through a 'consumer expenditure' schedule upto the eighteenth round (February 1963–January 1964), but through an 'Integrated Household Survey' schedule during the nineteenth through the twenty-fifth rounds. (The 'consumer expenditure schedule' was brought back with effect from the twenty-sixth round). In the 'Integrated Schedule' approach, data on various productive enterprises of the household and on several other aspects were collected in addition to data on consumer expenditure; also, the blocks for recording consumer expenditure data were slightly different from the corresponding blocks of earlier rounds. Earlier, during the tenth through the fourteenth rounds, the consumer expenditure schedule had been expanded to an 'Income and Expenditure' schedule by adding a few blocks for recording the receipts and disbursements of the household.

(c) The reference period to which the budget data relate varied in the early rounds. From the seventh round onwards, the last month reference period, except that for several groups, like clothing and durables, the reference period had been used for all times of the consumer budget. Data for the fourth and fifth rounds presented here are also based on the last month reference period was 'the last year'. The thirty-second round tried last month as well as last year for item-groups like clothing, but the available results relate to the last month reference period.

Tables I to IV present selected results on changes in level of living in rural India based on the NSS budget data. To save space, these results are given for the earliest and the latest rounds for which data are available, leaving out the intermediate rounds. Similar results for more NSS rounds are presented in Bhattacharya *et al.* (1985), which is referred to as the GLO study in Table IV. The results were obtained by interpolation from the available results of the NSS enquiries. By way of explanation, it may be mentioned that the decile groups were formed after arranging the sample households in increasing order of PCE (= per capita total consumer expenditure) and then grouping them in such a way that the first decile group comprised the poorest 10 per cent of the population (judged by PCE), the second decile group the next poorest 10 per cent, and so on; the tenth decile group included the richest 10 per cent of the rural population.

Table I shows little trend in real consumption per capita

TABLE I

Average PCE in real terms* for Selected Groups of Population in Rural India, by NSS rounds

NSS Round	Survey Period	average PCE (Rs per 30 days) by group						General Population
		Decile Group Number						
		1	2	3	9	10		
(1)	(2)	(3)	(4)	(5)	(6)	(7)		(8)
13	SEPT. 1957–MAY 1958	5.97	8.57	10.33	27.25	48.71		18.37
15	JULY 1959–JUNE 1960	6.74	9.53	11.24	26.70	44.71		18.32
16	JULY 1960–AUG. 1961	7.31	10.30	12.45	31.72	56.35		21.46
27	OCT. 1972–SEPT. 1973	6.90	9.64	11.42	26.85	46.07		18.67
28	OCT. 1973–JUNE 1974	7.49	10.33	12.44	28.65	47.28		19.83
32	JULY 1977–JUNE 1978	7.40	10.48	12.63	30.14	60.39		21.33

*The all-India rural CPI number for agricultural labourers was used for deflation.

TABLE II

Average Consumption of Cereals per person for Selected Groups of Population in Rural India, by NSS rounds

NSS Round	Survey Period	Average Quantity Consumed (kg per person/30 days) by group						General Population
		Decile Group Number						
		1	2	3	9	10		
(1)	(2)	(3)	(4)	(5)	(6)	(7)		(8)
4 AND 5	APRIL 1952–MARCH 1953	9.28	12.39	14.14	22.83	24.96		17.64
7	OCT. 1953–MARCH 1954	11.10	13.84	14.06	19.63	22.27		16.88
8	JULY 1954–MARCH 1955	10.37	12.79	14.25	20.78	21.60		16.81
27	OCT. 1972–SEPT. 1973	9.08	12.03	13.32	18.96	21.83		15.46
28	OCT. 1973–JUNE 1974	8.67	12.41	13.64	19.30	21.42		15.21
32	JULY 1977–JUNE 1978	9.72	12.44	13.63	18.45	20.59		15.40

*The estimates presented for these rounds are those based on the month reference period.

TABLE III

Average Consumption of Rice (r), Wheat (w) and Other Cereals (oc) per person for Selected Groups of Population in Rural India, by NSS rounds

		Average Quantity Consumed (kg per person/30 days) by group								
NSS Round	Survey Period	Decile Group 1			Decile Group 2			General Population		
		r	w	oc	r	w	oc	r	w	oc
(1)	(2)	(3)	(4)	(5)	(6)	(7)	(8)	(9)	(10)	(11)
8	JULY 1954–MARCH 1955	2.59	0.21	7.57	4.13	0.48	8.18	8.18	1.42	7.21
9	MAY-NOVEMBER 1955	2.65	0.43	8.29	3.55	0.91	8.73	7.48	2.58	7.72
13	SEPT. 1957-MAY 1958	3.04	0.38	5.83	4.32	0.80	7.49	7.10	2.28	7.27
27	OCT. 1972-SEPT. 1973	3.79	1.42	3.87	5.06	2.25	4.72	6.59	3.88	4.99
28	OCT. 1973-JUNE 1974	3.19	1.17	4.31	5.46	1.98	4.97	6.90	3.52	4.79
32	JULY 1977-JUNE 1978	3.76	1.57	4.40	5.46	2.43	4.56	7.12	4.05	4.23

TABLE IV

Indices of Absolute Poverty in Rural India based on distribution of Population by PCE, for selected NSS rounds

NSS Round	Survey Period	Head-Count Ratio			Sen's Index	
		Ahluwalia's Estimates I	Ahluwalia's Estimates II	ILO study	Ahluwalia's Estimates	ILO study
(1)	(2)	(3)	(4)	(5)	(6)	(7)
12	MARCH–AUGUST 1957	0.541	–	–	0.230	–
13	SEPT. 1957–MAY 1958	0.502	0.534	–	0.220	–
14	JULY 1958–JUNE 1959	0.465	–	–	0.190	–
15	JULY 1959–JUNE 1960	0.444	0.487	–	0.170	–
16	JULY 1960–AUGUST 1961	0.389	0.420	–	0.140	–
27	OCTOBER 1972–SEPTEMBER 1973	–	–	0.464	–	0.176
28	OCTOBER 1973–JUNE 1974	0.461	0.476	0.425	0.170	0.150
32	JULY 1977–JUNE 1978	–	–	0.402	–	0.143

taking all items of the household budget together. Table II presents a similar picture for per capita consumption of cereals in physical terms, which is a most important indicator of the level of living in rural India. The share of cereals in total consumer expenditure is typically over 40 per cent in rural India; it is as high as 60 per cent or even more for the lowest decile groups. Cereals supply about 80 per cent of the total calorie intake of persons in the bottom decile groups. Table II clearly shows that the cereal consumption is far from adequate for the three bottom decile groups covered in the table. A close look reveals some decline over time in the level of consumption of cereals for the top decile groups. This, as pointed out by Vaidyanathan (1986), throws doubt on the inter-temporal comparability of the data. The decline could have been caused by greater care in fieldwork and/or statistical processing exercised in the later rounds.

Table III shows the trends in consumption of three major components of cereals, namely rice, wheat and other cereals. It appears that the per capita consumption of rice and wheat, especially the latter, rose significantly over time for the bottom decile groups, while the corresponding figures for other cereals showed a clear decline over time. In this sense, there was some improvement over time in the domestic consumption standards of even the lowest decile groups.

In Table IV we present some indices of absolute poverty based on NSS data on distribution of population by PCE and a poverty line representing a subsistence level of living. These indices are available for a larger number of NSS rounds and show fairly wide fluctuations but little trend over time. These fluctuations have been shown to be related to factors like current and lagged per capita cereals production in the country (Bhattacharya *et al.*, 1985).

2.2 *Changes in housing conditions*

Compared to the NSS data on household budgets, the NSS data on housing conditions have attracted far less attention. This is quite unfortunate, as such data can be collected more cheaply and more accurately than data on household consumption, and, further, they show clear improvement over time in the level of living in rural India, unlike the data on household consumption.[2] It is a matter of great regret that there has been no fullfledged enquiry on housing conditions since the twenty-eighth round (1973–4).

The NSS conducted all-India enquiries on housing conditions, usually through some blocks added to the 'consumer expenditure' scheduled, during a large number of rounds (*vide* Table V).[3] The items of information covered in these enquiries varied a great deal across rounds, but broadly speaking the following items were included in one or more rounds.

The number of rooms, the number of living rooms, the floor space, the type of structure (i.e. materials of roof, wall and floor), the source of drinking water and its distance from the household, whether this source was in the exclusive use of the household or not, the type of latrine and whether or not it was in the exclusive use of the household, the type of ownership, the monthly rent (if any), whether electricity was used or not.

The materials used for floor, wall and roof were used for classifying houses into three broad categories—*pucca, semi-pucca* and *katcha*. Broadly speaking, pucca houses are those where both walls and roof are made of oven-burnt bricks, stone, cement concrete, jackboard (cement-plastered reeds), and timber. Tiles, galvanized iron, or asbestos cement sheets used in the construction of roofs were also regarded as pucca material. A semi-pucca house is one which is not pucca but where either plinth or wall or roof is made of oven-burnt bricks, stones, cement concrete or timber. A katcha house is one where the walls, roof and plinth are all made of unburnt bricks, bamboo, mud, grass or leaves, reeds and/or thatch.

Table V shows the changes over time in a number of indicators of housing conditions in rural India. Some of the figures look doubtful when compared to others. We refrain from examining them in detail in the light of what is known about their sampling errors. Several remarks may, however, be

[2] Similar remarks apply for data on availability of different kinds of facilities discussed in the following sub-section.

[3] Data were also collected in some other rounds (including some later than the twenty-eighth) on a few items of information, like source of drinking water, usually through the 'consumer expenditure' schedule.

made. First, the sample size was fairly small except for rounds 18, 19 and 28. Second, the relative neglect of the enquiry on housing conditions might have led to some amount of non-comparability of the data over time. Finally, tabulation by classes of PCE are regrettably absent for any of the rounds, and one can hardly examine the changes in housing standards for different sections of the population.

Anyway, taking the rural population of the country as a whole, it is clear from Table V that the percentage of households living in pucca houses rose appreciably over time, while the corresponding percentage for katcha houses declined; the percentage for semi-pucca houses (not shown) seemed to have remained relatively stable. The percentage of households with no built-up latrine declined somewhat. The use of drinking water from tap or tubewell also showed a rising trend, as did the use of electricity for lighting. However, even the position reached in the twenty-eighth round period (Oct. 1973–June 1974) is far from satisfactory by any standards, and most of the improvements in housing conditions had probably benefited the decile groups of population at the top.

2.3 Changes in the availability of public goods

The NSS conducted a large-scale survey on social consumption during its thirty-fifth round (July 1980–June 1981), but the results of this enquiry are not yet available. The results are expected to reveal the extent of use of public goods—health and education facilities, facilities for drinking water, etc.—by different segments of the population.[4]

In this connection it may be recalled that between 1955–6 and 1967–8 the NSS used to canvass a village schedule called 'village statistics' (Sch. 3.0) with a view to collecting data on different types of facilities available in each sample village (*vide* Table VIA). While the set of items varied from round to round, the

[4] Enquiries of this nature covering rural and urban areas of West Bengal were carried out during 1964–5 and again during 1976—*vide* Maitra *et al.* (1974) and Maitra (1985). Broadly speaking, Maitra found a significant rise in the availability and utilization of public health and education services in rural West Bengal between the two survey periods.

TABLE V

Selected Indicators of Housing Conditions in Rural India based on NSS enquiries

Indicator	NSS round number (survey period)							
	7 (Oct. 53– March 54)	10 (Dec. 55– May 56)	11 (Aug. 56– Jan. 57)	12 (March– Aug. 57)	15 (July 59– June 60)	18 (Feb. 63– Jan. 64)	19 (July 64– June 65)	28 (Oct. 73– June 74)
(1)	(2)	(3)	(4)	(5)	(6)	(7)	(8)	(9)
I. PERCENTAGE OF HOUSEHOLDS LIVING IN								
(A) PUCCA HOUSES	2.7	1.9	2.7	1.4	–	–	14.6	18.5
(B) KATCHA HOUSES	63.4	62.9	60.3	67.3	–	–	71.1	49.1
2. PERCENTAGE OF HOUSEHOLDS HAVING NO BUILT-UP LATRINE	95.1	94.6	95.1	96.7	–	–	–	92.4

3. PERCENTAGE OF
HOUSEHOLDS WITH SOURCE
OF DRINKING WATER

(A) TAP	0.4	–	–	–	2.6	2.2	4.7
(B) TUBEWELL	3.2	7.1	–	–	11.2	9.1	7.0
(C) WELL	70.7	67.2	–	–	68.1	86.0	65.8
4. PERCENTAGE OF HOUSEHOLDS HAVING ELECTRICITY FOR LIGHTING	–	–	–	1.0	–	–	6.6
NO. OF SAMPLE HOUSEHOLDS	4,181	1.616	7,255	5.292	7,700	21,710	15,041	139,680

Note: '–' means figure not available.

TABLE VIA

Percentage of Villages reporting different types of Facilities within the village based on 'Village Statistics' enquiries of different NSS rounds

Type of Facility	Percentage of villages by NSS round number (survey period)							
	10 (Dec. 55– May 56)	11 (Aug. 56– Jan. 57)	12 (March 57– Aug. 57)	13 (Sept. 57– May 58)	14 (July 58– June 59)	18 (Feb. 63– Jan. 64)	19 (July 64– June 65)	22 (July 67– June 68)
(1)	(2)	(3)	(4)	(5)	(6)	(7)	(8)	(9)
PRIMARY SCHOOL	39.6	43.5	42.9	–	38.8	51.3	51.3	–
HIGH SCHOOL	1.0	2.0	1.5	3.5	1.3	2.7	3.7	–
POST OFFICE	7.5	10.3	9.6	–	9.3	14.6	15.1	18.3
HOSPITAL	1.3	2.3	1.6	4.8	0.7	1.4	2.0	–
HEALTH CENTRE	–	–	–	–	1.2	2.7	4.5	–
VETERINARY HOSPITAL	–	–	–	0.5	1.6	2.0	3.1	–
BUS STOP	–	–	–	–	–	11.3	12.6	–
MARKET	–	–	–	–	–	3.6 }	6.1 }	7.2
HAAT	–	–	–	–	–	8.5 }	– }	–
ELECTRICITY	–	–	–	–	4.3	8.4	11.7	–
RAILWAY STATION	0.9	0.9	–	–	0.7	0.7	1.8	–
SCHEDULED BANK	–	–	–	–	–	–	5.2	–
NO. OF SAMPLE VILLAGES	1584	1788	1794	1829	2594	7716	8319	8544

Note: '–' means figure not available.

following items were covered, broadly speaking, in one or more rounds:

The availability of different facilities within the village, e.g. primary, middle and high school, post office, hospital, health centre, veterinary hospital, police station, railway station, market, *haat*, metalled road, bus stop, electricity, scheduled bank; the distances to these facilities from the village, the condition of the road leading to them and the usual means of conveyance; the availability of medical practitioners by type (system of medicine, graduate/licentiate/others); sources of drinking water, etc.

While such data cannot reveal the extent of use of different facilities by *different* socio-economic groups of the rural population, they certainly throw considerable light on the level of living in rural India. It is therefore regrettable that the NSS assigned low weightage to such data after the twenty-second round (1967–8). In some of the later rounds, especially the thirty-fifth, which was devoted to an enquiry on social consumption, some data of this nature were collected in the schedule 0.0 used for preparing lists of all households in sample villages, but such data have never been tabulated so far.

Table VIA presents some time series of indicators of social consumption based on these 'village statistics' enquiries of the NSS. For the sake of interest, Table VIB sets out some figures based on the later NSS enquiries of this type against corresponding figures based on complete enumeration carried out in the Economic Census of 1977. (Incidentally, similar information was collected and tabulated in the population censuses of 1971 and 1981.) A few of the NSS-based figures are clearly wrong and need scrutiny and revision. Such instances would probably have been fewer if adequate attention had been paid to such time series thrown up by the NSS. It should, however, be pointed out that pps selection of sample villages was adopted in most of the NSS rounds, except the fourteenth, where the selection was done with equal probability; the former technique tends to select larger villages, on the whole. Anyway, these tables clearly depict an increase over time in the availability of different facilities, though the rate of increase was markedly different for different facilities. It is important to note that in spite of a few wrong and erratic results, the sample-survey approach followed

TABLE VIB

Percentage of Villages reporting different types of Facilities within specified distances from the village, based on 'Village Statistics' enquiries of selected NSS rounds and on Economic Census (EC) 1977

Type of facility (distance from the nearest centre)	Percentage of villages by NSS round/Economic Census			
	18th round (Feb 63–Jan 64)	19th round (July 64–June 65)	22nd round (July 67–June 68)	EC 1977
(1)	(2)	(3)	(4)	(5)
Primary school (2 km)	75.9	76.1	–	90.1[a]
High school (5 km)	31.8	33.3	–	20.9
Post office (2 km)	33.8	33.6	35.7	53.2
Hospital (5 km)	19.3	18.7	–	35.5
Health centre (2 km)	7.8	8.7	–	12.0
Electricity (5 km)	28.1	35.1	–	33.4[b]
Veterinary hospital (5 km)	22.7	24.1	–	45.2
Market (2 km)	10.5	–	–	14.8
Haat (2 km)	18.9	15.3	15.9	26.8
Bus stop (2 km)	24.7	23.8	–	40.3
Railway station (5 km)	14.2	15.0	–	18.3
Scheduled bank (5 km)	–	11.3	–	39.9
Drinking water (within village)	–	–	76.3	92.6
Fertilizer depot (5 km)	–	–	18.8	43.9

[a] primary or junior basic
[b] distance not mentioned
Note: '–' means figure not available.

by the NSS is capable of revealing improvements over time in the availability of public goods.

2.4 *Changes in mortality rates*

There has been a marked reduction in mortality rates in India since independence. Thus, the expectation of life at birth for males increased from 32.5 to 53.2 between 1951 and 1981, while the corresponding figures for females were 31.7 and 51.8. Such figures are not, however, available separately for rural India. To what extent sample surveys of the NSS type can measure such decline in mortality rates is an unsettled question, as will appear from the following account.

Data on current death events began to be collected on an exploratory basis in the seventh round (October 1953–March 1954) of the NSS, but the crude death rates estimated from all the NSS rounds prior to the fourteenth (July 1958–June 1959) were clear underestimates when judged against rates based on decennial population censuses. The first large-scale effort for estimation of (birth and) death rates through the NSS was made during the fourteenth round at the instance of the Planning Commission. The data were collected in two phases. During the first four months of the survey period, the population of each sample village was completely enumerated through the enumeration schedule (Sch. 12.1) which also recorded data on (birth and) death events occurring in every household during the last two years. Later, the population of the same sample villages was completely re-enumerated through the re-enumeration schedule (Sch. 12.1.1) during the last four months of the survey, i.e. after an interval of eight months, on an average. Data on (birth and) death events occurring in the household and changes in household membership during the intervening period were also collected through the re-enumeration schedule. The estimates thrown up by the fourteenth round enquiry were fairly plausible and were corroborated later by the 1961 census results. The census estimates of the crude death rate were 27.4 and 22.4 (per 1000) for the decades 1941–51 and 1951–61, respectively. The fourteenth round estimate for rural India was 19.0 per 1000 based on the enumeration schedule and 21.2 per 1000 based on the re-enumeration schedule.[5]

[5] The natural growth rate of 19.2 per 1000 estimated from the NSS fourteenth round was the first indication of increased growth rate in the country and considerably influenced national planning and policy-making. It was later confirmed by the decadal rate of 18.9 per 1000 for 1951–61, estimated from census data. See Das and Bhattacharya, 1977, for further details.

The approach of re-enumeration mentioned above was dropped in subsequent rounds of the NSS, and the death rates based on the enumeration approach declined sharply and unrealistically after the fourteenth round, presumably due to lack of adequate attention and control over the survey operations. Some of the available estimates of annual death rates for rural India are shown in Table VIIA. On the whole the NSS estimates of death rates are clear underestimates due to serious under-reporting of death events in the NSS-type enquiries. Deaths of infants as well as of adults seem to be under-reported, partly through recall lapse, but partly due to other factors. (The effect is less serious for birth events.) The estimates are based on the events reported to have occurred in the sample households during the last year (i.e. the last 365 days) preceding the date of enquiry. Detailed examination has shown that an increasing proportion of events are not reported as the recall period—the gap between the date of the event and the date of interview—increasès from 1 to 52 weeks (*vide* Das, 1981). The death rates are fairly plausible when the recall period is 1, 2 . . . 10 weeks, but progressively declines as the recall period is increased beyond 10 weeks, roughly speaking. The rates based on a one-year reference period are therefore on the low side. They would increase by 25 to 30 per cent and would become acceptable if the NSS employed the reference period of the last two or three months. Anyway, the current NSS programme is to conduct an enquiry on popula-

TABLE VIIA

Crude Death Rates (annual) estimated for Rural India, for selected NSS rounds

NSS Round	Survey Period	Death Rate (per 1000)
(1)	(2)	(3)
14	July 1958 – June 1959	19.0
15	July 1959 – June 1960	15.1
18	February 1963 – January 1964	12.4
19	July 1964 – June 1965	13.0

tion, births and deaths once in ten years following the fourteenth round approach of enumeration and re-enumeration, which should yield satisfactory results. This was followed in the thirty-ninth round (January–June 1984).

Plausible estimates of life expectancy at birth have nevertheless been obtained by careful analysis of the NSS estimate. Of the following estimates for rural India, only the nineteenth round figure for females appears to be on the high side:

	14th round		19th round	
	males	*females*	*males*	*females*
e_0^0 (years)	45.2	46.6	49.3	52.2

Table VIIB presents the crude death rates for rural India estimated from the Sample Registration System (SRS). A clear decline is observed after the mid seventies.

It should be noted that the SRS procedure is somewhat different from that of a typical sample survey. Data are collected from sample areas which are villages or segments of villages in rural areas. Part-time enumerators keep a continuous record of (birth and) death events, as they occur; and once in six months supervisory staff, mostly full-time, conduct a retrospective survey to prepare an independent list of vital events. The enumerators' and supervisors' records are compared and re-

TABLE VIIB

SRS estimates of Annual Crude Death Rates in Rural India

Year	CDR (per 1000)	Year	CDR (per 1000)
1968	16.8	1976	16.3
1969	19.1	1977	16.0
1970	17.3	1978	15.3
1971	16.4	1979	14.1
1972	18.9	1980	13.7
1973	17.0	1981	13.7
1974	15.9	1982	13.1
1975	17.3		

verified, if necessary, in the field, to arrive at a final list of events.

The retrospective survey conducted by supervisors resembles the birth and death enquiries of most of the NSS rounds. The SRS combines this with the approach of continuous registration of (birth and) death events. This is, admittedly a reasonable combination of approaches. The possibility however remains that the retrospective survey alone could yield satisfactory results if adequate precautions were taken against and adjustments made for recall lapse.[6] The NSS fourteenth round approach seems to be even safer, in retrospect.

3. STRENGTHS AND WEAKNESSES OF THE NSS AND OTHER SAMPLE SURVEYS

The merits of large-scale survey data on level of living may be briefly enumerated. Such data are collected from households selected by a fully specified probability scheme and they represent the country and its various regions satisfactorily. In principle, it is possible to assess the magnitudes of sampling errors of various estimates through calculation of SEs. Coverage error due to failure to cover inaccessible areas or due to lack of response is generally negligible. The fieldworkers typically have permanent jobs. In the NSS, most of the investigators hold a master's degree. They use structured questionnaires and follow elaborate printed instructions which are explained to them (in the relevant regional language) through regular training conferences. Seminars are sometimes organized for discussions among fieldworkers on how to reduce non-sampling errors arising in field data collection. This ensures uniformity of concepts, definitions and procedures to be followed by all fieldworkers spread over the country. Supervision is in-built. In the NSS, there is one Assistant Superintendent over every two Investigators, and the Assistant Superintendent

[6] A more sophisticated approach would be to tabulate the death rates by recall period, to fit a mathematical curve to the rates, treating the rate as a function of the recall period, and to quote the limiting rate as the recall period tends to zero (Som, 1966). This has the merit of utilizing the entire volume of data collected for a one-year reference period.

is required to tour continually and check a good proportion of the primary work done by the Investigators. Supervisory Officers at higher levels also function in the same way. Statisticians in the planning and analysis groups pay visits to the field to exercise control over the quality of fieldwork. The filled-up forms are scrutinized at various stages for the elimination of erroneous and doubtful data—in the field offices, soon after the forms have been filled, in the data processing centres before transcription of data on to punched cards/magnetic tapes, and again on the electronic computor. Errors detected in the field scrutiny are sought to be eliminated by recall or revisits, to the extent possible. Even the scrutiny checks to be applied are fully documented. Sampling errors being measurable, the main risk seems to be the response biases due to conscious/ unconscious misreporting of facts by respondents, such as the concealment of income. This, however, does not appear to be serious for many of the components of level of living if an appropriate reference period (recall period) has been chosen for the enquiries.

Indeed, it would appear from the critical survey of findings made in Section 2 above that sample-survey data also reveal significant improvements in level of living in rural India, especially if one examines aspects other than domestic consumption. The findings of the micro studies carried out by anthropologists are corroborative rather than contradictory.

The criticisms made by anthropologists of the sample-survey approach and its results are, nevertheless, justified to a considerable extent, and economic statisticians would do well to pay serious attention to these criticisms.

First and foremost, very little work has been done, or at least documented, on the reliability and validity of sample-survey data collected in India by less motivated investigators through interviews lasting a few hours per household. There is thus a great need of methodological studies in the field, and also of careful analysis of survey data, including external checks, to assess the magnitude of different types of errors that might have crept into the data collected on various items. Such studies have been few and far between even for NSS household budget data used extensively for a variety of purposes, in spite of the serious doubts expressed by economic statisticians themselves about the validity and inter-temporal comparability of these data.[7] The data collected by the anthropological approach may on occasion be more accurate and may, in suitably designed field studies, serve as the standard against which the sample survey data could be judged.

Anthropologists are understandably sceptical about the quality of primary data collected in large-scale socio-economic sample surveys (Srinivas *et al.*, 1979; Hill, 1982). However, the response errors may contain a large random component that gets eliminated in the process of averaging over sample households. The crucial question is to what extent the response errors contain a systematic component—the non-sampling *bias*—that cannot be eliminated by averaging over sample households. Such non-sampling bias (response bias) may be best examined for different socio-economic groups of households through collaborative studies undertaken by anthropologists and survey statisticians. However, even if such studies show that the survey data are appreciably biased, these data may be useful for many comparisons if the bias is more or less constant over time or across regions and socio-economic groups.

Second, compared to the micro approach of anthropologists, the sample-survey approach has often failed to take a comprehensive view of the level of living. Thus, the NSS has emphasized consumer expenditure and neglected, in a relative sense, aspects like housing conditions, stocks of consumer durables, and availability and consumption of public goods. Observations on the lack of attention paid to housing conditions and consumption of public goods have been made earlier in sub-sections 2.2 and 2.3. As regards stocks of consumer durables the data collected in some rounds have hardly been tabulated. The problems of data collection through sample surveys could in fact be less serious for some of these aspects than for consumer expenditure. As pointed out in sub-section 2.4, the sample-survey approach should also be capable of detecting the decline in mortality rates.

Third, the tabulation and analysis of sample-survey data have

---

[7] It may be stated, however, that the NSS organization has lately taken up a series of field studies designed to settle these issues, to the extent possible.

generally been incomplete and unsatisfactory. Not many results are furnished for regions smaller than states, on considerations of inadequacy of sample size. So far as the NSS is concerned we have a long way to go before the central and the state samples are pooled to overcome this problem of sample size, and before region-wise estimates are built. Such estimates would no doubt meet a variety of important needs of the government. Apart from this, only some broad tables are prepared from the voluminous data collected in any sample survey and much valuable information is left unutilized. With the advent of computerization, it should be possible to extract more information from survey data through further cross-tabulations of the data, and through regression analyses and other model-building techniques. To cite just one example, NSS household budget data have seldom been tabulated by social group, such as scheduled castes, scheduled tribes, etc., or by household occupation, or by size and classes of land possessed by the household. The variation in PCE across sample households has yet to be satisfactorily explained in terms of various factors. The work done by anthropologists can provide valuable insights and throw up interesting hypotheses that can help in the fuller statistical analysis of sample-survey data.

Finally, most sample-survey organizations in India have fought shy of one simple step which is well known in the literature on sample surveys—that of revisiting the same sample units (here villages and households) in the repeated surveys. This reluctance may be partly due to the fear of increased resistance from respondents and partly to complications created by migration, births and deaths, household splits, etc. These problems can be overcome, and are being overcome, especially in the developed countries, where panel data are collected for different types of enquiries. The great merit of repeated visits to the same villages/households is that *changes* over time can be more precisely measured through repeated visits to the same units than if the samples for successive surveys are drawn completely independently of one another. The work of anthropologists based on revisits to the same villages suggests very strongly that economic statisticians in India should give a serious trial to this idea which is stressed in their own literature.

The micro studies of anthropologists are too expensive to be carried out in a large sample of villages. They cannot therefore meet all the demands placed on the sample-survey data. They can, however, serve very well as pilot enquiries, in a broad sense, and help in planning and improving the analysis and reporting of large-scale sample surveys (*vide* contributions to this volume by Appadurai, Wadley and Derr, for illuminating observations bearing on these aspects).

Before concluding, we may put on record a few additional points regarding Indian National Sample Survey data bearing on measurements of the level of living. The NSS socio-economic enquiries seem to have been missing a not very small proportion (say 5 to 10 per cent) of the rural population. This cannot be explained by the exclusion of the institutional population living in jails, military cantonments, etc., or by the failure to cover remote and inaccessible areas. However, the degree of underenumeration of the rural population might have narrowed to some extent in the last ten years or so. The reasons for such underenumeration and for the reduction in the extent of underenumeration are not at all clear, nor has anyone any definite idea as to the types of persons escaping the NSS net. One can only conjecture that nomadic and houseless people, especially those living in inaccessible areas, are likely to be missed relatively often.

It is sometimes said that the NSS enquiries have tended to under-represent richer sections of the population. This question has never been investigated in depth. The underenumeration of the population points in the opposite direction, i.e. to the under-sampling of the poor.

The NSS enquiries have been based on rigorously selected probability samples of households. In general, no attempt has been made to over-sample the rich households, and so the estimates for the rich have been based on relatively few households. But this does not make these estimates *biased*. Bias could arise only through response and non-response errors. There are no hard data on the extent of non-response, but it appears from discussions with the experts of the NSS that the proportion of sample villages which were substituted or became casualties has generally been quite small, and the same is said of the proportion of sample households chosen for interviewing.

Only in exceptional circumstances could sizeable fractions of villages not be surveyed, owing to shortage of staff. In general, in such cases, a valid sub-sample of the allotted sample was covered by the survey team. Really serious instances of coverage error have been rare, like failure to cover tribal areas of Tripura during the thirty-eighth round (1983) owing to serious political disturbances.

In this connection, it should be noted that substitution of a sample household was allowed in the earlier rounds only when a sampled household had temporarily left the village. In later rounds, such substitution was allowed on one additional ground, that of serious non-co-operation from the sample household.

Incidentally, an attempt to oversample the rich in rural and urban areas will be made for the first time during the forty-third round, to be conducted during July 1987–June 1988.

Data on stocks of all types of consumer durables—e.g. domestic utensils and furniture held on the date of survey— were collected in some of the early rounds of the NSS, but such data have seldom been tabulated. There is a view supported by some isolated results that *purchases* of luxury durables are under-reported in this kind of survey (Rudra, 1972). The downward bias is revealed through comparisons with supply figures based on production and import statistics. This bias may arise due to the undersampling of rich households or due to under-reporting by rich households. *Stocks* of such articles are also likely to be understated.

Exploratory studies on morbidity were carried out in a number of NSS rounds between the seventh (October 1953- March 1954) and the twenty-eighth (October 1973-June 1974), but the methodology does not seem to have been finalized through these explorations. The incidence and prevalence rates were found to be much lower than the corresponding rates for developed countries. This could be partly due to the low level of health consciousness in India, contributing to the under- reporting of spells of sickness. As regards data on causes of sickness, too many cases fell in 'undiagnosed' categories like 'other fevers' and 'stomach troubles'. The latter difficulty can be overcome only through diagnostic surveys employing fully equipped medical teams.

4. A RESURVEY OF NSS VILLAGES AND HOUSEHOLDS: SOME PRELIMINARY RESULTS[8]

The present authors, in collaboration with Professor Ashok Rudra, have undertaken a survey project in rural areas of three districts of West Bengal—Burdwan, Birbhum and Purulia. The fieldwork was conducted during July 1985-June 1986. The aim was to examine the extent to which the approach of large-scale socio-economic sample surveys can measure changes in level of living if the idea of revisits to the same villages and households is fully exploited. The survey design had two main components:

(a) All the sample households canvassed for the NSS twenty-eighth round (October 1973-June 1974) enquiry on housing conditions (through Schedule 1.2) in the rural areas of the three districts mentioned above were revisited for a repeat survey on housing conditions.[9] This repeat survey covered 1153 sample households in 72 sample villages. Data were also collected from these households on stocks of consumer durables and changes therein in recent years. A village schedule was filled up for each village; as no such schedule had been canvassed in the twenty-eighth round, information on *changes* in infra-structural facilities in the village over time, especially during the last ten years, was sought to be collected through this village schedule, sometimes relying on the memory of knowledgeable persons in or around the village.

(b) The sample households interviewed for the NSS twenty-seventh round (October 1972–September 1973) enquiry on consumer expenditure were revisited for a repeat survey on consumer expenditure. Here again, only a randomly chosen subset of the original sample was actually covered for the resurvey. The twenty-seventh round enquiry was arranged in the form of four quarterly sub-rounds (seasons) and, in general,

---

[8] More results on this resurvey project have been published in the *Economic and Political Weekly*, Bombay (*vide* references).

[9] More precisely speaking, the resurvey covered only those households which had been surveyed in the first and the third of the three three-month sub-rounds (i.e. seasons) of the NSS 28th round. The first subround was conducted during October-December 1973 and the third subround, during April–June 1974. This should not vitiate the results since the data on housing conditions are hardly affected by seasonal variation.

each household was revisited in the same season as in the twenty-seventh round enquiry. The sample size came to 67 villages and 790 households.

It may be stated that West Bengal had experienced the so-called Green Revolution to some extent between the early seventies and the mid-eighties, and this had raised the intensity of cropping and the production of major crops like rice and wheat. Of the three districts named, Burdwan had prospered the most through this revolution and Purulia the least. It would naturally be of interest to check whether the resurvey can detect these differential effects.

It this section we briefly present some provisional results of this resurvey. They are generally based on the entire sample covered for the resurvey.

The sampling design of the NSS enquiries and hence of the resurvey was fairly complicated, but there was provision for two independent and interpenetrating sub-samples in the design. The divergence between sub-sample results indicates the margin of uncertainty associated with the combined sample estimate. We refrain from presenting sub-samplewise results, for reasons of space. In general, the conclusions drawn here would be supported by statistical tests of significance.

For reasons of space, again, we present only a few two-way tables showing the joint distribution of households by variate-values/forms of attributes ascertained during the earlier NSS enquiry and during the resurvey. Such distributions reveal considerable scatter. Also, changes in the characteristics during the period of more than one decade were far from unidirectional—while they showed improvements in living standards in many cases, instances of deterioration were also quite plentiful. These changes have yet to be examined and fully understood. It is possible that some of the curious changes are due to household splits which were quite frequent (see below) or to the devastating flood of 1978. Anyway, some of the tables presented below are one-way tables which present a summary picture of these changes.

The first point to note is the proportion of households in the earlier sample which could not be resurveyed, either because they had left the village or were not traceable at all, and the proportion of households which had been split during the intervening period with all or some of the fragments residing in the original village, etc. Table VIII shows that household splits were quite frequent—brothers had often separated after the death of parent(s)—and that, broadly speaking, a resurvey

TABLE VIII

Number of Sample Households Covered or Missed in the Resurvey, by Reasons

Category of Households	27th round consumer exp. (sub-rounds 4 and 1)	28th round housing consumer exp. (sub-rounds 1 and 3
(1)	*(2)*	*(3)*
UNCHANGED HOUSEHOLDS		
RESURVEYED	432	743
EXTINCT THROUGH DEATH	17	27
LEFT VILLAGE	49	40
SPLIT HOUSEHOLDS		
ORIGINAL HOUSEHOLDS	160	181
FRAGMENTS FORMED	382	442
FRAGMENTS RE–SURVEYED	358	410
" LEFT VILLAGE	24	32
OTHER HOUSEHOLDS		
NOT TRACED	18	5
REFUSED	1	0
NOT AVAILABLE AT THE TIME OF SURVEY	–	4
HHS IN ORIGINAL SAMPLE	667	1000
HHS EXPECTED IN RESURVEY	882	1234
HHS ACTUALLY RESURVEYED	790	1153

TABLE IX

Source of Drinking Water during NSS twenty-eighth round, sub-rounds 1 and 3 combined (October-December 1973 and April-June 1974) and during the Resurvey (July' 85-March' 86)

Source during Original Enquiry	No of households by source during the resurvey								
	tap		tubewell		well		tank	river	total
	private	public	private	public	private	public	private	public	
(1)	(2)	(3)	(4)	(5)	(6)	(7)	(8)	(9)	(10)
TAP PRIVATE	8								8
TAP PUBLIC	1	1		1					3
TUBEWELL PRIVATE		2	55	14					71
TUBEWELL PUBLIC	3	5	126	440	3	2			579
WELL PRIVATE		3	4	19	11	8			45
WELL PUBLIC	2	29	12	168	21	119			351
TANK PRIVATE				48	1				49
TANK PUBLIC		1	2	16	1	15	1		36
RIVER PUBLIC			1					1	2
OTHERS PRIVATE				1					1
OTHERS PUBLIC									
NOT KNOWN			4	4					8
TOTAL	14	41	204	711	37	144	1	1	1153

would miss roughly about 10 per cent of the original households or their fragments.[10]

Table IX shows, as expected, some improvement in the availability of safe drinking water. Thus, sources like tanks and rivers virtually disappeared over time and there was a shift from wells to tubewells, broadly speaking, and from public wells/ tubewells to private ones. Here, as in other two-way tables, some shifts in the opposite direction can be noticed. Such contrary movements were probably caused by the devastating flood of 1978. Splits of the original sample households did not explain most of these shifts.

Table X shows, in the main, a shift from kerosene to electricity as the source of lighting for a little over 5 per cent of the households.

TABLE X

Type of Domestic Lighting during NSS 28th round, Subrounds 1 and 3 (October-December 1973 and April-June 1974) and during the Resurvey (July 1985–March 1986)

Type of lighting: Original enquiry	No. of households by type of lighting: resurvey				
	No arrangement	Kerosene	Electricity	Bio-gas	Total
(1)	(2)	(3)	(4)	(5)	(6)
NO ARRANGEMENT		3	1		4
KEROSENE	1	1054	63	3	1121
ELECTRICITY		5	16		21
BIO–GAS		0			2
NOT KNOWN		7			7
TOTAL	1	1069	80	3	1153

[10] The sample design for the enquiry on housing conditions and hence of village facilities was a self–weighting one, so that unweighted counts, average, etc., constitute fully valid and final estimates. The design for the enquiry on consumer expenditure was not, however, self-weighting.

Table XI shows some rise in the percentage of pucca houses but a greater rise in the percentage of katcha houses over the period. The proportion of semi-pucca houses naturally went down appreciably. The increase in the proportion of katcha houses was mainly due to the severe flood of 1978 which particularly affected the districts of Burdwan and Birbhum.

TABLE XI

Type of Structure of Residential House during NSS 28th round, Subrounds 1 and 3 (October-December 1973 and April-June 1974) and during the Resurvey (July 1985-March 1986)*

	No. of sample households by type of structure				
	Katcha	Semi-pucca	Pucca	Type not known	Total
ORIGINAL ENQUIRY	813	228	105	7	1153
RESURVEY	895	116	136	6	1153

* For definition of the three categories of house structure, see subsection 2.2 above.

Table XII shows that on an average, during the last ten years, there had been a net addition to the stocks of a wide variety of consumer durables representing groups like furniture, utensils and various types of modern gadgets. A comparison of figures in columns 3 and 4 reveals that the net additions during the last ten years formed a sizeable fraction of the number possessed on the date of survey for items like radio/transistor, torch light, wrist watch, bicycle, folding umbrellas and also for stainless steel dining plates. Improvements for traditional items like bell-metal dining plates are found to be less impressive.

Table XIII shows the number of sample villages out of the 72 covered for the 'village schedule' reporting different types of facilities within 2 km from the village during the resurvey. It may be seen that there had been appreciable increase after 1975

TABLE XII

Possession on Date of Survey and Net Addition to Stock during the last ten years, for selected items of Consumer Durables, based on Resurvey of Households covered in NSS 28th round (Subrounds 1 and 3) enquiry on Housing Conditions

Item	Percentage of hhs reporting possession	Average no. possessed per hh.	Net number added per hh
(1)	(2)	(3)	(4)
BEDSTEAD	33.4	0.55	0.06
RADIO/TRANSISTOR	29.9	0.30	0.18
DINING PLATE			
BELL–METAL	50.8	2.12	0.06
STAINLESS STEEL	20.5	0.80	0.66
ALUMINIUM	88.0	4.72	1.31
BUCKET IRON	51.8	0.81	0.18
LANTERN	58.8	0.86	0.16
TORCH LIGHT	49.1	0.54	0.22
WRIST WATCH	31.7	0.43	0.25
BICYCLE	34.4	0.38	0.17
UMBRELLA FOLDING	10.7	0.14	0.06
UMBRELLA ORDINARY	41.2	0.56	0.18
MOSQUITO NET	54.1	1.08	0.32

in the proportion of villages with facilities like health–care institution, banks, manure shops and public libraries.

As regards domestic consumption standards, we provide two tables that present figures for per capita consumption in physical terms. Table XIV relates to the crucial indicator of the level of living in rural India, namely per capita consumption of cereal items (rice, wheat, etc.) in physical terms. Table XV covers a wide variety of items, namely food, beverages, tobacco and fuel groups of the household budget. Both tables point to stagnation in living standards so far as domestic consumption is concerned.

TABLE XIII

Number of Sample Villages (out of 72 surveyed) reporting different types of Facilities within 2 km during the Resurvey by Year of Establishment

| Type of facility | No. of villages reporting facility by year of establishment | | |
	before 1975	after 1975	total
(1)	(2)	(3)	(4)
PRIMARY SCHOOL	66	5	71
HEALTH CENTRE	5	3	8
HEALTH SUB-CENTRE	8	11	19
MATERNITY HOME	2	4	6
DOCTOR'S CHAMBER (ALLOPATH)	19	5	24
METALLED ROAD	34	7	41
BUS STOP	36	3	39
POST OFFICE	45	9	54
BANK	5	19	24
MANURE SHOP	17	15	32
CINEMA HALL	5	2	7
PUBLIC LIBRARY	25	12	37

The figures for sugar and gur (cane) in Table XV show some shift from *gur* (unrefined sugar) to sugar; and the consumption of tea seems to have gone up. But these improvements are of minor consequence.

To sum up, the resurvey yielded encouraging results in the sense that a comparative analysis of NSS data for the early seventies and the resurvey data for 1985–6 showed some improvement in living standards in those aspects where one expects to find some improvement, namely infrastructural facilities in the villages, some aspects of housing conditions, and stocks of consumer durables. In contrast, one finds stagnation in domestic consumption per capita, at least for food items, which

TABLE XIV

Average per capita Consumption of Cereals per 30 days in physical terms during July–June in Rural Areas by Districts

District	No. of sample households in resurvey	Average cereals consumption/person/30 days (kg)	
		NSS 27th round	Resurvey
(1)	(2)	(3)	(4)
BURDWAN	382	14.58	14.26
BIRBHUM	199	15.05	14.23
PURULIA	209	13.83	14.68
TOTAL	790	14.43	14.42

TABLE XV

Average per capita Physical Consumption of Selected Items per 30 days during July-June in Rural Areas of the three Districts

Item	Unit of quantity	Average per capita consumption/30 days	
		NSS 27th round 1972–73	Resurvey 1985–86
(1)	(2)	(3)	(4)
PULSES	kg	0.33	0.36
MILK	litre	0.93	1.65
EDIBLE OIL	kg	0.26	0.27
MEAT	kg	0.07	0.06
EGG	no.	0.50	0.31
FISH (FRESH)	kg	0.22	0.28
POTATO	kg	1.17	1.17

| Item | Unit of quantity | Average per capita consumption/30 days | |
		NSS 27th round 1972–73	Resurvey 1985–86
(1)	(2)	(3)	(4)
SUGAR	kg	0.17	0.32
GUR (CANE)	kg	0.33	0.13
TEA (CUPS)	no.	1.25	2.09
TEA (LEAF)	kg	0.02	0.02
COOKED MEAL	no	·0.47	0.39
BIRI	no.	60.82	49.23
KEROSENE	litre	0.49	0.43

has been the pattern for rural India ever since the NSS started its enquiries on consumer expenditure in the fifties. The improvements noticed are by no means dramatic—again as expected. That samples of about one thousand households (or of 72 villages) can reveal such moderate improvements should not be missed by sample survey statisticians and their opponents.

5. SUMMARY AND CONCLUSION

The survey of NSS results bearing on the level of living in rural India and the results of the resurvey reported in section 4 reveal several things:

(a) The relative stagnation over time in living standards is observed mainly for the component of domestic consumption. Significant improvements over time are discernible in other components of level of living, e.g. some aspects of housing conditions and availability/consumption of public goods (such as education and health services). Data on such components collected by the NSS and other agencies have been relatively unnoticed in comparison with the data on household consumption. The increasing availability of public goods has benefited even the poorer sections of the rural population.

(b) The sample-survey data on different aspects of the level of living are certainly open to serious doubts and criticisms. It is imperative to carry out intensive field studies as well as analytic studies to assess the reliability and validity of data collected by current approaches and to evolve more satisfactory data collection procedures, if necessary. Collaboration with anthropologists may prove to be highly beneficial for such studies.

(c) The available sample-survey data have not at all been exploited fully for analytic purposes. With the advent of computerization, it should be possible to utilize them properly for thorough statistical analyses through further cross-tabulations, regression analyses, etc. Attempts should also be made to publish more and more *disaggregated* results for small regions, selected socio-economic groups, etc.

(d) The NSS and other sample-survey organizations should adopt sampling designs where some or all of the sample households are revisited after a suitable number of years. Some technical problems will, no doubt, arise, but changes over time are likely to be better estimated with such designs than if completely independent samples of villages/households are drawn for different rounds of enquiry (i.e. years).

We refrain from reviewing the results of the micro studies. It appears that these are not really divergent from those of the macro approach (*vide* Bhattacharya, Chakravarti and Chattopadhyay, 1985). Many of them indicate little improvement over time, ŏr even a lowering of living standards for the poorer sections of the population (e.g. agricultural labourers—Etienne, 1982; Freeman, 1977); it is only for the richer sections that one finds increasing prosperity over time. Anyway, such studies can hardly replace the sample surveys in view of their limited geographical coverage and the purposive selection of villages.[11] They can, however, play a major role if one is interested in improving data collection and analysis by the sample-survey approach. Thus, they can provide useful data against which the

[11] Both Appadurai and Harriss (*vide* contributions to this volume) concede that the set of villages chosen by anthropologists might form a biased sample. There is also the suggestion—see also Jodha (this volume)—that the improvement in level of living noted by anthropologists occurred not so much in income/domestic consumption, but affected aspects like the use of new commodities or the extent of reliance on traditional patrons.

data collected in the field studies proposed in (b) above may be checked. More importantly, the anthropological studies may serve as pilot studies for planning the sample surveys, for designing the survey instruments and for suggesting interesting hypotheses and lines of analysis—*vide* (c) above—which may be tried out and tested with sample-survey data. In short, economic statisticians can profit greatly through collaboration with anthropologists following their traditional approach.

Anthropological studies like those reported in the present volume show that interesting and important aspects of the level of living are being missed by economic statisticians in their large-scale surveys. Thus, the paper by Wadley and Derr demonstrates the value of caste (=*jati*) as an analytical tool and depicts the erosion of the *jajmani* system over time. There is no doubt that the anthropologist can gain considerable insight into the trends and processes of social and economic change provided he 'sees correctly' and collects and utilizes solid statistical data on various characteristics of the population (*vide* Wadley and Derr, this volume).

The well-known study by Bardhan and Rudra (1978) shows how the scope of statistical surveys can be widened to cover linkages or relations and processes. Longitudinal studies based on the panel approach can investigate the dynamics of, say, the size distribution of landholdings. Even a one-shot enquiry can make an effort in the same direction, by say, collecting data on all land transfers that occurred during the past ten years. However, statistical surveys may not do very well for softer, not-easily quantifiable, items like those mentioned by Appadurai (this volume)—'the perception of security in livelihood, the sense of freedom from harassment . . . the feeling of dignity in day-to-day relations, etc.'—or those connected with intra-household relations. Anthropological studies are more appropriate for such aspects. They also help in interpreting the data collected from large-scale surveys.

REFERENCES

A. DOMESTIC CONSUMPTION

Ahluwalia, Montek S. 'Rural poverty and Agricultural Performance in India,' *Journal of Development Studies*, vol. 14, no. 3, pp. 298–323. 1978.

Bardhan, P. K. 'On the minimum level of living and the rural poor,' *Indian Economic Review*, 1970.

———, 'On the minimum level of living and the rural poor: A further note,' *Indian Economic Review*, April 1971.

———, 'On the incidence of poverty in rural India in the sixties,'. in Srinivasan, T. N. and Bardhan, P. K. (eds.). *Poverty and Income Distribution in India*, Statistical Publishing Society, Calcutta, 1974.

Bhattacharya, N., 'A study on consumer behaviour in India', in Iyengar, N. S. and Bhattacharya, N. (eds.), *A Survey of Research in Economics*, vol. 7, Allied Publishers, Bombay, pp. 170–232, 1978.

Bhattacharya, N. and Mahalanobis, B. 'Regional disparities in household consumption in India,' *Journal of American Statistical Association*, vol. 62, 1967.

Bhattacharya, N. and Chatterjee, G. S. 'On rural-urban differentials in consumer prices and per capita household consumption in India, by levels of living,' *Sankhyā*, series B, 33. 1971.

Bhattacharya, N., Coondoo, D., Maiti, P. and Mukherjee, R. *Relative Price of Food and the Rural Poor—The Case of India*, Economic Research Unit, Indian Statistical Institute, Calcutta (study sponsored by International Labour Office, Geneva). 1985.

Bhattacharya, N., Chattopadhyay, M., and Rudra, A. 'Changes in Level of Living in Rural West Bengal: Private Consumption,' *Economic and Political Weekly*, vol. 29, 11 July 1987a.

———, 'Changes in Level of Living in Rural West Bengal: Consumer Durables, Clothing and Footwear,' *Economic and Political Weekly*, vol. 29, 31 October 1987b.

———, 'Changes in Level of Living in Rural West Bengal:

Perceptions of the People,' *Economic and Political Weekly*, vol. 29, November, 1987c.

————, 'Changes in Level of Living in Rural West Bengal: Variations Across Socio-Economic Groups,' *Economic and Political Weekly*, vol. 30, 28 May 1988.

Bhatty, I. Z. 'Inequality and poverty in rural India,' in Srinivasan, T. N. and Bardhan, P. K. (eds.), *Poverty and Income Distribution in India*, Statistical Publishing Society, Calcutta 1974.

Chatterjee, G. S. and Bhattacharya, N. 'Some observations on NSS household budget data,' in Dandekar, V. M. and Venkataramaiah, P. (eds), *Data Base of Indian Economy*, vol. II Statistical Publishing Society, Calcutta 1974a.

————, 'On disparities in per capita household consumption in India', in Srinivasan, T. N. and Bardhan, P. K. (eds.), *Poverty and Income Distribution in India*, Statistical Publishing Society, Calcutta 1974b.

Chatterjee, G. S., Sarkar, D. and Paul, G. 'A preliminary study on the dietary levels of households in rural India.' in Srinivasan, T. N. and Bardhan, P. K. (eds.), *Poverty and Income Distribution in India*, Statistical Publishing Society, Calcutta 1974.

Dandekar, V. M. and Rath, N. *Poverty in India*, Indian School of Political Economy, Pune 1971.

Iyengar, N. S. 'A study of differential prices movements and consumer behaviour,' *Indian Economic Review*, October 1967.

Iyengar, N. S. and Bhattacharya, N. 'On the effect of differentials in consumer price index on measure of inequality,' *Sankhyā*, series B 1965.

Iyengar, N. S. and Mukherjee, M. 'A note on the derivation of income distribution from a given distribution of consumer expenditure,' paper presented to the Second Econometric Conference 1961.

Kansal, S. M. 'Structural changes in consumption expenditure in India, 1950–51 to 1965–66,' paper presented at 6th Conference of the Indian Association for Research in National Income and Wealth 1968.

Mahalanobis, P. C. 'A preliminary note on the consumption of cereals in India,' *Bull. Int. Stat. Inst.*, part 4, 1962.

Minhas, B. S., 'Rural poverty, land distribution and development,' *Indian Economic Review*, April 1970.

———, 'Rural poverty and minimum level of living: A reply,' *Indian Economic Review*, April 1971.

Mukherjee, M. 'Size and areal distributions of the level of living in India,' *Sankhyā*, series B 3, parts 3 and 4, 1969.

Mukherjee, M. and Saha, S. 'Reliability of National Income and Allied Estimates,' *Journal of Income and Wealth*, vol. 5, no. 2, 1981.

Mukherjee M. and Chatterjee, G. S. 'On the validity of NSS estimates of consumption expenditure,' *Artha Vijnana*, June 1972.

Oja, P. D. 'A configuration of Indian poverty: Inequality and levels of living,' *Reserve Bank of India Bulletin*, January 1970.

———, 'Pattern of Income Distribution in India: 1953–55 to 1963–65,' in Srinivasan, T. N. and Bardhan, P. K. (eds.), *Poverty and Income Distribution in India*, Statistical Publishing Society, Calcutta 1974.

Radhakrishnan, P. N., Srinivasan, T. N. and Vaidyanathan, A. 'Data on distribution of consumption expenditure: An evaluation,' in Srinivasan, T. N. and Bardhan, P. K. (eds.), *Poverty and Income Distribution in India*, Statistical Publishing Society, Calcutta 1974.

Rao, V. K. R. V. *Food, Nutrition and Poverty in India*, Vikas Publishing House Pvt. Ltd., New Delhi 1982.

Rudra, Ashok 'Savings, investment and consumption,' in Rao, C. R. (ed.), *Data Base of the Indian Economy*, vol. 1, Statistical Publishing Society, Calcutta 1972.

Rudra, A. 'Minimum level of living—statistical examination,' in Srinivasan, T. N. and Bardhan, P. K. (eds.) *Poverty and Income Distribution in India*, Statistical Publishing Society, Calcutta 1974.

Sen, A. K., 'Poverty, inequality and unemployment,' *Economic and Political Weekly*, Special number, August 1973.

Sukhatme, P. V., *Feeding India's Growing Millions*, Asia Publishing· House, Bombay 1965.

———, *Nutrition and Poverty*, Lal Bahadur Shastri Memorial Lecture, Indian Council of Agricultural Research, New Delhi 1977.

Sundaram, K. and Tendulkar, S. D. 'Towards an explanation of inter-regional variation in poverty and unemployment in rural India,' Working Paper No. 237, Delhi School of Economics 1983.

Vaidyanathan, A., 'Some aspects of inequalities in living standards in rural India,' in Srinivasan, T. N. and Bardhan, P. K. (eds.), *Poverty and Income Distribution in India*, Statistical Publishing Society, Calcutta 1974.

Visaria, P., 'Poverty and living standards in Asia,' *Population and Development Review*, vol. 6, no. 2, 1980.

B. HOUSING CONDITIONS

ICSSR (Indian Council of Social Science Research) and CSO (Central Statistical Organization). *Social Information of India: Trends and Structure*, Hindustan Publishing Corporation, Delhi 1983.

Kumar, K., 'An appraisal of housing statistics,' in Dandekar, V. M. and Venkataramaiah, P. (eds.), *Data Base of Indian Economy*, vol. II, Statistical Publishing Society, Calcutta, 1974.

Bhattacharya, N., Chattopadhyay, M. and Rudra, A. 'Changes in Level of Living in Rural West Bengal: Housing Conditions,' *Economic and Political Weekly*, vol. 29, 5–12, 1987.

C. CONSUMPTION OF PUBLIC GOODS

Bhattacharya, N. and Dey, B. 'Distribution of public health and education services,' *Economic Weekly*, 5 June 1965.

Bhattacharya, N., Chattopadhyay, M. and Rudra, A. 'Changes in Level of Living in Rural West Bengal: Social Consumption,' *Economic and Political Weekly*, vol. 29, 15 August 1987.

Maitra, T., Dey, B. and Bhattacharya, N. 'An enquiry on the distribution of public education and health services in West Bengal,' in Srinivasan, T. N. and Bardhan, P. K. (eds.), *Poverty and Income Distribution in India*, Statistical Publishing Society, Calcutta 1974.

Maitra, T., *Public Services, in India: An Analysis of Their Consumption in West Bengal*, Mittal Publication, Delhi 1985.

Reddy, K. K., 'The distribution of the benefits of public expenditure: significance, conceptual and empirical framework,' *The Journal of Income and Wealth*, vol. 4, no. 2 1980.

D. MORTALITY

Das, N. C. and Bhattacharya, N. 'National Sample Survey—An appraisal of demographic data,' in Bose, A., Gupta, D. B. and Raychaudhuri, G. (eds.), *Data Base of Indian Economy, Vol. III, Population Statistics in India*, Vikas Publishing House Pvt. Ltd., New Delhi 1977.

Das, Nitai Chandra 'A note on the NSS—enquiries to estimate vital rates,' *Sankhyā*, 38, series C, pts 1 and 3, pp. 155–76, 1981.

Mazumdar, M., 'Estimation of vital rates in the Indian National Sample Survey,' *World Population Conference*, Belgrade, 1965.

Som, R. K., *Recall Lapse in Demographic Enquiries*, United Nations Economic Commission for Africa, Ethiopia 1966.

E. MICRO STUDIES

Aggarwal, P. C. *The Green Revolution and Rural Labour: A Study in Ludhiana*, New India Press, New Delhi 1973.

Chattopadhyay, M. *Mahalanobis Survey Revisited: Prospects of Agrarian Change in West Bengal*, Indo Overseas Publications, Calcutta 1982.

Danda, A. K. and Danda, D. G. *Development and Change in Basudha: A West Bengal Village*, National Institute of Community Development, Hyderabad.

Epstein, T. S. *South India: Yesterday, Today, Tomorrow: Mysore*

Villages Revisited, The Macmillan Press Pvt. Ltd., London 1973.

Etienne, G. *India's Changing Rural Scene: 1963–73*, Oxford University Press, Delhi 1982.

Freeman, J. M. *Scarcity and Opportunity in an Indian Village*, Cummings Publishing Co. 1977.

Hill P. *Dry Grain Farming Families: Hausaland (Nigeria) and Karnataka (India) Compared*, Cambridge University Press, Cambridge 1982.

Mukherjee, R. *Six Villages of Bengal*, Popular Prakashan, Bombay 1971.

Srinivas, M. N. *The Remembered Village*, Oxford University Press, New Delhi 1976.

F. GENERAL

Bardhan, P. and Rudra, A. 'Interlinkage of Land, Labour and Credit Relations: An Analysis of Village Survey Data in East India,' *Economic and Political Weekly*, February 1978.

Bhattacharya, N., Chakravarti, P. and Chattopadhyay, M. 'Time Trends in Level of Living in Rural India—A Critical Survey of Literature,' Paper presented to a Workshop on *Rural Economic Change in South Asia: Differences in Approach and in Results between Large-Scale Surveys and Intensive Micro Studies*, organised by Social Science Research Council, New York, at Bangalore, during 5–8 August 1985.

Leach, E. R., 'An Anthropologist's Reflections on a Social Survey,' in Jongman, D. G. and Gutkind, P. C. W. (eds.), *Anthropologists in the Field*, Van Goreum, 1967.

Mukherjee, M., 'Statistical Information on Final Consumption in India and the National Sample Survey,' *Economic and Political Weekly*, vol. 21, no 5, 1 February, pp. 206–9. 1986.

Srinivas, M. N., Shah, A. M. and Ramaswamy, E. A. *The Fieldworker and the Field: Problems and Challenges in Sociological Investigation*, Oxford University Press, 1979.

Vaidyanathan, A., 'On the Validity of NSS Consumption Data,' *Economic and Political Weekly*, vol. 21, no. 3, 18 January 1986.

Chapter 4: Karimpur 1925–1984: Understanding Rural India Through Restudies

SUSAN S. WADLEY and BRUCE W. DERR

> But the condition of our [Brahman] people was better [in 1925]. Now the village people are not so good. . . . But theirs [other castes] was bad, their condition has improved. Only ours has become worse.
>
> —Brahman headman, Karimpur,
> 10 December 1985[1]

In 1925 Karimpur, a village in western Uttar Pradesh, was owned by absentee zamindars and effectively controlled by the

[1] This interview was conducted and transcribed by our research assistant, Umesh Chandra Pandey, who willingly and graciously asked further questions upon receiving our queries from the US. Research in 1983–4 was conducted by Bruce W. Derr and Susan S. Wadley with funding from the Smithsonian Institution and the US Department of Education. They were assisted by Monisha Behal, Umesh Chandra Pandey, Nanhe Khan, Ant Ram Batham, Ambika and Rajani Pandey. Three earlier research endeavours also contribute to this paper. William and Charlotte Wiser worked in Karimpur from 1925 to 1930 and their records and writings from that period provide a significant baseline for the later work in Karimpur. Susan S. Wadley did doctoral dissertation research in Karimpur in 1967–9 with funding from the National Science Foundation. Finally , Bruce W. Derr and Susan S. Wadley worked in Karimpur in 1974–5 with funding from the American Institute of Indian Studies. We wish to thank all these agencies and individuals for their support of our efforts to understand various facets of Karimpur lives. We would also like to express our gratitude to the villagers of Karimpur, who have so graciously assisted us in our attempts to understand their ways of life.

Brahman caste, which had primary tenancy rights to 74 per cent of the land. Moreover, the *jajmani* system—defining patron (*jajman*)–client (*kamin*) ties between service castes and landowners—was a significant feature of Karimpur life. Few men (or women) worked out of the village, and most villagers were tied both to agriculture and the Brahman landlords for survival. The village school had only first and second classes, no one had ever attained a college diploma, not a single brick house existed, all water had to be drawn from open wells, and electricity was still far in the future. Trucks, tractors, motorcycles and even bicycles were not owned by villagers, nor were there radios, tape-recorders or watches. Local *hakims* (traditional *ayurvedic* practitioners) treated illnesses, the Dhanuk caste provided midwives, and early deaths were common for both men and women.

By 1984 there is schooling through to class eight in the village, several men have MAs, and (even) a daughter is finishing her BA. A large number of houses have at least one brick room, while many are all brick. The wealthier families generally have a handpump or well in their courtyard, and five houses and the co-operative bank and seed store have electrical connections. One villager owns a truck, another a tractor and a third a motorcycle. There are many bicycles and watches, a few radios, a rare tape-recorder (but as yet no TV or video recorder). A private 'doctor' resides in the village, as does a government appointed compounder. A maternity clinic is nominally open and a government midwife available on call. People are living longer and child-mortality rates are down significantly.

Despite these manifest material changes, to the Brahmans of Karimpur these differences over the past sixty years are viewed as bad. Following zamindari abolition, land ceilings, and land consolidation, the Brahmans own only 58.1 per cent of the land; they regularly employ only a few kamins; and they see both their sons and the men of the traditional service-providing castes looking elsewhere for employment. With the decline in agricultural employment and jajmani relationships, the Brahmans now perceive their economic and political control of the village as being eroded. They see their condition as having worsened, while that of the 'other' castes is perceived as having disproportionately improved. This opinion from the Brahmans, as stated here by the elected village headman—himself a Brahman and a manifest symbol of Brahman political control—is in marked contrast to other studies of South Asian communities which suggest that the wealthier peasants have benefited from the Green Revolution and other structural changes, while the poor have become 'poorer' (see Freeman 1977, Van Schendel 1984, Etienne 1982). We must ask whether the old rich in Karimpur are in fact worse off than before, and if so by what criteria. Further, we must seek the factors that lead them, despite better material living conditions, to perceive their lot as worse. More importantly, we must attempt to discover if the old poor are in fact better off in the 1980s then before. These questions can only be answered through a detailed study of Karimpur life in the period 1925 to 1984.

Fortunately, the materials for such a study exist. Karimpur, best known as the village 'behind mud walls' described by William and Charlotte Wiser in their 1930 classic, has been more thoroughly researched over time than almost any other community in India. As such, we have an opportunity to examine the merits of doing re-studies of small local communities for the purpose of comprehending socio-economic change in rural India.

THE METHODOLOGY RESTUDIES

The term restudies is used generally to refer to anthropological micro studies over a period of time, or at two (or more) points in time.[2] It should.be noted that economists and others, such as T. Scarlett Epstein (1973, 1979), use the anthropological approach of an intensive micro study of a small community from a different disciplinary perspective. By reflecting the anthropological bias of a small community study, the restudy does not lend itself to large-scale generalizations, but it can provide insight into the trends and processes of social change as manifested in one limited locale.

[2] This term should be distinguished from resurveys, a very different approach conceptually and analytically. See Campbell (1984) and Wadley (1986) for discussions of survey versus intensive field studies in the South Asian context.

In many respects the scholar doing a restudy is using the methodology of the historian, except that instead of having to reconstruct a prior situation, at least some detailed statistical and, more critically, qualitative baseline data are available.[3] Furthermore, the true long-term study, with repeated field trips over a period of time, allows the researcher to see what actually happens at different points in time. To the extent that the anthropological fieldworker 'sees' correctly, itself a major methodological issue, considerable insight into the processes of change is possible.

Restudies are not without problems. While representing an effective methodology for micro-level studies of socioeconomic change, a restudy is only as good as its initial as well as follow-up data. Willem Van Schendel, in his restudies of three communities in Bangladesh, was unable to gain access to the original field notes relating to two communities and had to rely on published data. Unfortunately, the questions asked by one scholar at one point in time are not often those asked by a second scholar later. Hence, reliance on published materials is often frustrating. Van Schendel, for example, had difficulty finding published materials that provided household-level data (1984: 25).

A second problem which commonly faces the scholar doing a restudy is the often limited amount of field time for the second trip. While there are several long-term studies being conducted in Africa and South America (see Lee 1979, Scudder and Colson 1979, Vogt 1979), this has not been the case in South Asia, perhaps because of the distances involved. Two of the major studies where the fieldwork was conducted by the same scholar at two points in time (thus far in print) for South Asia are both based on brief second trips—Epstein (1973) for five weeks to her Mysore villages, and Leaf (1984) for eight weeks to his Punjab community. Two more recent longer-term village restudies are those conducted in 1983–4 by Ullrich and Harper in Totagadde, and by Mahar and Kolenda in Khalapur: as yet, however, only preliminary analyses have been reported in conference papers (Harper 1984, Kolenda 1984, Mahar 1984, Ullrich 1984). More senior scholars, committed to academic institutions abroad and

[3] The classic village study by a historian is Kessinger 1974.

to new research projects, often find it difficult to relocate families and selves to remote rural areas for extended periods of time. One result is that some restudies are done by other younger scholars (see Das Gupta 1977).

There is no doubt that the restudy is strongly affected by the research interests and personalities of the scholars involved. For a single scholar, theoretical interests vary over time, perhaps shifting from a focus on behavioural issues to symbolic systems. These shifting interests can lead to serious methodological problems as adequate baseline data for issues such as health care may not be available when, for example, the original scholar was studying caste relationships. When a different scholar is doing the restudy, the issue of shifting theoretical interests remains, compounded by a different personality, approach and outlook, and the differing reactions of the subjects to the investigator. The differences that Redfield (1930) and Lewis (1951) found in the Mexican village of Tepoztlan highlight this issue.

Even when a sole researcher does his/her own restudy, 'personality' is changed when the young graduate student returns as a mature scholar, possibly accompanied by family. While the return may be joyous (see e.g. Epstein 1979: 217 and Leaf 1984: 10–15), and rapport rapidly regained—so that research can commence almost immediately—the 'person' is not the same and the community is well aware of the changed status. These changed statuses often redefine friendships and alliances, potentially altering one's view of a community. Some of these handicaps can be overcome if the individuals writing about restudies are explicit about their own field situations and theoretical orientations as contrasted to those of previous scholars, including themselves at earlier times.

Given these issues, what makes a restudy successful? Most essential is a set of core baseline data, with comparable data from later points in time. Foster *et al.,* in their discussion of long-term research, suggest a set of minimum core data, including

maps, vital statistics, census material (including marital and parental status, social and residential units of affiliation, occupations, education, and religion); resource base (minimal descriptive data on ecological and economic categories); and sociopolitical differentiation. . . . Generally we felt that solid, factual data of earlier years, whether garnered by the current researcher or a predecessor, have proven to be more valuable than the theoretical interests of the person who gathered them (1979: 333).

It is this 'solid factual data' left by the Wisers and augmented at several points in time by us that allows a restudy of Karimpur. Censuses, land records, and accounts of the number of families tied in whatever manner to jajmani provide the core data around which a restudy of Karimpur can be built.

Restudying Karimpur

In 1925, after a half dozen years in India as a teacher in the agricultural college in Allahabad, William Wiser sought permission from the Presbyterian mission to do a survey of a farming community in order to better understand the agricultural conditions and life-styles facing his students. With his family, he pitched tents in a mango grove near the village later called Karimpur.[4] The survey turned into a detailed study of Indian village life, extending over six camping seasons from 1925 to 1930 and culminating in four manuscripts: *Behind Mud Walls*, first published in 1930; 'Social Institutions of a Hindu Village in North India,' a doctoral dissertation in rural sociology submitted to Cornell University in 1933; *The Hindu Jajmani System*, 1936, and, by Charlotte Wiser, *The Foods of an Indian Village*, published in Allahabad in 1936. These works form the core of published baseline materials on Karimpur for 1925–30.

After working for thirty years in India Village Service in Etah district to the north, the Wisers decided to retire to Karimpur. As their house neared completion, William became seriously ill and saw it only once. Later Charlotte returned, and, living in Karimpur periodically from 1962 to 1971, continued to investigate and write about village lives. Her publications from this period include two new chapters to *Behind Mud Walls* (1960, 1971) and the monograph *Four Families of Karimpur* (1978). Her

---

[4] Karimpur as studied here is not coterminous with the revenue village of which it is the administrative centre. The studied village is composed of three hamlets, all understood by their inhabitants to constitute the village 'Karimpur'. These understood boundaries are demonstrated both ritually and behaviourally.

notes and tapes from this period appear to be missing, but a partial census from 1964 exists.

After gaining access to the Wiser Collection of Oral Traditions, Susan S. Wadley, then a student at the University of Chicago, began to do fieldwork on oral traditions in Karimpur in 1967. Wadley worked in Karimpur from December 1967 to March 1969, focusing primarily on oral traditions as keys to Karimpur belief-systems concerning religion. She also collected basic core data, including a household census, land records and maps, and data on jajmani relationships. Her notes provide further information on politics and agriculture.

In 1974–5, Bruce W. Derr went to Karimpur to do research on agriculture and socio-economic change. This work was specifically to be a restudy of land tenure patterns, but difficulty with access to land records transformed it into a study of farming practices and reactions to agricultural change and population growth. He focused on detailed interviews with selected farmers, in addition to collecting a new census, production figures, etc. His findings are reported in 'The growing Abundance of Food and Poverty in a North Indian Village: Karimpur 1925–1975,' a doctoral dissertation submitted to Syracuse University, as well as numerous papers.

Finally, in 1983–4, Derr and Wadley returned to Karimpur to do a study of social change, focusing on men's and women's life histories. In addition to life history materials from a variety of villagers, they did a complete village census, collected retrospective fertility histories from all women who were ever married, updated Wadley's collection of oral traditions, did time studies of men and women's work, and obtained land records and maps for twelve points in time between 1940 and 1984.

Each of these field trips took place under vastly different circumstances. William and Charlotte Wiser were Christian missionaries studying Karimpur during the British raj. They chose Karimpur because the Mainpuri church had contact with Christians there. They lived in tents outside the village, and had a car and access to government officials. Both Wisers spoke careful standard Hindi, but neither read Devanagari. They were assisted by a clerk, who did some transcriptions from Devanagari to Roman script, and some translations. Their yearly census was done in three days every December with the help of village boys. It is probable that, except for the Bhangis who were Christians at that time, they had little contact with other low castes: their main informants were members of the Brahman caste groups.

In contrast to the Wisers' Christian mission presence and, by 1967, Charlotte's elderly presence, Wadley went to Karimpur as a twenty-four-year-old graduate student. She was thought by most villagers (despite endless denials) to be (a) 16 years old, and (b) Charlotte's granddaughter.[5] Wadley worked alone, seldom using an interpreter and gaining some mastery of the village dialect, though some women and most fights are beyond her comprehension even today. Her census was collected through personal visits to every house over the period of research. Like Charlotte, she lived with a Brahman family, a fact which sometimes proved to be a detriment to her work.

In 1974–5, Wadley and Derr returned to Karimpur as a married couple, providing a status not present earlier. Their residence remained the old Wiser house and its Brahman inhabitants. Derr, with good comprehension of Standard Hindi but less speaking ability, used interpreters (either a Brahman or a Muslim male) for much of his work. Derr's census was collected primarily through group discussions with men in the various neighbourhoods of the village.

The 1983–4 trip was dramatically different. Returning with their two daughters, an American tutor, a research assistant from Delhi, their old cook, and a car with driver, Wadley and Derr took rooms in Mainpuri and commuted to the village daily, spending nights there for festivals, weddings or other events. When in Karimpur, the old Wiser house, now rebuilt with their help, served as their headquarters. Derr worked with the same interpreters, using his Muslim colleague for all low-caste interviews. Wadley generally worked alone, using one of the other assistants when necessary. The census was collected immediately upon arrival in the field, through visits

[5] The individual persons of Charlotte and Susan are now combined in the folklore of the region, so that now people tell the story of a '*rani sahib*' who comes periodically to the village of Karimpur to help people there. We heard the story only after the SSP's wife in Mainpuri heard it from one of her servants and had him repeat it to us!

to every house, and was corrected and updated throughout the year.

Aside from the differences in age, status, personality and 'role' (missionary, graduate student, faculty), all the research endeavours in Karimpur have had markedly different theoretical bases. Wiser wrote one of the first dissertations on village India—and on peasants—in the US. (*Behind Mud Walls* was published the same year as Redfield's first Mexican work.) His writings reflect the textual bias of Indian scholarship in the 1920s. *The Hindu Jajmani System* provides an interpretation of patron-client relationships in twentieth-century rural India based on the *Laws of Manu*. While there is surely continuity over the 1800-year period between Manu and Karimpur of the 1920s, most scholars today find it a curious interpretation of a politically and economically exploitative system. Fortunately, as in all good scholarship, Wiser's theoretical bias did not mask his detailed charts and descriptions of the economic transactions occurring in jajmani. It is this rich statistical and descriptive data that facilitates a restudy.

Wadley's work from 1967 until recently has all focused on symbolic aspects of Indian society, including women's ritual, song and epic. It is Wadley's 1968 census and materials on jajmani, land and politics that are most critical to the current endeavour.

Derr's work in 1974–5 is most allied to Wiser's initial description of Karimpur social life, although from a vastly different orientation. Derr's planned study of the devolution of land among families turned into an exegesis on the social organization of agriculture and the initial response of that system to the elements of the Green Revolution that were just taking hold. He sought to explain the observed situation of a growing abundance of food coexisting with a growing abundance of hunger and poverty in the village. He also viewed traditional agricultural practices as essentially rational, a perspective just gaining strength in social science writings (see Nair 1979). Much of the research highlighted the tensions that existed in the village between the wealthy landowners (mostly Brahman) and the less privileged sharecroppers and landless.

Wadley and Derr's work in 1983–4 was most profoundly influenced by their experiences in the field of women's studies

during the years between field trips. It was this experience that
lead to the focus on life histories as an avenue of investigating
social change. The concerns of feminist anthropology to
understand the disadvantaged, whether male or female, as well
as the politically dominant and economically powerful were
congruent with their feelings of how the research should be
carried out. We felt that life histories would be a method of
capturing the voices of those not usually heard, especially
women and lower-caste men. This attitude was found to be in
explicit contrast to the style of research William Wiser evinced
in his exploration of the working of the *jajmani* system, which
not only shows a textual reliance on Brahmanical texts for
interpretation but also reliance on Karimpur Brahmans as his
main source of ethnographic data. Despite this different
theoretical perspective, we recognized the value of replicating as
much of the Wiser's core data as possible, and did so.

Given these points of similarity and difference among various
scholars and their field situations in Karimpur, is there any
comparability? Fortunately, yes. The following types of data
exist for all Karimpur research periods: population and demographic information on sex, age, education, marital status, place
of birth, household composition and family type; land records
(*khasra* and *khatauni*) and maps; house types and size; occupational information for village men; jajmani ties and interfamily
relationships. In addition, complete animal censuses were
collected in 1929, 1975, and 1984; data on material possessions
were collected in 1968 and 1984, and less reliably and completely
in 1925–30 and 1975. Agricultural practices and implements
were thoroughly surveyed in 1975 and 1984, irregularly in 1968,
and no data exist (that we are aware of) on this topic from the
Wiser period.

Some problems in comparability exist. The Wiser censuses
report all persons in the village on the day of the census,
including visitors. Any permanent resident not present on the
day of census was reported as absent and was not included in the
total population figures. We have not attempted to correct the
Wiser data, although it is possible because of the yearly nature of
the records.

A major problem remains: Karimpur reporting of ages, either
of currently living persons or of the dead, reflects an all-India

bias towards inaccuracy, as the current 'real' age of persons is simply not an important concern in village life. For example, women's ages are reported as 15, 20, 25, 30, 40, 50 or 'very old, probably ninety'. These biases towards ages ending in 5 or 0 are apparent in all the census done in Karimpur, from the 1920s to the 1980s. Unless other evidence was available, we used the age of first census as the basis for the person's age for all further censuses. Fortunately, many men were born during the Wiser's period of residence in the 1920s, so that we have a more accurate fix on older ages than would otherwise be possible. Wives' ages were adjusted to fit husbands,' depending on their reported age differences at marriage. But no age data given for Karimpur should be taken as 'accurate' by western standards.

Wadley's data from 1968 notes kamins for each family, but contains little data on the strength of those ties. In contrast, we know the extent of kamin–jajman ties in 1984, but not the specifics of each family's patrons and clients.

Fortunately Wiser used a definition of family still currently in use: that a family is based on the sharing of a cooking hearth and food supplies. Karimpur residents recognize separation of a joint family by the term *nyare*. If they considered a family nyare, so did we, even if some joint property, such as land and tools, remained undivided. In most cases, ritual separation did not occur for many years after the physical separation of foodstuffs and cooking areas (see Wadley and Derr, forthcoming).

Occupational data for men is reliable across time, but that for women is not, prior to 1984. Wadley, Derr and Wiser paid little attention to women's work prior to the 1984 trip, although all noted female household heads who worked as labourers. None of these materials contain detailed income or consumption data, or information on days worked (over whatever period of time).[6]

Given these larger methodological issues and problems, let us now examine some aspects of socio-economic change in Karimpur to gain further insight into the restudy methodology and its problems.

[6] Wiser in *The Hindu Jajmani System* provides information that indicates that such records were kept for at least some workers, but these are lost (see 1936: 43).

KARIMPUR 1925–84

It is the economic fabric of Karimpur bound up in the 1920s in the jajmani system and agriculture that has most altered over time. By 1984, jajmani functioned only for a few services, outside of ritual activities. And whereas every Karimpur family in 1925 lived by agriculture, either directly or through jajmani relationships to landowners, by the 1980s 30 per cent of the families received their primary income from non-agricultural occupations. Finally, the distribution of land shifted from 74.3 per cent controlled by Brahmans in 1925 to only 58.1 per cent in Brahman control in 1984. Meanwhile the village population had exploded: in 1925 Karimpur had 754 individuals living in 161 family units. By 1984 there were 2047 individuals in 327 families (see Table I).[7] Attempts to understand these issues of change lead, however, to serious methodological problems of comparison.

Methodological Issues of Comparison

First, it is necessary to note that all families living in the village at each time period were studied. There was minimal out-migration, and none among the landowning families. In the late 1970s one Brahman landlord/schoolteacher moved part of his family to Mainpuri, but spent several days a week in Karimpur and considered running for headman in 1988. Most poor people take jobs in urban areas, leaving their wives and children in Karimpur.

In attempting to document shifts in land-distribution patterns, occupation, and population, particularly as they contribute to the headman's earlier claim of the disproportionate Brahman loss over time, it is necessary to examine relative economic status. Looking at economic status took us immediately to the issue of caste as an analytic tool for status designation. As is common in older studies of Indian villages,

[7] The village identified as Karimpur, both ritually, socially and economically by its residents and hence by those studying it, is not coterminus with the British Revenue village used for the census. The revenue village includes five other locally-conceived distinct villages. Hence no direct comparison to census data is possible.

TABLE I
Population and Family: 1925, 1968, 1975, 1984

Caste	Total Population				Total Families			
	1925	1968	1975	1984	1925	1968	1975	1984
BANYA (Shopkeeper)	14	19	24	38	3	2	4	5
BARHAI (Carpenter)	42	57	64	76	8	8	10	11
BHANGI (Sweeper)	35	89	109	118	8	14	18	19
BHURJI (Grain Parcher)	10	18	22	29	1	4	4	4
BRAHMAN (Priest)	188	332	384	443	41	43	51	62
CHAMAR (Leatherworker)	29	80	87	96	8	13	15	16
DARZI (Tailor)	21	15	21	28	5	3	3	4
DHANUK (Midwife; Mat Maker)	28	105	116	167	7	17	20	30

DHOBI (Washerperson)	6	15	12	9	1	3	2	3
DHUNA (Cotton Carder)	9	25	31	38	1	5	5	5
FAQIR (Beggar)	22	46	66	71	8	12	13	13
GARARIYA (Shepherd)	26	78	85	107	6	17	19	20
KACCHI (Vegetable Grower)	152	284	348	415	26	46	48	59
KAHAR (Watercarrier)	83	191	195	236	19	35	38	45
KAYASTHA (Accountant)	6	31	33	25	1	2	4	3
KUMHAR (Potter)	9	10	11	10	3	3	3	3
LODHI (Rice Grower)·	6	17	22	14	1	3	3	2
MALI (Gardener)	17	19	29	20	1	3	4	3
MANIHAR (Bangle Seller)	10	12	16	24	2	3	3	5
NAI (Barber)	2	—	—	—	1	—	—	—

TABLE I (Contd.)

Caste	Total Population				Total Families			
	1925	1968	1975	1984	1925	1968	1975	1984
NAT (Entertainer)	–	–	6	7	–	–	1	1
RAY (Bard)	15	14	13	16	2	2	2	2
SUNAR (Goldsmith)	11	8	10	–	2	2	2	–
TAWAIF (Dancing Girl)	3	–	–	–	2	–	–	–
TELI (Oil Presser)	10	39	44	55	4	6	9	11
THAKUR (Farmer)	–	–	5	6	–	–	1	1
Totals	754	1504	1753	2048	161	246	282	327

caste served as the analytic base for economic groupings in both the Wisers' and Derr's early work. In the past, caste was strongly correlated with land tenancy, the major source of income, and, with jajmani relationships, a subsidiary source of income. But this is no longer true, and was not true for all families even in 1925.

Jati (caste) designates an individual's birth group, marking him or her as a certain kind of individual with given physical and moral characteristics (see Marriott and Inden 1974). Jati has also been associated with the 'traditional' occupation of that group, whether or not members of a given jati do in fact practice that occupation. Finally, the jatis in a given community are ranked by the community, these rankings being manifested in food and other transactions.

There were 24 Karimpur jatis in the 1920s, 20 Hindu and 4 Muslim. All families in 18 of these jatis were practising the traditional occupation, while as few as 7 per cent of families in the other 6 jatis were following the traditional occupation. Overall 49 per cent (80 of 161) of Karimpur families in 1925 followed their traditional occupation for some portion of their income. By 1984, only 3 jatis had all families practising the traditional occupation as their major source of subsistence.[8]

Closely tied to the concept of caste and traditional occupation is the economic system called 'the Hindu Jajmani system' by Wiser.

These service relationships reveal that the priest, bard, accountant, goldsmith, florist, vegetable grower, etc., etc., are served by all of the other castes. They are the jajmans of these other castes. In turn each of these castes has a form of service to perform for the others. In this manner the various castes of a Hindu village in North India are interrelated in a service capacity. Each serves the others. Each in turn is master. Each in turn is servant: Each has his own clientele comprising members of different castes which is his 'jajmani' or '*birt*'. This system of interrelatedness in service within the Hindu community is called the Hindu 'Jajmani system' (Wiser 1936: xxi).

Those individuals who serve others are called kamins or *kam karne wale*. Their patrons are jajmans.

In the 1920s, 32 of 161 Karimpur families (19.9 per cent)

[8] These jatis are Dhobi, Nat and Kumhar.

derived the bulk of their income from jajmani ties (Wiser 1936 : 120–1). The other families in Karimpur were, however, used as kamins for some services. Ultimately, every family in the village was tied into the system either as a kamin or jajman, if not both. The benefits of being a kamin were many. Wiser lists these:

In return for the various services rendered, there are payments in cash and in kind made daily, monthly, bi-yearly, per piece of work, and on special occasions, depending on the type of service rendered and in part on the goodwill of the jajman. The strength of the system depends, however, not on the actual payments made but on the concessions granted to the different occupational groups. These may be listed as:

a.   Free residence site
b.   Free food for family
c.   Free clothing
d.   Free food for animals
e.   Free timber
f.   Free dung
g.   Rent-free land
h.   Credit facilities
i.   Opportunities for supplementary employment
j.   Free use of tools, implements and draft animals
k.   Free use of raw materials
l.   Free hides
m.   Free funeral pyre plot
n.   Casual leave
o.   Aid in litigation
p.   Variety in diet
q.   Healthful location

(Wiser 1936: xxiv)

Despite these benefits, most families who were primarily kamins were poor: Wiser got a prosperous Brahman man to rate the economic standing of every family actively involved in jajmani relationships as a kamin: 16 of the 80 kamin families enjoyed a good economic status, 11 had a fair economic status and 51 had a poor economic status.[9] No information on the economic status of families independent of jajmani is offered.

[9] The figures given by Wiser in the table on page 118–19 of *Hindu Jajmani System* do not always match each other. We have used the totals achieved by adding the figures in the columns.

Jati in the 1920s was largely correlated with traditional occupations and (discounting the Brahman landlords and the Kacchi farmers [the primary *jajmans*]), only 16 Karimpur families derived their main income outside jajmani. But despite the close linkage between jati membership and occupation, and hence jajmani relationships, we still do not know the extent to which jati relationship and economic status are correlated.

If jati in the 1920s was correlated with occupation, and hence to jajmani relationships, was it also correlated with land tenancy rights, the major source of income in those days? Table II provides figures on the provisional jati distribution of land in Karimpur in 1925, 1968, 1975 and 1984.[10] In 1925, land records clearly showed the Brahman, Kacchi and Kahar jatis as having tenancy rights in excess of the rest of the community. While everything we know of Karimpur suggests that the Brahmans and Kacchis should control land, the 36.01 acres of the Kahars is surprising, as Wiser discusses them only as watercarriers tied into jajmani. But in fact only 11 of 18 Kahar families are kamins, while the other 7 families have primary tenancy rights to 32.99 acres of the land. Here we have a significant discrepancy between jati as an indicator of economic status and actual status based on land tenancy rights. The situation with Brahmans is reversed. Brahmans are the primary jajmans and the main controllers of land in Karimpur, but 6 Brahman families have no tenancy rights and another three have less than 2 acres, while 6 have between 2 and 10 acres and the rest 10 or more (up to 73.36 acres).

Jati, then, used as a criterion for economic ranking, hid significant variation in economic status among families of some jati groups. The correlation between jati and economic status becomes even more questionable as we turn to the most recent data.

In his studies of Karimpur in the 1920s Wiser created three groupings based on his vision of jajmani as the key to Karimpur economic life. Group I was those jatis who in 1925 constituted

[10] This table is based on land records collected by Wiser in 1926; a summary of ownership collected by Wadley in 1968 and by Derr in 1975, and on a preliminary translation and summation of 1984 land records collected in 1984. These data are called provisional because official land records covering the period from 1940 to 1984 were obtained in 1984—these have yet to be fully translated and analysed.

TABLE II

Distribution of Land in Karimpur by Jati. 1925–84

	Total land (Acres)			
Caste	1925	1968	1975	1984
BANYA	0.28	5.20	39.90	39.90
BARHAI	16.81	13.80	14.80	14.00
BHANGI	3.21	1.60	1.60	3.40
BHURJI	0.00	4.80	4.80	5.60
BRAHMAN	721.02	572.60	551.30	562.90
CHAMAR	6.51	12.40	15.40	12.80
DARZI	1.09	2.80	2.80	3.00
DHANUK	3.79	10.60	8.60	43.30
DHOBI	0.04	0.20	0.20	0.00
DHUNA	0.00	2.00	2.00	3.00
FAQIR	7.14	2.80	2.80	0.12
GARARIYA	1.28	19.80	19.80	23.10
KACCHI	150.26	209.60	210.90	167.14
KAHAR	36.01	45.00	42.60	45.92
KAYASTHA	3.54	7.40	7.40	7.60
KUMHAR	0.00	0.00	0.00	0.50
LODHI	11.75	13.60	13.60	10.00
MALI	4.95	4.20	4.20	5.46
MANIHAR	0.00	0.40	0.40	0.00
NAI	0.81	—	—	—
NAT	—	—	0.00	0.00
RAY	1.72	14.80	14.80	10.00
SUNAR	0.00	0.00	0.80	—
TAWAIF	0.00	—	—	—
TELI	0.30	10.00	10.00	10.80
THAKUR	—	—	0.00	0.00
TOTAL	970.51	953.60	968.70	968.54

the jajmans of the village; Group II was those jatis whose members were the 'more favoured kamins' (i.e. those who received fixed semi-annual payments); and Group III was the less favoured kamins. In parts of his analysis of Karimpur socioeconomic change, Derr continued these same three groupings, redefining them slightly:

Group I: Brahman, Kacchi, Ray, Sunar, Kayastha and Lodhi
Group II: Banya, Bhurji, Manihar, Kumhar, Thakur
Group III: Kahar, Dhobi, Bhangi, Dhanuk, Chamar, Garariya, Faqir,
           Teli, Dhuna, Mali, Nat and Darzi[11]

(Derr 1979: 137–8)

Group I remained unchanged from Wiser's grouping, Group II
was made up of three jatis which were essentially independent
of direct jajmani support in the past plus the Barhais and
Kumhars—who were still quite dependent upon jajmans—
and the Thakur who had moved in. Group III consisted of the
'less favoured' kamins of the 1920s, plus the Kahars and
Dhobis, both groups clearly struggling, and the Nats who had
immigrated.

A further refinement is needed for 1984. An economic index,
based on landownership, wage labour income and other
income-generating activities (selling cow-dung cakes, renting a
tonga) has been created for every Karimpur family in 1984 (see
Appendix A). Ranking these groups by median economic index
shows that the current top group is composed of three jati
(Brahman, Lodhi, Ray) from Wiser's Group I, with the Banya
added and the Sunar dropped because of emigration. The
Kacchis and Kayasthas are not in the top five economically.
Then a new group of marginal jati families can be seen, but they
are not the 'favoured kamins' of the past. Moreover, we now
find a wide variation in economic level within most jatis, with
some families well below the poverty line, whether Brahman or
untouchable, and others far above it. Hence a jati-based analysis
no longer reflects the true economic situation of Karimpur, if in
fact it ever did.[12]

Any correlations that existed between jati and economic
status in the 1920s were largely gone by the 1980s. But Wiser's
use of caste as his analytic tool means that by retaining his
categories the only current comparisons would also have to be

[11] We had missed the presence of the Nat and Thakur families during
fieldwork in 1974–5. Upon learning in 1984 that they had moved to
Karimpur prior to 1975, we have altered Derr's analysis accordingly. Both
the 1968 and 1975 censuses have been retrospectively revised to reflect
knowledge gained in 1984.

[12] This point is reinforced by Table IX, showing percentage of families
below subsistence for each jati.

by jati. Yet a jati based interpretation of Karimpur economic life in 1984 is blatantly false. Our solution was to recreate for 1925, 1968 and 1975 an economic index for each family based on landownership or tenancy rights, occupation, and other income. While these are not fully comparable (land is both worth more today and yields more), they provide a measure for studying changing economic conditions that we otherwise lack. Details regarding the creation of these indices are found in Appendix A.

Despite the fact that jati-based analysis hides significant economic variation within the jati categories, jati membership and identity remain salient features of Karimpur life. While recognizing that jati is not the most applicable tool for designating analytic categories for studying some aspects of Karimpur economic life, jati remains a critical category for understanding Karimpur social norms and political life. As we shall see below, behaviour regarding such things as fertility is more jati based than economically based. The following discussion alternates between our more etic economic index and the emic category of jati as a basis of analysis.

Economic Status: Karimpur 1925–84

Using the economic indices determined for each family for 1925, 1968, 1975 and 1984 allows us to see the increase in poor in Karimpur over time. We have distinguished four categories of economic well being: the very poor, those eking out a bare subsistence living, those with a slight excess, and the affluent. In 1984, the characteristics of these groups differ from earlier periods, but offer some insight into each group.

Group A is the affluent, the richer landowners, with an economic index of 6.5 and above (see below and Appendix). They often own more than 10 acres of land, in addition to having well-educated sons in service jobs. One owns a tractor, another a truck, a third a motorcycle. These families live in brick houses, a few have electricity, they are knowledgeable about health-care facilities, give large dowries for their daughters and receive equally large ones for their sons (see Table III).

Group B represents families who sometimes manage a surplus over their subsistence needs, having an economic index

TABLE III

Characteristics of Karimpur Economic Groups, 1984

Economic Group	# Families	Family Type Data*								Average Family Size	Per cent Population	Average Land (ac)	Per cent Educated**
		Nuclear		Joint		Other							
		#	%	#	%	#	%						
A (6.5+)	45	24	53	17	38	4	9			6.51	14	10.68	47.5
B (3.6–6.5)	83	44	53	34	41	5	6			7.14	29	4.01	29.2
C (2.6–3.5)	80	30	38	28	35	22	27			6.59	26	1.24	20.3
D (0–2.5)	119	87	73	12	10	20	17			5.33	31	0.47	15.3

* Nuclear includes supplemented nuclear; other includes other, single person, sub-nuclear, and supplemented sub-nuclear. See Kolenda 1968 and Wadley and Derr forthcoming for an explication of these categories.

** This is the per cent of all children born to mothers of each group. It is NOT, at this point, a figure that represents educational status of the whole population of the group. Sample size is 2308 children.

of 3.6 to 6.5. Many own small plots of land, some have men working in regularly paid jobs. a few are in the military. These families rarely, if ever, face hunger. Many have well-educated sons and daughters.

Those barely managing to feed themselves without real hunger form Group C. These are families with an economic index of 2.6 to 3.5. Some men are labourers, others farm their own small plots and sharecrop for richer farmers. Most manage semi-regular meals, a change of clothes is common, and children and adults receive better and more frequent health care. Education for males is saved for, and sometimes managed, but few girls go to school, and never past the fifth class.

Group D, the very poor, are those families with an economic index of 2.5 or below. The men are labourers and some women work as field workers, cut grass, maintain low-paying jajmani ties, etc. Few families own any land. Most are nuclear families.[13] These are families where hunger is common, adequate warm bedding for the cold January nights is exceptional, a change of clothing rare, and health care minimal. Education is a luxury most cannot afford.

As Table IV shows, Karimpur's population has become

TABLE IV

The Distribution of Karimpur Families by Economic Group
1925–84

Economic Group	1925 #	1925 %	1968 #	1968 %	1975 #	1975 %	1984 #	1984 %
A	46	28.6	44	17.9	46	16.3	45	13.8
B	35	21.7	62	25.2	64	22.7	83	25.4
C	46	28.6	55	22.4	67	23.4	80	24.5
D	34	21.1	83	33.7	106	37.6	119	36.4

[13] While family size is not strongly correlated with economic class, it is correlated with jati defined categories. Using the Wiser/Derr jati grouping based on jajmani ties, we discovered that the jajmans have an average

increasingly poor over time, although the percentage of families in Group D, the very poor, has not increased in the last ten years. What is most marked is the drop in the percentage of families that are affluent, from 28.6 in 1925 to 13.8 in 1984. Both Groups B and C have remained proportionally rather consistent over time. In order to better comprehend these shifts in economic status, we now turn to changes in population, land ownership, and occupation.

Population Growth, 1925–84

Between 1925 and 1984 Karimpur's population grew by 171 per cent. This growth, however, was not evenly distributed among Karimpur social groups: most importantly, the population of Karimpur has become increasingly poor and male. First, the poor of Karimpur have had higher growth rates than the rich. Second, over the years both the juvenile and overall sex ratios have shown a marked trend towards male dominance.

We saw above that the percentage of families in the lower economic groups in Karimpur has increased, while the percentage of families that are affluent has fallen. These figures represent not merely a shift in economic status from rich to poor, but also a dramatic population explosion among the poor. Table V shows the percentage increase in population growth over time of families belonging to each economic group in 1925, based on the economic indices calculated as outlined in Appendix A.

Even more marked, however, is a jati-based analysis of population growth, using Derr's modification of Wiser's groupings of jajmans, favoured kamins, and less favoured kamins. In such an analysis the less favoured kamins grew by 255 per cent, while the jajmans grew by 149 per cent and the favoured kamins by only 108 per cent. The jati-based pattern of population growth is also most consistent over time. We suggest that there is a jati ethic or code of conduct, that cuts across economic lines, which often affects behaviour, including

---

family size in 1984 of 7.1; the favoured kamins of 6.3; and the less favoured kamins of 5.6. Here again we see the effect of jati norms overriding more purely economic considerations.

TABLE V

Per cent Population Increase among Families according to Economic Groups of 1925, 1925–84

Economic Group (1925)	Percentage of Population Increase*
A	204.0
B	218.5
C	216.4
D	251.4

* Increases are calculated on the total population descended from members of each economic group in 1925, no matter what group they may currently fall into. Due to out-migration and families dying out, these figures are higher than the absolute growth rate of Karimpur during this period.

fertility behaviour, in Karimpur.[14] Further, these figures, whether calculated by jati or economic class, show a trend of population growth which varies inversely with economic security: that is, as the economic position of the group becomes less secure, their growth tends to increase.

A second aspect of Karimpur population growth is the trend towards male–dominant sex ratios. As Table VI demonstrates, the juvenile sex ratios have become increasingly male-favourable over time, with the adult sex ratio less consistently showing a male trend.

A masculine sex ratio is generally understood to be the result of a relatively low valuation of females. Here we see (i) a marked male trend in Groups C and D, those who are poor or bordering on subsistence, and (ii) a shift to a more equal sex ratio in Groups A and B (where Group B in 1984 includes many

[14] Other instances of a jati code of conduct that are relevant here are rules for marriage, including marriage payments, direction and distance of marriage, age and timing of consummation of marriage, and widow remarriage.

Susan S. Wadley and Bruce W. Derr 101

TABLE VI

Karimpur Sex Ratios by Economic Group 1925–84

Economic Group	Sex Ratio Females/1000 Males			
	1925	1968	1975	1984
A	895	888	928	928
B	849	844	799	963
C	891	769	769	694
D	817	1024	860	751*
Village	866	890	836	816
Adult	842	943	908	826
Juvenile	913	832	750	802

* Male migrants who consider their homes to be in Karimpur are counted as residents.

families who were in Group A before). Several factors contribute to the increasingly negative valuation of women represented by these figures. First, there has been a shift to dowry marriages from bride-price marriages (actual payment by the groom's family to the bride's family for a bride) in most jatis heavily represented in these two groups (the Bhangis and Telis have had bride-price marriages since 1980: no others were reported).[15]

Second, the jatis represented in Groups C and D are primarily traditional service-providing castes, some with female service occupations (such as the Kahars [watercarriers] or Dhanuks [midwives]). With the decline in jajmani ties, more and more men of these jatis have sought employment outside agriculture, usually out of the village. And the demand for female service

[15] Also, a marriage called dola was common among service castes prior to the 1960s: here the actual marriage took place in the groom's house, with his family paying all marriage expenses. Now marriages in these jatis cost at least Rs 900/1000, and most expect to pay more.

occupations has declined. It is these groups that do not keep
daughters alive.[16]

Land and Agriculture in Karimpur, 1925–84

Prior to the Mainpuri area being ceded by the Nawab of Oudh
to the British in 1801, Karimpur Brahmans had held tenancy
rights granted to them by the legendary Khan Bahadur, who
they say is the founder of the modern village. Under early
British policy the Brahmans were unable to meet the revenue
demands so rights to Karimpur were sold to a Brahman from
Farrukhabad. He fell into arrears in 1891 and the revenue rights
then went to two Banyas. A few years later, one portion went
to the Raja of Awa, from Etah district, and the other remained
with a Banya from Kanpur. The revenue rights to Karimpur
belonged to these two men during the Wisers' initial research.

Under these two *lambardars* in 1925, the Brahmans held
tenancy rights to 74.3 per cent of Karimpur land.[17] As the
Brahmans then constituted 24.9 per cent of the population, this
was a disproportionate share of land. The overwhelming
dominance in land control by landholders of the Brahman jati
was the primary basis of their power in Karimpur. The only jati
close to them in terms of land was the Kacchis, whose share was
significantly smaller than that of the Brahmans. The Kacchis
represented only a slightly smaller proportion of the population.

Two developments after Independence altered Karimpur
landholding patterns.[18] First, the Uttar Pradesh Zamindari
Abolition and Land Reforms Act, 1950, was enacted to create,
among other things, new tenures with 'possession to the tillers
of the soil' (Singh and Misra 1964: 3). In conjunction with land
ceilings, the effect of the Zamindari Act in Karimpur was

[16] See Wadley and Derr 1986 for details on these issues of female survival
in Karimpur.

[17] See Derr 1979: 105–24 for a fuller discussion of land holding in
Karimpur in 1925.

[18] Changes in the role of the state in Karimpur life, and the significance
of the state as the driving force of agrarian change is muted in this paper,
which focuses on the impact of these changes. For a fuller explication of the
changing role of the state, especially as viewed from the village level, see
Wadley 1988.

twofold: absentee zamindars were eliminated and Karimpur farmers were able to acquire land as their own, with full rights of disposal. Second, the ceilings led to a redistribution of land that gave ownership to a greater number of non-Brahman families. The results of these shifts are seen in the figures for 1968 in Table II.[19]

A second and important development was land consolidation, which occurred in Karimpur during the period 1967–70. The object of consolidation was to regroup the holdings of small landowners into one single plot, and those of larger landowners into two or three (or more) plots. The process was tedious, as each plot was inspected and valued, and then new plots of an equal total value assigned. Other elements such as ownership of wells and trees also had to be calculated. There was much opportunity to influence the Land Consolidation Officers, and general opinion agreed that the richer farmers gained through consolidation, either in amount of land or quality or both. Land figures by jati for 1975 reflect the minor shifts resulting from consolidation.

Karimpur farmers also benefited from a series of innovations that led to higher yields, and ultimately a better standard of living. These include installation of a government tube well in 1952 that provided irrigation for approximately a third of the village agricultural land.[20] Agricultural implements changed, with mechanical fodder-cutters and threshing machines, new ploughs, cultivators, and Persian wheels all present by the early 1960s. Tractors and tubewell sets, both diesel and electric, were added in the 1970s. A government seed store and co-operative bank opened in the 1960s which aided the distribution of new seed varieties and fertilizers, although membership of the co-operative has always been dominated by the richer farmers.

In 1964 a drainage canal was constructed through the fields lying to the west of the village, and turned previously poor land into some of the best-quality land in the village. A cold storage

[19] Nevertheless, many Brahman families retained more land than they could farm and sharecropping was, and is, common, with landlords being careful to shift the fields cultivated by any given sharecropper so that he develops no rights to that land.

[20] Nearly all the land in this area was in Brahman hands at the time of installation.

plant opened in Mainpuri, seven miles away, permitting the
storage of potatoes and wheat. The new high-yielding wheat
varieties were first planted in 1965 and virtually every farmer
was using them by 1975. Land consolidation facilitated the
installation of private tubewells, with five by 1975 and 39 by
1984,[21] by which time no one lacked water for irrigation.

In addition to planting high-yielding varieties of wheat, by
the mid 1970s Karimpur farmers had recognized the value of
new cash crops for the local market. While the lack of a
processing plant cut into sugarcane production, and cotton and
peas had all but disappeared by 1984, peanuts, garlic, fennel and
potatoes were expanding.

Meanwhile the value of land had increased and a lively land
market developed, aided in part by the use of land as collateral.
This furthered the redistribution of land among families and
social classes.

While the figures in Table III showed the very poor have
essentially no land, and the rich have over 10 acres per family,
there are changes over time. As Table VII demonstrates, the

TABLE VII

Size of Holding and Number of Families 1925–84

Holding Size (acres)	Number of Families (per cent)			
	1925 (n=161)	1968 (n=246)	1975 (n=282)	1984 (n=327)
0.0	73 (45)	99 (40)	121 (43)	92 (28)
0.01–4.99	40 (25)	94 (38)	102 (36)	173 (53)
5.00–9.99	15 (9)	29 (12)	31 (11)	36 (11)
10.00–	33 (21)	24 (10)	28 (10)	26 (8)
Totals	161	246	282	327

[21] The 1975 tubewells were all fixed, whereas in 1984 few were
permanently installed. This means that one tubewell pump can effectively
irrigate wherever there is a well head.

percentage of landless families has actually decreased since 1925, with a sharp decline since 1975. Meanwhile, the percentage of families owning over 10 acres has dropped from 21 to 8, while the percentage of families with 5–10 acres has remained nearly stable. There is a sharp increase seen in the percentage of families owning 0.01–4.99 acres. Further, between 1925 and 1984 the Gini coefficient went from .584 to .498, marking a shift towards land equity. Critically, too, the average acres per household went from 6 in 1925 to 3 in 1984.

Families owning less than 5 acres have increased by 333 per cent since 1925. Many of those added to this category between 1975 and 1984 have benefited from government schemes to redistribute village common lands to the landless or near landless. Due to the influence of the Dhanuk *uppradhan* (assistant headman) during this period, the Dhanuk jati in Karimpur was most affected by these schemes.[22] The increase in families with less than 5 acres is most disturbing, however, because families with less then 3–4 acres are unable to subsist by farming alone. Aside from the landless, 50 per cent of Karimpur families in 1984 had less than 4 acres. If we include the landless, 255 Karimpur families (78 per cent) must seek other employment to live. In 1925, 107 families (66 per cent) were land poor. Meanwhile, employment opportunities in agriculture elsewhere in the village have declined as farm families, with their own population increases, specifically adult sons, have turned away from hiring agricultural labourers and sharecroppers to farm their own land.

Let us now turn to an examination of jajmani and occupational change in Karimpur since 1925.

Changes in Jajmani and Occupation, 1925–84

Though an essential component of Karimpur's economic life in 1925, the 'Hindu jajmani system' was largely inactive by 1984. In 1984 only 3 Karimpur families out of 327 derived their

---

[22] The land represented by these figures is often poor, but cultivable. A more recent effort has resulted in poor families being given uncultivable *usar* land. We have not included these latter grants in any land figures used in this paper.

primary income from traditional jajmani relationships—two Dhobi (washerman) families and one Barhai (carpenter). While others were following their traditional occupations, jajmani-based income was either supplemental, or the inherited aspect of fixed ties between two families had been lost. Many services formerly provided by kamins were now obtained in the nearby market town. The Chamars, who in 1925 were essentially bonded labourers, were freed of their servitude. The land-rich/labour-poor jajman/farmers of the 1920s were now themselves labour-rich. Those kamins who had been peripheral to the services of the jajmani systems (Garariya, Mali, Dhanuk, Darji) had been extensively employed as labourers in the 1920s: now they are not.

By 1968 only 71 families (of 246) gave semi-annual payments to kamins, these payments being the primary payments for most kamins. Most importantly, only 22 of 40 landed Brahman families and 11 of 43 landed Kacchi families gave semi-annual payments. With the jajman/farmers beginning to deny their jajmani ties through non-payment, the 'classical' system described by Wiser was certain to change further.

The reasons for the jajman/farmer to opt out of the system are many. In the labour-rich situation of the late 1960s, a farmer no longer needed to maintain labourers who were obliged to work for him when called (whereas in the 1920s a farmer could call any of his kamins, whatever their real occupation, to work his fields when necessary). First, it was cheaper to hire labour by the day than it was to maintain annual payments. Furthermore, the traditional grain payment had acquired a monetary value, and it was now cheaper for the farmer/jajmans to pay for labour in cash than in grain.

Further, many services were no longer needed. Most rich farmers now had hand-pumps in their courtyards, so the Kahar watercarrier was made obsolete. In a curious shift, most Brahman wives now use the fields as a latrine, obviating the need for the daily services of the sweeper (Wiser reports 13 latrines in Brahman houses in the 1920s, none existed in the 1960s, a few were installed by 1984). The traditional occupation of the Telis had been eliminated by the installation of oil presses in Mainpuri. The richer farmers preferred the Dhobis in Mainpuri—with their soap powder, starch and irons—to the

Karimpur Dhobis, while their wives washed more of their own clothes with the water supplied by their new hand-pumps and the detergent purchased in the market.

In 1984 few kamins received regular semi-annual payments. Payments, when given, were for services rendered on specific occasions. Moreover, few families used daily services—a half dozen rich Brahmans still had a sweeper clean daily, while 2–3 houses often used a watercarrier to help the women scrub pots. The Dhobis visited the wealthier families every one or two weeks, and the poorer ones only at childbirth or when clothes were polluted. These services continued to be hereditary, with fixed ties between jajman and kamin families. The one carpenter still working in the village and the Darjis, now augmented by men of other jatis who had learned tailoring, no longer served traditional patrons but were chosen by need and skill, although the carpenter did have some hereditary patrons remaining.

For weddings, childbirth, death, and yearly festivals kamins continue to provide ritual services. But here too payment is by the event, not by yearly subsidies. It is the ritual aspects of jajmani that have been the focus of earlier discussions of the endurance of the jajmani system (Beidelman 1959, Elder 1970, Gould 1964; see also Commander 1983 for an overview). And while ritual services will continue to be offered and utilized without doubt into the next century, they are not in fact the most valued components of jajmani as manifested in Karimpur during the 1970s and 1980s.

Looking at the non-ritual services that continue in Karimpur, one factor stands out: almost all are services primarily utilized by women or the poor—those who, for cultural or economic reasons, have little access to the services provided in the nearby market town. The Dhanuks, Bhangis, Dhobis, Malis, Kahars, even the Darjis, all provide services accessible to upper-class women in purdah. A few other services, such as those of the Nai, are utilized in the village by poorer men, being less expensive than in Mainpuri, and also readily available for those who have less need to visit the town. But the rich farmers and their school-going sons get their hair cut, their carpentry done, and their clothes washed in Mainpuri. Their wives, however, are cut off from the services of the market economy by restrictions on mobility, and hence patronize village kamins. It

is not only the development of a market that has influenced
modern jajmani practices: cultural norms for female behaviour
have been equally influential.

The occupational structure of an Indian village is a complex
involving many varied tasks and has been, until recently,
intricately linked to the jati system. The nature of the jati system
is such that village men, and to a lesser extent women, have
tended to follow the occupations their parents and grandparents
pursued. The result is epitomized in the jajmani system
discussed above. When jati occupations were insufficient to
provide for families, supplementary jobs were necessary. Given
jati restrictions (no one but a Bhangi would sweep, only a
Dhobi would wash clothes) and limited education, farming was
the one job open to all. In the 1920s no individual held a
non-traditional occupation that took him outside the village.
Those few who held non-traditional occupations did so within
the village—police watchman, zamindar's agent.

By the 1970s there was an expansion in the total number of
workers and in the incidence of non-traditional and extra-village
sources of income. Whereas all but 14 families, landless or
landed, in the 1920s were engaged in agriculture, only 16 of the
village's 106 landless families worked in agriculture in 1975.
Some villagers now have bicycle-repair shops to fix the cycles of
their affluent neighbours, others drive tongas or rickshaws,
both to town and within town. Small shops have sprung up at
the bus-stop to offer cigarettes, water and other wares to the
frequent passers-by. A few men have received training that
allows them to be machinists, radio repairmen, or schoolteachers. Many families invest in educating their sons in the
hope that somewhere, somehow, a service job will be found.
Some never work; others end up driving rickshaws.

Table VIII shows the distribution of jobs in Karimpur in
1925, 1975 and 1984. Farming remains the occupation of the
majority of the men, but that majority declined from 72 per cent
in 1925 to 51 per cent in 1984, as reliance on other income
sources has grown. There is a diversification of jobs at all levels,
with both rich and poor shifting from agriculture, though the
landed continue to work their fields. Further, there is some caste
specialization in the new occupations.

Several other trends are revealing. Looking first at outside

TABLE VIII

Men's Occupations in Karimpur 1925, 1975, 1984

Number of Men and Primacy of the Occupation

Occupation	1925		1975		1984	
	Primary	Secondary	Primary	Secondary	Primary	Secondary
FARMING	191	44	236	17	258	38
LABOUR						
—INTERNAL	20	65	45	111	39	25
—EXTERNAL	—	—	2	15	84	15
TRADITIONAL	37	18	14	36	22*	18
SERVICE						
—INTERNAL	—	3	1	3	5*	1
—EXTERNAL	8	1	42*	—	54*	5
SHOPKEEPING						
—INTERNAL	7	3	7	11	23	2
—EXTERNAL	—	—	—	—	6	—
MILKSELLING	—	10	6	10	16	9
PROSTITUTION	3**	2	—	—	—	—
TOTAL	266	146	353	203	507	113***

* Includes one woman.
** All three are women.
*** More men were fully employed in 1984, leading to a decline in secondary occupation.

employment, workers whose primary income comes from service (counted as any permanent regularly paid work, including factory workers, peons and schoolteachers) have risen from 8 in 1925 to 54 in 1984. In 1925 service jobs were held by the poor—by the untouchable sweepers working in Calcutta. By 1984 service jobs had become the desired occupation of the wealthier families: there were 15 Brahmans, 9 Kahars, 4 Kayasthas and 6 Kacchis, in addition to 8 Bhangis and a variety of others, in service jobs. Whereas earlier farming and jajmani ties had served the need of Karimpur's families, they now regularly sought jobs in the wider urban market. And another two dozen educated men were seeking work, but found no jobs.

Over time more and more people had opened their own shops, whether cycle-repairing, tailoring or selling basics like soap and cigarettes. Many landowning families see shops as a way of employing educated sons while adding a small amount to the family income. For others, their shops provide basic subsistence. Equally important, six men now have shops in Mainpuri—bicycle-repair, radio, and bangle selling. Another occupation that shows a new orientation to the urban market is milkselling. Sixteen men, primarily Garariyas and Kahars, now collect milk in Karimpur and nearby villages and sell it in Mainpuri.[23] Some see milkselling as a supplement to farm incomes; for others it is a full-time occupation. For those willing to work hard, this is a lucrative business and several have prospered. Milkselling has a detrimental effect, however, on village nutrition as more and more families now sell their milk to supplement family incomes rather than retaining it for family use.

Meanwhile the poor have shifted from agricultural employment to outside labour jobs, in both the 1920s and 1970s. The number of men whose primary occupation involves labour outside Karimpur has risen dramatically since 1975, from 2 to 84. These men drive rickshaws, carry bags of grain for mills,

[23] As we were leaving in 1984, the milksellers were beginning to feel the effects of new inspection measures designed to cut down on the watering and adulteration of milk between the villages and the cities. New regulations were also being promulgated that would require milksellers to be licensed. Such measures will undoubtedly affect the popularity of this source of income in the future.

load brick kilns, unload trucks, work in construction, or do any other of the many labour-intensive jobs that one finds in India. Even without an industrial base, the nearby district town provides jobs for those willing to seek them: having no land and no education, their bodies are their only resource. In 1975 this shift in labour had not yet occurred, as there were 111 men working part-time in Karimpur itself, hoping to get jobs that no longer existed, and contributing to Derr's pessimistic view of Karimpur at that time as a place facing a growing abundance of food and a growing abundance of poverty.

In fact the 1975 study becomes crucial to understanding economic life in Karimpur and its changes over time. At that point the 'Green Revolution' was just taking off, and the population had certainly exploded. Compared to 1925, there was less employment and more poverty. If a restudy had only been done in 1984, we could reach the same conclusion. But that is not the true case: as Table IV and Table IX show, there has been a levelling off in the increase in poverty since the 1970s. We saw in Table IV that the percentage of families in Group D had declined slightly in the period of 1975–84, while those in Group C had risen only slightly. Likewise, Table IX demonstrates that the percentage of population below subsistence has declined since 1975. Thus the proportion of the population that is poor has not risen in the past decade, although the actual number of poor has, of course, increased.

Many of the poor told us that things had not really changed; a few feel that conditions now are worse, while others, especially those in Groups B and C, actually think their lives are better. The rationale offered was based not on hunger or poverty, but on personal freedom. Derr paraphrased the feelings of many *chhoti* jati men in his field notes:

They [Brahmans] say they kept us like *maa-baap* [like they were our parents], that all we had to do was go to them and we would receive. But to maa-baap one must show respect and humbleness, we would go with folded hands and we might receive, if we were properly humble. They helped us in the courts or with officials, surely. They could read, *they* had time to go to school because *we* were working in their fields for them. By keeping us illiterate they could keep us unaware of our rights—they could take advantage of us if we went against them because they knew the workings of government, they

TABLE IX

Karimpur Families Below Subsistence by Caste 1925–84

	Families Below Subsistence Level							
	Percentage of Families				Percentage of Population			
Caste	1925	1968	1975	1984	1925	1968	1975	1984
BANYA	66.7	0.0	0.0	40.0	71.4	0.0	0.0	26.3*
BARHAI	12.5	25.0	40.0	54.5	21.4	38.6	45.3	69.7
BHANGI	37.5	64.3	72.2	78.9	40.0	75.3	81.7	74.6
BHURJI	0.0	50.0	25.0	25.0	0.0	38.9	13.6	20.7
BRAHMAN	7.3	7.0	11.8	8.1	6.9	5.1	9.9	2.9
CHAMAR	37.5	61.5	80.0	75.0	41.4	57.5	85.1	71.9
DARZI	0.0	66.7	33.3	50.0	0.0	66.7	52.4	50.0
DHANUK	0.0	70.6	70.0	56.7	0.0	76.2	74.1	62.3
DHOBI	0.0	66.7	50.0	100.0	0.0	66.7	41.7	100.0
DHUNA	100.0	80.0	80.0	80.0	100.0	80.0	83.9	84.2
FAQIR	87.5	83.3	84.6	92.3	86.4	91.3	93.9	91.5
GARARIYA	33.3	23.5	31.6	35.0	46.2	27.3	44.7	37.4
KACCHI	34.6	32.6	35.4	35.6	25.0	30.0	35.6	29.9
KAHAR	26.3	48.6	52.6	51.1	36.1	48.2	47.2	48.3
KAYASTHA	0.0	50.0	75.0	66.7	0.0	77.4	75.8	60.0
KUMHAR	0.0	66.7	66.7	0.0	0.0	90.0	90.9	0.0
LODHI	0.0	33.3	33.3	0.0	0.0	29.4	27.3	0.0
MALI	0.0	33.3	75.0	0.0	0.0	5.3	75.9	0.0
MANIHAR	0.0	33.3	33.3	100.0	0.0	58.3	62.5	100.0
NAI	0.0	—	—	—	0.0	—	—	—
NAT	—	—	0.0	0.0	—	—	0.0	0.0
RAY	100.0	0.0	0.0	0.0	100.0	0.0	0.0	0.0
SUNAR	0.0	0.0	0.0	—	0.0	0.0	0.0	—
TAWAIF	50.0	—	—	—	66.7	—	—	—
TELI	50.0	83.3	88.9	72.7	80.0	92.3	93.2	74.5
THAKUR	—	—	—	100.0	—	—	—	100.0
Total	25.5	41.1	45.4	44.6	25.3	40.1	45.1	40.4
(n=	41.	101	128	146	191	602	791	827)

* This caste has a bifurcated economic situation, with three families very wealthy and two families (non in-migrant) very poor.

knew the officials, and they had the money to pay bribes. They were maa-baap, and sometimes they showed the love that maa-baap are to have for their children, but sometimes they beat us just as maa-baap sometimes beat their children. (BWD Field Notes, 1983–4, Book 4, pp. 290–1)

A group of men from the Kahar jati agreed: 'Now we are free, we do not have to work for them because we can go outside, we are educated and know our rights.' (Interview, 5 November 1983). This sense of freedom parallels Jodha's findings (this volume) of the terms by which villagers accounted for economic change, particularly the importance of a reduced reliance by the poor on traditional patrons.

On the upper end of the scale, we find that the rich farmers have lost, as their lands have been divided among sons. But this is a paradoxical picture, for those acres do yield more produce following the advances of the Green Revolution. There is no doubt that the standard of living in Karimpur is better now than in 1925, and also better than in 1968. If we look at health care or mortality rates, quality of housing, source of water, quality of clothing, educational levels, or consumer goods (watches, radios, cycles, etc.), the village has prospered. Yet there are many whose families have seen none of this increased prosperity. Their standard of living is comparable to that of their grandfathers in the 1920s, and some may even be hungrier. As one elderly Chamar stated, 'The condition of our house is the same as before. There is difficulty all the time: there is no rest' (Interview, 6 October 1983).

Part of the paradox of change in Karimpur is that in the 1920s the rich ate better than the poor (see Wiser 1936) and certainly had political and economic clout over the poor, but otherwise everyone shared in a poor standard of living. Now everyone may in fact eat less well (e.g. the back of milk) but other differences are visible. Now the rich live in brick houses while the poor still have mud huts; now the sons of the rich receive MAs while the poor are illiterate; now the rich daughters wear 200- and 300-rupee saris at weddings while the poor are still in tatters. Certainly there is a greater visible disparity between rich and poor than before.

Yet the Brahman *pradhan* claimed, the Brahmans are now worse off than before. But the data in Table IX shows that fewer Brahmans are below subsistence than in 1925. There *has* been a decline in families in Group A, a factor affecting primarily the Brahman landlords. And their share of the land is less. Meanwhile, many are heavily in debt, having over-extended themselves with easily accessible government loans that they cannot repay (see Derr 1984). But surely they can see their brick houses and well-dressed offspring?

Two factors are involved: first, as Sharma discusses for Brahmans in a village in Himachal Pradesh,

with no other source of income he [the .Brahman migrant] would certainly forgo the surplus which enables him to be a hirer of labour, a patron of poorer men, a giver of feasts and dowries. The standard of living which he is seeking to maintain is not some absolute standard of wealth but a particular position in relation to other groups with whom he is in the habit of comparing himself (1977: 295).

The Brahmans of Karimpur are used to comparing themselves to the Kacchis, Kahars and other kamins of Karimpur, as well as to their kin in nearby villages and urban areas. They see their economic control of the old kamins eroded. One Brahman family used to feed the whole Kahar jati at Holi: this is no longer possible. They also see their political superiority melting away, as the kamin jatis, having no economic ties to the Brahman landlords, no longer abide by their political wishes. In addition, the disproportionate population growth of the poor has given them a greater voice in Karimpur elections. Most people concurred that the Brahman headman won the last election through fraud: the election should have gone, they say, to a Kacchi.

At the same time, their greater connections to urban areas have made the Brahman families aware of the possibility of an even better life-style, one filled with gas stoves, videos and cars. Some of their daughters cook on gas stoves, others have relatives with large houses in Agra. The Karimpur Brahmans are caught between the economic and political challenge of their old kamins and the disparity between themselves and the urban middle class. Looking either way, they see themselves as having lost.

MEASURING SOCIO-ECONOMIC CHANGE THROUGH RESTUDIES

There are many ways to measure change in India—we could count calories or protein, sets of clothes or crop yields, calculate mortality rates or the age of marriage. In this paper we have attempted to measure changes in the relative number of rich and poor in a village in Uttar Pradesh over the period 1925–84, showing how these are connected to changing patterns of landownership and occupation.

Several lessons come from this exercise. First, we could not 'measure' the different standards of living represented by being poor or rich at each period. Poverty is always relative to what is defined as 'wealthy' at any given point in time. Our suspicion is that the very poor (in Group D) today have a style of life comparable to their poor ancestors fifty years ago, while everyone else has a better 'style/standard' of life, despite their perceptions to the contrary.[24]

We also learned the difficulties of measuring the 'same' thing, using four different sets of data. Wiser counted population by an individual's presence in the village on a given day: we counted it by who 'belonged' to the village (all wives who had their *gauna*, all married daughters who had not had their gauna, men who worked outside, etc.). Derr had calculated occupation in 1975 by full-time or part-time, while Wiser looked at primary and secondary sources of income (as did the 1984 census). Even the 'minimal core data' advocated by Foster *et. al.* (see above) can prove to be troublesome in later interpretations.

Next, the importance of jati as an analytic category was reinforced. Jati in India is not merely an occupational designation or a marker or ritual status. It defines codes of conduct that influence decisions regarding a range of behaviour, from number and spacing of children to acceptable levels of debt. Any micro-level study of socio-economic change in rural India will have to take into account the cultural codes associated with jati membership: only then can we move beyond 'measurement' to an understanding of the human decisions that have led to the patterns measured.

Agrarian change takes place in a particular cultural context

[24] Even the very poor have drastically lower child mortality rates and longer life spans.

and people's actions are informed by their understanding of the way the world is or should be. People act within frameworks of meaning, and perhaps the anthropological methodology is most useful in its attempt to provide a picture of the larger world view in which agrarian change is enacted. It is not that the well-trained survey worker is not sensitive to his informants and the implications of his questionaire (see Srinivasan in this volume), but that his goal is to mute the individual actor's voice in the final analytic product. The value of the anthropological endeavour is the explicit goal of highlighting the voice, for it is actors who are the agents of social change. The gross measures of poverty, *pucca* houses, electrical connections, etc. are only the products of people acting within specific cultural contexts. Hence this paper is framed by the voices of Karimpur residents, articulating their understanding of change in their communities.

Finally, the value of restudy as a methodology was reinforced. First, the length of time covered by this study was itself significant. The Wiser materials from the 1920s are valuable not only for their rarity, but because they present a detailed picture of a village community that did change. We could not have understood the significance of those changes without the historical baseline given in their writings. For example, Elder (1970) writes about the jajmani system in a village in Lucknow district as he found it in 1957, using district records and Wiser's writings to reconstruct it as it might have been in the 1930s. If our baseline had been the 1950s, seeing the jajmani system as Elder found it, much of the significance of occupational change that we discovered would have been lost.

Second, while our primary focus has been change between 1925 and 1984, the intervening trips proved immensely useful. In a small population, the statistics of any one year may hide long-term trends (see the sex ratio for Group D in 1968, Table VI). The trends that emerged across time, despite some apparent anomalies, are more legitimate because of their repeated documentation.

Third, many studies of agrarian change, even by field-based anthropologists, attempt 'history' through recollections of the past, as understood in the context of the present. Wiser's writings give us interpretations at various points in time, as well as recollections of the past. These aid the ultimate endeavour of the anthropologist to interpret that past.

Fourth, the value of our own familiarity with Karimpur cannot be underestimated. It is a familiarity based on months of living and working in the village, at several points in time. It is the many interviews, the sharing of jokes, the long gossip sessions, the participation in marriages, the sharing in births and deaths, and the raucous celebration of Holi that ultimately legitimates, for us at least, this attempt at measurement.

APPENDIX A

Economic Index

An economic index was developed for each household in the village in each time period. The following factors were considered: land ownership, employment of men, women and children, jajmani relationships that lead to income, sharecropping, income-producing animals (cows, water buffaloes, goats, pigs, chickens, horses and donkeys), money-lending, and income producing machines (tongas, rickshaws, pump-sets rented out for irrigation, tractors, electric threshers, mills, trucks). Employment and other income was scaled by contribution to subsistence. The total income or the land equivalent of income for each family was divided by the numbers of persons in the household. Using the village calculation of 3 *bighas* (0.6 acre) as minimal subsistence per person, the poverty line is seen as an index of 3.0 (so a family of five receiving all income from land would need 15 bighas or three acres for subsistence). A day labourer with a family of five regularly employed earning Rs 400 per month [Rs 15–20 per day] also received an index of 3. The Planning Commission set the poverty line in 1977–8 at Rs 65 per capita per month. Our figure, six years later, is a monthly per capita of Rs 80. The range for 1984 is 0.6 to 25, with 44.6 per cent of Karimpur households falling below the poverty line. Data on caste and economic status for 1925–84 are found in Table A. 1.

Reconstructing an economic index for non-landowning families of the 1920s was tricky at best. But it is our only choice if we wish to understand the changes in family economic status

TABLE A.I

Median Economic Index by Caste 1925-84

Caste	Economic Index			
	1925	1968	1975	1984
BANYA	2.3	4.2	12.0	9.0
BARHAI	4.0	3.4	3.4	2.8
BHANGI	3.5	2.4	2.35	1.9
BHURJI	4.0	3.2	3.05	3.55
BRAHMAN	16.5	5.6	7.7	6.5
CHAMAR	3.0	2.3	2.1	2.5
DARZI	3.5	2.4	3.0	3.0
DHANUK	3.0	2.3	2.1	2.85
DHOBI	3.5	2.5	2.75	1.5
DHUNA	1.4	1.0	1.6	2.0
FAQIR	2.5	2.0	1.6	1.8
GARARIYA	3.0	3.6	3.6	3.1
KACCHI	4.05	3.85	3.25	3.5
KAHAR	3.5	3.0	2.6	2.9
KAYASTHA	4.6	3.6	2.3	2.6
KUMHAR	3.6	2.5	2.5	3.1
LODHI	9.8	5.6	4.2	6.2
MALI	4.5	3.4	2.7	3.8
MANIHAR	4.0	3.3	3.0	2.5
NAI	4.5	—	—	—
NAT	—	—	3.0	3.7
RAY	2.55	7.2	7.7	5.3
SUNAR	4.1	5.05	7.05	—
TAWAIF	2.75	—	—	—
TELI	2.75	2.55	2.0	2.4
THAKUR	—	—	—	—
VILLAGE	3.6	3.1	3.0	3.1

over time, as jati clearly is inadequate as a guide to economic
status for all families. Fortunately, Wiser provides numerous
clues to the economic situation of many. For example, in
discussing the Bhangis (sweepers) he says, 'each family has a

sufficiently large jajmani either in the village or in nearby hamlets to give them the subsidy they require for their simple style of living. They, more than any other group in Karimpur, are familiar with what a city can offer in a larger cash income, but most of them prefer what the village grants them' (Wiser 1936: 35).[25] Later, in a chart on the economic condition of each caste, he notes that the condition of one Bhangi family is good, and that of seven poor (Wiser 1936: 119). In determining an economic index for each family we interpreted these statements to mean that the Bhangi families with husbands in Calcutta were doing better, while the others are placed at a minimal subsistence level. We could not, however, identify the one family thought to be far above the rest.

Likewise, in discussing the Kahars (watercarriers) he says, 'Most of the Kahar men are employed as day labourers in the fields. Some of the best among them are regularly employed. Others are more ambitious and cultivate their own fields. Those who are not prepared to supplement their jajmani rights, eke out a miserable existence.' (Wiser 1936: 23) Later he states that eight Kahar families are independent of jajmani, while of the eleven dependent upon it two are in the economic condition of 'fair' and nine are 'poor'. In assigning an economic index to each Kahar family we tried to determine through our knowledge of current inherited jajmani ties those families which had been independent of jajmani in the 1920s. Then we used occupational categories and notes from the census to attempt to identify those families which were 'more ambitious' in farming, and hence better off.

With an economic index based largely on land, transformations over time in land productivity and value skew the results when the same value is placed on land at all times. Land quality appears consistent over the 60-year period considered here. But land productivity increased slightly from 1925 to 1968, markedly from 1968 to 1975, and has been largely consistent since 1975. Land values have risen, but inputs have also increased. Considering these factors, we feel that for the farmer with 25–50 bighas that can be farmed by family labour, our scale is

[25] In fact, 5 of 8 Bhangi families had men serving in Calcutta or elsewhere in 1925.

skewed downward, i.e. he is probably better off than the index suggests. The land-rich farmer, who must give land on shares, bears more of a burden of increased inputs and less return for that portion of his land on shares.

A second source of possible error within each time period is family size. Each individual was considered an equal consumption unit. Recognizing this bias, the index is skewed too low, for the percentage of juveniles in the population of each economic group is highest among the poor, especially in recent times. Currently, 50 per cent of Group D is juvenile, while only 37 per cent of Group A is juvenile (comparable figures for 1925 are 39 per cent and 29 per cent). On the other hand a greater proportion of landed families have unproductive elders: in 1984, 50 per cent of Group A families had persons 60 or older while only 24 per cent of Group D families had persons 60 or older. Finally, to the extent that a large family is more economic, our index is skewed too low, for the larger families belong primarily with the wealthier households.

As a final qualifier, we note that for the 1975 to 1984 interval, there should be little skewing, although at each point in time the figures might be skewed downwards, especially for the poor. Without detailed income and consumption data over time for each family in the village, we can at best estimate. Our purpose in creating the index, and hence the attempt to quantify, is to trends to be used in suggesting further avenues of exploration and explanation.

REFERENCES

Akhtar, Rais., A Note on the Nutritional Geography of Karimganj Village. In *The National Geographic Journal Of India*, 207–14. (Based on research done in Karimpur during six months in 1970. This work has many factual errors. 1971).

Beidelman, Thomas O., *A Comparative Analysis of the Jajmani System*. Monographs of the Association for Asian Studies VIII. Locust Valley, N.Y.: J.J. Augustin Inc. (1959).

Campbell, J. Gabriel, and Linda Stone. The Use and Misuse of Surveys in International Development: An Experiment From Nepal. *Human Organization* 43: 27–37. (1984).

Commander, Simon., The Jajmani System in North India: An Examination of its Logic and Status across Two Centuries. *Modern Asian Studies* 17 (2): 283–311. (1983).

Das Gupta, Monica., From a Closed to an Open System: Fertility Behavior in a Changing Indian Village. In T. S. Epstein and D. Jackson, eds., *The Feasibility of Fertility Planning: Micro-Perspectives.* Oxford: Pergamon Press, pp. 97–121. (1977).

Derr, Bruce W., The Illiterate Peasant Farmer: A Misunderstood Expert. New York State Conference on Asian Studies, Albany. (1976).

—— The Growing Abundance of Food and Poverty: A Fifty Year Perspective on Karimpur. Sixth Annual Conference on South Asia, Madison. (1977).

—— More People, More Food, More Poverty: Karimpur 1925–1975. Annual Meeting of the North India Studies Association in conjunction with the Annual Meeting of the Association for Asian Studies, New York City. (1977).

—— The Growing Abundance of Food and Poverty in a North Indian Village: Karimpur 1925–1975. Unpublished doctoral dissertation, Department of Anthropology, Syracuse University. (1979).

—— Karimpur Kids: Economic and Demographic Aspects of Population Growth in Karimpur. Eighth Annual Conference on South Asia, Madison. (1979).

—— Jajmani in Karimpur: Fifty Years After Wiser. Ninth Annual Conference of South Asia, Madison. (1980).

—— Sharecropping in Karimpur: Contemporary Forms and Tendencies in *Proceedings of Second International Symposium on Asian Studies, 1980.* Hong Kong: Asian Research Service. (1981).

—— Farmers at the Edge of Subsistence. Annual Meeting of the Association for Asian Studies, Toronto. (1981).

—— *Ham Garibi Log*: The 'new poor' in Karimpur. Thirteenth Annual Conference on South Asia, Madison. (1984).

Elder, Joseph W., Rajpur: Change in the Jajmani System of an Uttar Pradesh Village. In K. Ishwaran (ed.), *Change and*

Continuity in India's Villages. New York: Columbia Univ. Press. (1970).

Epstein, T. Scarlett., *South India, yesterday, today, and tomorrow: Mysore villages revisited*. New York: Holmes and Meier. (1973).

———— Mysore Villages Revisited. In Foster, George M. *et al.*, *Long Term Field Research in Social Anthropology*. New York: Academic Press, pp. 209–26. (1979).

Etienne, Gilbert., *India's Changing Rural Scene 1963–1979*. Delhi: Oxford University Press. (1982).

Foster, George M., Thayer Scudder, Elizabeth Colson, Robert V. Kemper., Conclusion: The Long-Term Perspective. In Foster, George M. *et al.*, *Long Term Field Research in Social Anthropology*. New York: Academic Press, pp. 323–48. (1979).

Freeman, James M., *Scarcity and Opportunity in an Indian Village*. Menlo Park, CA: Cummings Publishing Co. (1977).

Gould, Harold A., A Jajmani System of North India: Its Structure, Magnitude and Meaning. *Ethnology* 3: 12–41. (1964).

Harper, Louise, 'Return to India'. Paper presented at the Wisconsin South Asia Conference, Madison. (1984).

Kessinger, Tom G., *Vilyatpur: 1848–1968*. Berkeley: University of California Press. (1974).

Kolenda, Pauline M., Region, Caste, and Family Structure: A Comparative Study of the Indian 'Joint' Family. In M. Singer and B. Cohn (eds), *Structure and Change in Indian Society*, pp. 339–96. Chicago: Aldine Publishing Co. (1968).

———— Status of Women in Khalapur. Thirteenth Annual Conference on South Asia, Madison. (1984).

Lawrence, J. H., What Vocabulary Shall We Use? In *Indian Standard*. (Published at Saharanpur, U.P.) 38(2): 29–37, February. (Based on fieldwork in Karimpur. 1927).

Leaf. Murray J., *Song of Hope: The Green Revolution in a Panjab Village*. New Brunswick, N. J.: Rutgers University Press. (1984).

Lee, Richard B., Hunter-Gatherers in Process: The Kalahari Research Project, 1963–1976. In Foster, George M., *et al.*,

Long Term Field Research in Social Anthropology. New York: Academic Press, pp. 303–21. (1979).

Lewis, Oscar., *Life in a Mexican Village: Tepoztlan Revisited.* Urbana: University of Illinois Press. (1951).

Mahar, Michael., Shifting Patterns of Employment: Khalapur 1954–1984. Thirteenth Annual Conference on South Asia, Madison. (1984).

Marriott, McKim, and Ronald Inden., Caste Systems. In *Encyclopedia Britannica*, 15th ed. (1974).

Nair, Kusum., *In Defense of the Irrational Peasant.* Chicago: The University of Chicago Press. (1979).

Redfield, Robert., *Tepoztlan, A Mexican Village: A Study of Folklife.* Chicago: University of Chicago Press. (1930).

Scudder, Thayer., and Elizabeth Colson., Long-Term Research in Gwembe Valley, Zambia. In Foster, George, M., *et al.*, *Long Term Field Research in Social Anthropology.* New York: Academic Press, pp. 227–254. (1979).

Sharma, Ursula M., Migration from an Indian Village: An Anthropological Approach. *Sociologia Ruralis*, XVII (4): 282–303. (1977).

Singh, B., and S. Misra., *A Study of Land Reforms in U.P.* Delhi: Oxford Book Co. (1964).

Ullrich, Helen., Depression Differentials in pre- and post-puberty marriages among Havik Brahmin Women. Thirteenth Annual Conference on South Asia, Madison. (1984).

van Schendel, Willem., *Peasant Mobility: The odds of life in rural Bangladesh.* Assen: Van Gorcum. (1984).

Vogt, Evon Z., The Harvard Chiapas Project: 1957–1975. In Foster, George M., *et al.*, *Long Term Field Research in Social Anthropology.* New York: Academic Press, pp. 279–301. (1979).

Wadley, Susan Snow., *Shakti: Power in the Conceptual Structure of Karimpur Religion.* University of Chicago Studies in Anthropology: Series in Social, Cultural, and Linguistic Anthropology, No. 2. Department of Anthropology, University of Chicago. (Reprinted by Munshiram Manoharlal, New Delhi.) (1975, 1985).

———: Folk Literature in Karimpur: A Catalogue of Types. *Journal of South Asian Literature*, 11: 7–17, (1975).

———: Brothers, Husbands and Sometimes Sons: Kinsmen in North Indian Ritual. *Eastern Anthropologist*, 29: 149–70, (1976).

———: The Spirit 'Rides' or the Spirit 'Comes': Possession in a North Indian Village. In A. Bharati, ed., *Rituals, Cults and Shamanism: The Realm of the Extrahuman*. The Hague: Mouton, pp. 233–51, (1976).

———: Power in Hindu Ideology and Practices. In K. David, ed., *The New Wind: Changing Identities in South Asia*. The Hague: Mouton, pp. 134–57, (1977).

———: Texts in Contexts: Oral Traditions and the Study of Religion in Karimpur. In S. Vatuk, ed., *American Studies in the Anthropology of India*. New Delhi: Manohar, pp. 309–41, (1978).

———: The Ritual Neglect of Daughters in India: A North and South Comparison. Eighth Annual Wisconsin Conference on South Asia, Madison, (1979).

———: Women's Family and Household Rites in a North Indian Village. In Nancy Falk and Rita Gross, Eds., *Unspoken Worlds: Women's Religious Lives in Non-Western Cultures*. New York: Harper and Row, pp. 94–109, (1980).

———: Women's Songs, Music and the Seasons in a North Indian Village. Annual Meeting of the Society for Ethnomusicology, Bloomington, Indiana, (1980).

———: Women as Mothers, Wives and Daughters in North Indian Folklore. *Asian Thought and Society*, 6: 4–24, (1981).

———: Cunning in the Courtyard: Women in Karimpur Folktales. Annual Meeting of the Association for Asian Studies, Toronto, (1981).

———: She's Called 'the Village Indira': The Life Story of a Brahman Widow. Paper presented at the 13th Annual Wisconsin Conference on South Asia. Madison, Wisconsin, (1984).

———: Singing For the Audience: Aesthetic Demands and the Creation of Oral Epics. Annual Meeting of the American Folklore Society, Cincinnati, (1985).

———: Widows: Forced Independence for Some. Symposium on Widowhood, Remarriage, Divorce and Dowry in India. University of Toronto, (1985).

———: The Katha of Sakat: Two Tellings. In A. K. Ramanujan and S. Blackburn, eds., *Another Harmony: New Approaches to Indian Folklore*. Berkeley: University of California Press, (1986).

———: Survey Research or Intensive Field Studies? A Review of the Debate with Special Reference to South Asia. *Journal of Social Studies*, no. 33: 19–34, (1986).

———: The Domination of the Landlord and the Domination of Indira: Changing World Views in Karimpur, A North Indian Village. Presented at the Seminar: Voices of Authority and Protest, Center for Asian Studies, University of Texas, Austin, (1988).

———: Choosing a Path: Performance Strategies in The North Indian Epic Dhola. In Blackburn, Wadley, *et al.*, eds., *Oral Epics in India*. Berkeley: University of California Press, (1989).

———, Bruce W. Derr, Introduction, in *Four Families of Karimpur*, by Charlotte V. Wiser. Foreign and Comparative Studies Program, Series in South Asia, No. 3 Syracuse University, Syracuse, New York, (1978).

———, Demographic Change and Family Structure in Karimpur 1925–1984. Fourteenth Annual Conference on South Asia, Madison, (1985).

———, Child Survival and Economic Status in a North Indian Village. Ninth European Conference on Modern South Asian Studies, Heidelberg, W. Germany, (1986).

———, Death by Fire: Eating One's Sins in Karimpur. In Moffat, Wadley and Marriott, eds. *Toward an Ethnosociology of India*, special issue, *Contributions to Indian Sociology*, (1989).

———, Karimpur Families over Sixty Years. *South Asian Anthropologist*, M. S. A. Rao Memorial Issue. (In press)

Wiser, William H., Social Institutions of a Hindu Village in North India. Unpublished Doctoral Dissertation. Cornell University, 1933.

————, *The Hindu Jajmani System*. Lucknow: Lucknow Publishing House, (1936).

Wiser, William H., and Charlotte V. Wiser, *Behind Mud Walls 1930–1960 with a Sequel: The Village in 1970*. (Berkeley: University of California Press, 1971).

Wiser, Charlotte V., A Hindu Village Home in North India. *International Review of Missions*, London, July, (1929).

————: *The Foods of a Hindu Village of North India*. Allahabad: Superintendent, Printing and Stationery, United Provinces, (1936).

————: *Four Families of Karimpur*. Foreign and Comparative Studies Program, South Asian Series, No. 3, Syracuse University, (1978).

————: Time Perspectives in Village India. P. Reining and B. Lenkerd, eds. *Village Viability in Contemporary Society*. AAS Selected Symposium 34. Boulder: Westview Press. (1980).

Chapter 5: Extension of Scale in Fieldwork: From Village to Region in Southern Gujarat

JAN BREMAN

The focus in my research on labour relationships in western India shifted from village to region with the course of time. In this short methodological paper I want to list the reasons why, as well as touch on the problems produced by this shift in level of analysis.

I. THE TERRITORIALITY OF PARTICIPANT OBSERVATION

I started my fieldwork in South Gujarat in 1962–3 with the intention of identifying the changes which had come about in the relationships between local landlords and landless labourers. The subjects of study required a prolonged stay in one or more villages to collect data by observing and participating in village life. According to the notion then prevalent fieldwork in a peasant society couldn't be anything other than a community study—such was the instruction with which young anthropologists were sent off. Only there, in the village, could an encounter with social reality come about. In retrospect, it seems no exaggeration to say that even the formulation of this problem was upon the premise that the village community be studied within what was considered the basic social framework of the peasant order. That is to say, the method of investigation (fieldwork) dictated the location of analysis (the village), and was decisive, if not for the choice, at least for the elaboration of the theme of investigation.

I had made up my mind from the start to make no contribution to the series of village monographs which were being published around this time. My investigations, instead of being directed towards a systematic and all-encompassing inventory of a local community—a major ambition of most village studies—was concentrated on a more specific theme: the nature of the agrarian labour regime. Further, it was expressly not my intention to present the locality of my research as a more or less autonomous circuit whose dynamic, as far as it was present, could be explained only from internal mechanisms. Although the image of a closed village system had become effectively obsolete as indicator of a traditional setting since the early 1960s, many fieldwork reports still stressed the locality as the small world which contained the mass of the population and as the boundary of social horizons. Compatible with the line of thought was the notion that social dynamics had their origin in higher realms, from which they gradually trickled down to lower levels in society. Seen in this way the village was pre-eminently the framework for studying the impact of processes of change initiated from outside and above.

The penetration of institutions such as state and market points to a further extension in scale of the local system in connection with a more pronounced structural differentiation. This finding appears to be a common result in the publications of a team of Dutch investigators involved in the first fieldwork in South Gujarat in the early sixties. As a consequence, in preparation for a second research project, emphasis was given to the analysis of a number of institutional frameworks, e.g. bureaucratic machinery, political setting, trade and industry, elite clubs, migration, labour market, agrarian policy, education. These, it was thought, would provide ways to observe changes at the local level in their more specific context. The object was to make a study of social dynamics closer to the starting point than to the end point, implying a choice, at the same time, for a supra-local level of analysis. Thus, in the plan of research, the district town and its vicinity substituted for the village as the location of fieldwork. The basic assumption was that the district could be considered as being a strategic middle level, the main town its centre. From here, all kinds of processes of change originating higher up on the macro-level, whether directed by public policies or not, reached the surrounding countryside. This was the plan of study for Valsad district which was carried out by a team of Dutch and Indian sociologists from 1970 to 1972.[1]

The approach chosen cannot be seen apart from the modernization theories which, around this time, dominated development theory—albeit that more critical ideas also emerged in the elaboration of sub-themes in the research, in accordance with the centre-periphery model. The similarity was that both notions emphasized the hierarchical insertion of local-level phenomena into larger social settings, pointing to the region as the integrative mechanism in this process of expansion. The assumption in the further operationalization of the study in South Gujarat was that Valsad town functioned as a centre of control and focus of action (and also as a meeting place of contradictions) on what was thought of as an intermediate level in society.

The results of the investigation did not confirm this premise. Corrections were necessary in different respects. It was only to an extremely limited degree, for example, that the district centre functioned as the locus of power and activities in the region, initiating processes of change and channelling them to lower levels. Further, the usual stereotype of mobilization and incorporation from above, with its suggestion of the base of society as the controlled, essentially passive, element in an expanding system, seemed to rest on a misconception. Different partial studies showed the dynamic of forces 'from below', as appears not only from the active use of new possibilities at the local level and the entryway to a wider social network, but also from the subjection of external institutions to local interests.

It is possible that while reporting on the second project in South Gujarat, too little attention was paid to a finding which is quite striking: the inadequacy of describing the region as a separate level between the macro and micro systems. A policy of decentralization was underway, it is true, bolstering the political and bureaucratic weight of the district as a unit. But it would be going too far to derive from this the proof of the emergence of an intermediate circuit with the urban centre at its core. On the contrary, there was every reason to stress the intricate complexity of town and hinterland in Valsad itself, and

[1] S .D. Pillai and C. Baks (eds.), *Winners and Losers; Styles of Development and Change in an Indian Region* (Bombay, 1979).

the supremacy of the latter over the former in a number of respects. Additionally the different processes of change which can be distinguished analytically (economic, political, social, etc.), except regarding space and time, also show a great deal of discordance with regard to level of operation. All sorts of relationship patterns tied to different social spheres do not synchronize *vis-à-vis* distribution, and are not constructed according to a simple pattern of hierarchic or concentric stratification. Moreover, with regard to different sub-categories of the population, space is as little uniform a notion as are past and future. The horizon, measured both as to time and location, depends on social class. Generally, the higher it is the greater its reach, and the lower it is the more limited the distance.

On the basis of my involvement in the Valsad study, I have reached the conclusion that no institutional condensation occurs within a territorially demarcated zone which links the top and the base of society. Such a construction actually presupposes a type of society in accordance with the principle of spatial distribution, and this with the attendant suggestion of a direct and simple connection between the different layers: local–regional–national. In actual reasearch such an articulation cannot be recognized, nor when transposed into the terms micro, meso and macro. For what this reduction of social reality really implies is a vague conceptualization under which region is understood to be all that is, on the one hand, sub-national, and on the other, supra-local.

II. PROBLEMS IN THE DESCRIPTION OF A SPATIAL FRAMEWORK

My critical remarks about the region concept stem from experience in empirical research in southern Gujarat. The complication here was that fieldwork was adhered to as a research method in a situation which, spatially speaking, did not permit itself to be unequivocally defined. The great advantage of a systematic study of the interrelationships of a number of phenomena and actors vanishes, however, if the study loses its small-scale focus and reach. If a village or another concrete setting is abandoned as unit of analysis, it is still necessary to narrow the field of study to make fieldwork, in the anthropological sense, possible. Without a local base, the setting and focus of fieldwork seem to lose their territorial character. Fieldwork assumes a small-scale network—not necessarily contained within a well-defined space but certainly with a restricted, survey-able radius of action.

Does it follow from this that fieldwork and participant observation actually exclude each other at the regional level? Not when the pretension is dropped that the region can be covered and mapped as a complete system by means of this method. That would be an unfeasible task. But with a more modest plan which postulates the analysis of an institutional complex, fieldwork also acquires a significance which deviates from the usual understanding of the term in the literature. In my case this was the composition and operation of the market for non-agrarian labour in Valsad district. Let me amplify this further in the light of my own research practices.

During prolonged stays in two villages in South Gujarat in the beginning of the sixties, I restricted myself mainly to gathering data about local landlords, landless labourers and the relationships between these two classes. In the course of time the chosen loci became an intimate environment in which I was able to observe the investigated population close up, continuously and systematically, in the daily comings and goings of its members. After some time, each village had become a neatly ordered domain of research. Excursions out of the villages, which were periodically required, led to feelings of uncertainty which vanished when I returned. Only there, in my proper area of operation in the villages, could I 'place' the collected data, and comprehend as well as verify their background and drift. This was fieldwork which amounted to the colouring in of the framework I had sketched beforehand. The local system was a given in the research plan. Relationships which overstepped the borders were largely left out of analysis, even when their theme would have justified a greater interest. When I found out, for example, that the members of a very large number of households in one village went away annually for a period of many months, I did trace them to brickworks in the vicinity of Bombay but still paid insufficient attention to this phenomenon in my reporting. That is to say, rather than pursue the implications of seasonal migration for this rural proletariat, I was more content with presenting the consequences of their absence. Village study, however penetrating and exhaustively carried out, sets limitations to the representation of social reality. To obviate this drawback one must pay great attention to degree of representativity in selecting a location. I tried to give a broader tenor to the results of my first fieldwork by staying for a short time in a third village so as to point out similarities and variances. This attempt at generalization, however, still relates to what takes place at the lowest territorial level, the locality. A regional study is more than the common denominator of research findings in a number of villages. Suggestions to the contrary would give new fuel to the earlier anthropological fiction that the local system is a microcosm in which the total pattern of society repeats itself. The demand for representativity has a strongly horizontal bias. It bypasses the fact that in village studies, in the classic sense of the word, social complexity is reduced to the bottom segment— the lowest link of a chain whose length is not fixed and whose connecting points remain indistinct.

The choice of a greater territorial unit as the location for fieldwork (as in the second investigation in South Gujarat in which I took part) made it possible to observe social processes, mechanisms and networks over a greater distance. This time there was not the confinement to a smaller community which had forced me to emphasize the local interaction to the neglect of external relations and structures. The entire Valsad district was my territory for investigation; in it I could move freely while collecting information about the functionings of a regional labour market. The demarcation found in this study consisted of two components: an urban (informal labour sector) and a rural (labour contracting for seasonal migration), two terrains between which I commuted back and forth—in the literal sense of the word. My daily schedules reflected the greatly varied environments into which I had to get involved. It was not exceptional if a morning saw me visiting urban work sites, conducting interviews in government offices or with a union leader; or if midday saw me calling on several villages to meet seasonal migrants and their labour brokers; and if, of an evening, I sought out unskilled labourers in their hutments. The absence of a set rhythm and a fixed meeting place gave my fieldwork an extremely ambulatory character. The drawbacks are obvious.

In the first place the district forms a spatial framework so extensive that it is insufficiently discriminating for fieldwork. The investigator may easily get lost in this space. The blurring which shows up with increasing distance can only be partially compensated by the introduction of a thematic focus giving direction to the research. In journeys through the district the feeling regularly came over me of being adrift, especially because I saw no chance of linking up the levels on which I had gathered materials, and of making them align with the boundaries of this region. Usually I operated within the area, when engaged in analysis of the informal sector in the town of Valsad; sometimes I stepped outside, when following migrant workers to the brickworks and saltpans at the outskirts of Bombay. The region, understood as a hierarchically built system with a centre that blurs at the periphery, remains an elusive notion in terms of research. Thus the demarcation of a village study makes a more convincing impression at first sight. Here, however, the scale of the investigation—the possibility of operationalization within a surveyable and concrete area—plays an important role.

In the second place the theme of study in the event of a regional analysis also becomes characterized generally by a much greater complexity in the institutional framework. Where the labour system can still be observed in a local community as an aggregated whole, diffusion and disarticulation arise at a higher level. The situational diversity which comes about—the different spheres in which workers, employers, unions and governmental bodies operate—compels the fragmentation of fieldwork if, at the least, the theme of study is not narrowed down to one of the spheres concerned. In addition to a disjoined time schedule, this also made it imperative for the investigator to adapt himself alternatively to entirely divergent environments with which, however, he would never be completely familiar.

This fieldwork setting is characterized by superficial contacts with respondents who are approached to provide specific information connected with their roles. Questionnaires and interviews determine the manner in which data are collected. Participant observation no longer exists. In this sense the term fieldwork is a misnomer. Although still retaining the stamp of craftmanship—the investigator as an artisan—it is shorn of its original significance.

This was not a very satisfactory situation. It could easily have degenerated into a superficial, impressionistic style of research. In order to meet my own need for a more concrete operational base for my research, I sought out some local action sets. These were a limited number of work sites and neighbourhoods in both town and country, to which I returned regularly and from which I built up a network of broader contacts. I combined with this qualitative part of my research the collection of as much quantitative data at the district level as was possible: statistics, government reports and other source material. Together these formed the new raw material of my study. I remained alert, however, to the incompleteness of my data. This evoked the problem of validity and reliability and made me sharply aware of the lack of cohesion in my analysis.

III. THE NECESSITY OF A THEMATIC FOCUS

My experiences were not of such a nature as to make me turn back again to the local level, but I had no more reason to continue to start from a regional demarcation of my fieldwork. In the preparation for my third research project in south Gujarat—in the first half of 1977, with short follow-up visits in succeeding years—I did not tie myself down to a spatial framework in advance. Instead I let myself be led entirely by my gradually growing interest in the phenomena of seasonal migration. The starting point was the massive influx of temporary labour in a rural environment. For various reasons, which I have discussed elsewhere, I came to consider the surroundings of Bardoli in the hinterland of the city of Surat as my most suitable work base. I collected data about the massive seasonal employment of cane cutters who came great distances from neighbouring federal states. I collected data about the spontaneous influx of labour for other agricultural activities in this region, which had been transferred into an irrigated zone in the 1960s and 1970s.

The irony was that while I did not now begin with a regional analysis as such, the results of my investigations pointed much more strongly in this direction than had my second fieldwork.

This had to do with the economic, social and political dominance of the Kanbi Patidars who had emerged as a propertied peasant class in the previous decades.

My fieldwork was concentrated on a number of locations where the indigenous agricultural labourers and their competitors, the seasonal migrants, live. In these work camps which neighbour sugar factories, in shelters in the fields, and in the quarters within villages where the landless are set apart, they are at the disposal of their employers—whom they share in common. The employers belong mostly to the regional elite. In the sugar factories and other co-operatives which control economic production in the Bardoli region, it is they who set the tone. Their hegemony is also indisputable in the sphere of politics. This peasant lobby exerts strong pressure on the government to conduct a policy in agreement with its interests. Internal communication—at the time of my research even a monthly was published—reinforces the dominant caste feeling that, as landowners, they form the most important and deservedly privileged class. They are mobilized for all sorts of actions, such as rallies, campaigns or demonstrations.

Surat's hinterland was not all that dynamic at the beginning of this .century. The region was carved up very capriciously, territorially speaking. One part stood under British rule, another belonged to the principality of Baroda whose capital lay in central Gujarat. What lay behind the transformation into a region is a social movement which began in the colonial period. Since that time the awakening to consciousness of the region's dominant peasant class has accelerated. Region formation here went together with regionalism in a modernization process that came about along particularistic lines. The outcome is an organizational condensation in the region, a growing complexity of a number of institutional frameworks of an economic, political, social and educative nature—in which the controlling position of the leading landowners is expressed. Bardoli and its vicinity is quite obviously Patidar domain. They press so much of a stamp on life that the presence of other social classes, which jointly make up the majority of the population of the region, is hardly felt. This can be set right by fieldwork with a 'from below' perspective which then, however, bypasses local-regional differences. The conclusion that I want to draw from this is that, while doing fieldwork, regions as such are neither structures nor entities but rather analytical tools which may be employed or not, in accordance with the problematic which is the guiding principle of the research plan.

REFERENCES

Fieldwork-based publications of the author:

Patronage and Exploitation: Changing Agrarian Relations in South Gujarat, India (Berkeley and Delhi, 1974).

'Seasonal Migration and Co-operative Capitalism; Crushing of Cane and of Labour by Sugar Factories of Bardoli', *Economic & Political Weekly (EPW)*, XIII, August 1978, pp. 1317–60.

'Between Accumulation and Immiserization: The Partiality of Fieldwork in Rural India', *The Journal of Peasant Studies*, XIII–1, 1985, pp. 5–36.

'I am the Government Labour Officer . . . ', *EPW*, XX, June 1985, pp. 1043–56.

Of Peasants, Migrants and Paupers: Rural Labour Circulation and Capitalist Production in West India (Delhi, 1985).

Chapter 6: Knowing About Rural Economic Change: Problems Arising From a Comparison of the Results of 'Macro' and 'Micro' Research in Tamil Nadu*

JOHN HARRISS

"Much the same trends are apparent in Kirippur as in Kumbapettai . . . This suggests that the same processes are at work throughout the district and may perhaps be widespread in Tamil Nadu, if not elsewhere in India."

—Kathleen Gough

"What has happened is that in the absence of historical data a consensus has been built up on the basis of random insights . . . "

—Chris Bayly

"A plague o' both your houses!"

—Mercutio

PRELIMINARIES: WHAT ARE WE TALKING ABOUT?

Discussion of the methodology of agrarian research may be couched in terms of several oppositions: macro/micro; economic analysis/anthropological analysis; quantitative/qualitative. They are sometimes treated as being equivalent to each other. Thus it is argued implicitly that macro research=economic=

*I benefited from criticism of an earlier version of this paper by S. Guhan, C. T. Kurien and V. K. Ramachandran. I am sure they will like this version of the paper as little as they liked the first but I continue to believe that I have a point!

quantitative, and that micro=anthropological=qualitative. When put in this way the absurdity of treating the three oppositions as being equivalent to each other is apparent. Of course economists engage in micro-level research, and anthropologists can analyse societies at a level above that of a small village. But the discussion can become even more confused, because of a further tendency to equate the three oppositions referred to as more or less equivalent also to a fourth: survey/village study. And yet in terms of the methods employed many surveys and village studies are not clearly distinguished from each other at all. A lot of surveys involve the sending out of investigators armed with standard schedules of questions by the principal researchers; and so do many village studies, and both may suffer from the problems arising from bureaucratic organization referred to by Bardhan, Rudra and Vaidyanathan in their chapters in this book.

In the discussion which follows I shall be concerned with comparing some results of census and survey investigations with those derived from anthropological investigation. By this I mean those investigations in which 'data' are established not simply by asking direct questions, but also by observation of peoples' actions and by listening to what they say in circumstances other than those of a formal interview. The distinction is comparable with that which Geertz makes between 'convergent' as opposed to 'divergent' data:

By convergent data I mean descriptions, measures, observations, what you will, which are at once diverse, even rather miscellaneous, both as to type and degree of precision and generality, unstandardised facts, opportunistically collected and variously portrayed, which yet turn out to shed light on each other for the simple reason that the individuals they are descriptions, measures or observations of are directly involved in one another's lives . . . As such they differ from the sort of [divergent] data one gets from polls, or surveys or censuses, which yield facts about classes of individuals not otherwise related . . . (Geertz, 1983, 156)

Anthropological enquiry, on these lines, is disposed towards the relational perspective for which Appadurai appeals in his chapter. It is unfortunate, indeed, that so far very few anthropological studies of the rural economy of India have been undertaken, with the result that, as Vaidyanathan points out 'far too little is known of the nature and role of non-economic factors in relation to socio-economic change—the theoretical work on this interface is as yet rudimentary.' We should recognize, however, the achievements that there are in this field, including Wadley and Derr's demonstration of the enduring significance for economic activity of *jati* codes for conduct (in their chapter in this book) as well as Sundari's analysis of the relations of caste-class structure with rural labour markets. (Vaidyanathan refers to this; see also Harriss, 1989a, for a study of the powerful influence exerted on a rural labour market by variations in caste structure between villages).

I shall also be concerned, therefore, with comparing some of the results of village studies (without necessarily assuming that they are the products of 'anthropological' enquiry) with those of census and larger-scale survey research. Like other contributors (Rudra, Tendulkar, Jodha, Appadurai), I believe that 'micro-level' investigation (anthropological studies or small-scale surveys) can greatly improve the measurement of even elementary and apparently 'straightforward' (Bardhan) variables. Like Wadley and Derr I find that the establishment of standardized 'core' data is difficult and not at all unproblematic, and would caution against some of the claims made even by so experienced a fieldworker as Ashok Rudra when he says: 'there are certain things which are uniform within the village society . . . Thus, the daily wage rate of casual labourers is usually the same in a village . . . The marketing channels, the existence or otherwise of village moneylenders . . . are really information pertaining to the village and therefore do not vary from respondent to respondent. As I show here with reference to wages, such an assumption may be quite unfounded. The second major element in the argument for the interdependence of 'large-scale' and 'small-scale' investigation, about which the contributors to this book substantially agree, is that of interpretation. Here I, and others (Vaidyanathan, Appadurai) depart from the positivism of T. N. Srinivasan, for as Tendulkar says: 'LSS needs to be supplemented because the same observable end result can emerge from alternative causal forces'; and the same measurements can have different meanings, sometimes depending on the way they are used in aggregations (Appadurai). The aim of the comparisons that I make here, therefore, is, first, to evaluate the quality of the facts that we know about rural Tamil Nadu, and, second, to compare interpretations based on different modes of enquiry.

These objectives might be seen as contentious, in so far as they involve comparison of the results of survey and census investigations directed at delineating certain features of the rural economy of Tamil Nadu as a whole, with the results of 'anthropological' and/or village-level investigation. It might be pointed out that the different forms of inquiry investigate different objects, so that their results are not strictly comparable. My response to this anticipated objection is to emphasize that I am concerned, firstly, to use the results of 'micro' investigations (whether 'anthropological' or arising from village surveys) to raise questions about the quality of the factual information in censuses and large-scale surveys; and secondly, to raise questions about the interpretation of the 'facts'—the constructions that are placed upon them. The latter involves the assumption that 'micro' investigations help to elucidate processses which are effective on a wider scale, but it must avoid any claims of statistical generalizability. This is the problem with a statement like that of Kathleen Gough's, cited at the head of this essay. Observations in Kumbapettai and Kirippur do help us to understand processes, some of which have their origins elsewhere, or which obtain much more widely. But they cannot be used as the basis for generalizations of a statistical kind—and there is a strong hint of that in this particular statement (it is also a problem in the work of Gilbert Etienne, 1982. See review, Harriss 1984).

THE DIFFICULTY IN ESTABLISHING THE 'FACTS' ABOUT AGRARIAN CHANGE

In this section I will use three examples from research with which I have recently been involved in order to illustrate the difficulties of knowing about agrarian change. The problems recounted may be familiar to some, but in this case they will serve to remind such readers of just how problematic are the 'facts' with which we deal. The cases come from research on agrarian change in part of North Arcot district in northern Tamil Nadu, where I carried out 'anthropological' enquiries alongside survey teams in 1973–4 and again in 1982–4 (see Farmer, ed., 1977; and Hazell and Ramaswamy eds., forth-coming, for background ·and results).

(i) *Census villages and their populations:* in the 1973–4 survey in North Arcot a stratified random sample of eleven villages was drawn from the 1971 Census List of Villages, and the first operation to be conducted was to carry out complete household listing in each of them. The same eleven villages were studied in 1982–4. An elementary question to ask is about changes in village populations. Different answers to this sample question are shown in Table I.

Comparison of Census results for individual villages is made

TABLE I

Village Populations

	'71 Census	'73 Survey	'81 Census	'83 Survey	'71–81	'73–83
KALPATTU	1942	1537	2228	1393	14.7%	−9.4%
MEPPATHURAI	804	551	784	747	−2.5%	35.6%
VAYALUR	634	639	739	692	26.6%	8.5%
VEERASAMBANUR	540	565	560	620	3.7%	9.7%
VINAYAKAPURAM	784	750	846	814	7.9%	8.5%
RANDAM	1446	1388	1614	1487	11.6%	7.1%
AMUDUR	934	942	1121	986	20.0%	4.7%
VENGODU	1061	1046	1274	1165	20.1%	11.4%
DULI	450	456	617	538	37.1%	18.0%
SIRUNGATHUR	980	948	1172	1049	19.6%	10.7%
VEGAMANGALAM	1028	1023	1214	1062	20.7%	3.8%
TOTAL	10603	9845	12169	10553	14.8%	7.2%
EXCLUDING KALPATTU AND MEPPATHURAI	7857	7757	9157	8413	16.5%	5.5%

Note: For Kalpattu and Meppathurai there are particularly acute uncertain-ties as to the comparability of Survey and Census units, *and* the comparability of 1973 and 1983 Survey units.

difficult because of definitional and boundary changes. (This may account for the extreme results of − 2.5 per cent recorded for Meppathurai and +37.1 per cent for Duli, between 1971 and 1981, among the villages in the North Arcot sample.) Similar boundary problems also affect comparisons of survey results, and in this sample of villages we know of particularly acute problems in the cases of Meppathurai and of Kalpattu—where, in spite of repeated efforts in 1982–4, it proved impossible to establish comparability.

In each case (comparison of the 1973 survey results with the 1971 census, and of the 1983 results with 1981 census) it appears that the survey listings have tended to produce lower estimates of population than the immediately preceding census. In fact, the differences between the census and the survey figures are not statistically significant (as a helpful reviewer of an earlier version of this essay pointed out, in reporting the result of his application of the paired t-test). But the discrepancies are disturbing and do affect interpretations of agrarian change. In 1983–4, already aware of the discrepancies between census and survey figures, stringent efforts were made to check the accuracy of the data on village populations. Even after correction of initial household listing figures (which are expected to be on the low side because of the investigators' lack of familiarity with the villages) the disparities shown in Table I remained. The accuracy of the survey figures is confirmed by the independent measurement of the population of the main village of Randam in the course of my anthropological investigation. This showed an increase of 8.65 per cent between April/May 1976 and January/February 1984, corresponding quite closely with the 7.1 per cent increase shown by comparison of the survey results. There does seem to be a possibility that the census results for 1981 produced an overestimate of the village populations. Rather different estimates of the rate of population growth result from different modes of enquiry, with some effect on our understanding of the process of agrarian change.

(ii) *Labour Force Structure:* Another elementary question about agrarian change in North Arcot concerns trends in the structure of the labour force. Has the proportion of the labour force which is primarily engaged in and dependent upon agricultural wage labour increased or not? Data on this question, posed in terms of respondents' usual status, are given in Table II. This shows a considerable discrepancy between the results of survey investigation for Randam village, and those from anthropological enquiry. The latter shows a much lower number of agricultural wage labourers at both points in time, though it also suggests a rate of growth of the agricultural labourer population almost twice that of the surveys. The table also compares my independent estimates, from studies of samples of households, not from complete censuses, for three other villages. These suggest that the general increase in numbers of 'agricultural labourers' shown up in the comparison of the survey results may be the 'artifact' of underestimation in 1973 and overestimation in 1983 (note the case of Vinayakapuram, in particular). The point here is not to claim that the survey results are wrong and the independent findings right, but only to point out the difficulty of knowing about so fundamental a 'fact' as 'the incidence of agricultural wage labour'. The differences, both at one point in time, and between points in time, probably arise from the real difficulty of classifying individuals into a discrete

TABLE II

	1973 persons	%	1983 persons	%	independent sample or census estimates (see Harriss, 1989b)
KALPATTU	257	19.4	233	16.6	
MEPPATHURAI	89	16.2	128	17.1	
VAYALUR	166	26.0	110	15.9	
VEERASAMBANUR	158	28.0	131	21.1	1973:162; 1983:150
VINAYAKAPURAM	114	15.2	254	31.2	1973:145; 1983:110
RANDAM	355	25.6	376	25.3	1973:243; 1983:272
AMUDUR	275	29.2	357	36.0	
VENGODU	213	20.4	235	20.2	
DULI	90	19.8	137	25.5	1973:100; 1983:103
SIRUNGATHUR	179	18.9	310	29.6	
VEGAMANGALAM	216	21.1	246	23.2	
ALL VILLAGES	2153	21.9	2517	23.9	

category in circumstances of considerable occupational multi-plicity, and from variations between investigators in the ways in which they have classified women, especially. Some investiga-tors seem to have a tendency to consider that women's primary occupation is 'domestic work', with 'agricultural wage labour' as the subsidiary; others think the reverse. Differences of this kind may well be self-cancelling in a large sample. But there may be a systematic tendency to underestimate the importance of occupa-tions and activities other than cultivation and agricultural labour in censuses and surveys of rural economies in which these are the principal occupations. In these circumstances investigators perhaps tend to think in terms of the distinction between 'cultivator' and 'non-cultivator', and to equate 'non-cultivator' with 'agricultural labourer'. Certainly I suspect this to be the case in surveys in which the focus is on agriculture, as it was in the 1973 and 1983 North Arcot surveys. Jan Breman has reached a similar conclusion in his extensive fieldwork in south Gujarat: 'In fact, the concise questionnaire necessary to guarantee a reasonably reliable survey cannot do justice to the complexity of the actual employment pattern. For example, by pressing respondents to state only the principal source of external earnings over the preceding year, the individual variation in, or even combination of occupations is concealed.' (Breman, 1985, 300)

(iii) *Wages:* Another quite basic question about trends of change in an agrarian economy concerns wage rates. In the North Arcot case (as in much of Asia) there is first of all the problem that an important component of wages is in kind: kind payments in quantities of paddy for harvesting and threshing labour, and perquisites of food, and perhaps clothing or fuel. How these are to be measured and valued is of course a problem, and even more so when the attempt is made to compare data sets from different points in time.

In North Arcot harvesting payments may be made in the form of bunches of paddy on the stalk, or of a number of local volumetric measures. Threshing payments are also in terms of volumetric measures. The local 'measure' is of a slightly different size in different villages. Latterly there has been an attempt at standardization in terms of litres. The result has been that labourers and cultivators may say that they have received or paid a certain number of traditional measures, when the payment has been made out of a standard measure, or perhaps the other way round. People still refer to harvesting and threshing payments in terms of a particular number of measures. There is no clear evidence that these ideas of standard payments have changed (except perhaps in Vinayakapuram and Amudur: See Table VII). But the picture has been made even more complicated by a second consideration. This is that in the recent past there has been a shift away from the standard daily payments, which were still the norm in 1973–4, to much more employment of labour on the basis of various specific contracts. These mean that it is possible for the individual labourer to earn more than, or less than, the traditional rate for the day. In these circumstances (somewhat specific to the particular case perhaps, though surely not very unusual in the Asian context) it seems sensible to rely on comparisons of cash wages only. But here too we find sometimes quite considerable discrepancies between statements of the going wage rate in village labour markets on the one hand, and, on the other, statements of wages actually paid by cultivators (from plot data on the costs of cultivation), *pace* Ashok Rudra's suggestions as to the uniformity in daily wage rates of casual labourers in the same village. The point, again, is the sheer difficulty that is encountered in establishing quite basic 'facts' about an agrarian economy; and to emphasize both the importance and the difficulty of defining and measuring things in directly comparable ways when the attempt is made to establish trends from comparisons of data sets at different points in time.

The implications of these illustrations of the difficulty of knowing should be to make us extremely cautious about basic measures in agrarian economics, and even more about comparisons between data sets and between points in time.

RESULTS OF 'MACRO' RESEARCH ON TAMIL NADU: KURIEN'S FINDINGS

The most outstanding study of the macro-level sources on the agrarian economy of Tamil Nadu is that by Kurien (1980), referring to the period from 1950 to 1975. This analysis uses material from the various rounds of the National Sample Survey, the RBI All-India Rural Debt and Investment Surveys, the

Census of India, several All-India Labour Enquiries, Farm Management Surveys, and Tamil Nadu Government statistics—from Season and Crop Reports and the annual Economic Appraisal.

The principal theme of Kurien's study is that the rural economy of Tamil Nadu witnessed growth but without any 'structural transformation' between 1950 and 1975. There has, however, been an important but generally 'hidden' kind of structural transformation reflected in 'the tendency of small farmers to leave land and farming to join the ranks of the rural proletariat.' (1980, 389) The agricultural economy has shown dynamism but

these processes have also created some changes that were not desired. The pressure on small farmers to leave their land and to become agricultural labourers is one of them. The decline in the real wages of agricultural labour is another. And the tendency of mass poverty to continue and to increase is yet another . . . the development processes of the past have generated growth and affluence for the few and poverty and insecurity for the many. (1980, 389)

In short, he discerns what might be described as a process of 'proletarianization', but in circumstances in which proletarianized peasants move into very poorly remunerated activities. Some would consider this best described as 'marginalization'.

The key elements in the argument are as follows:

(i) Census data, after making allowance for the problems caused by changed definitions, show a definite shift of the labour force into agriculture between 1961 and 1971; and it is inferred that 'the decrease in the number of cultivators and the increase in the proportion of agricultural labourers is one of the most striking aspects of change in the economy of rural Tamil Nadu'. (1980, 371) This finding is confirmed by Subramaniam and Ramachandran in their study of census results on agricultural labourers in the working population of Tamil Nadu up to 1981. They note that the trend continued from 1971 to 1981, 'though there has been a considerable fall off in change as we defined it.' (Subramaniam and Ramachandran, 1982)

(ii) NSS data show that between 1961–2 and 1971–2 the percentage of households not owning land declined (from 24.2 to 17.01) while the percentage of households not operating land showed a marginal increase from 40 to 42. There does not seem to have been a lot of change in the distribution of land ownership, though there are indications of a modest shift of land from the biggest owners to the smallest (a trend which has perhaps increased, according to comparison of data from the Agricultural Censuses of 1970–1 and of 1976–7). But at the same time 'the evidence is that there is a very heavy concentration of assets in the hands of the wealthiest groups in the rural areas and that their relative share has increased over the decade.' (1980, 374)

(iii) In the 1950s there was an increase in the area under cultivation accompanied by some improvements in productivity; the 1960s saw stagnation in agriculture in terms of area, production and productivity, while the 1970s appear to have started an upward trend, especially in productivity (faltering again in the later 1970s, after the period which Kurien considered, according to data given in recent issues of 'Tamil Nadu: an economic appraisal', published annually by the Government of Tamil Nadu). During the entire period a shift of land from dry to wet crops is discernible.

(iv) The Annual Wage Rate Series constructed by the Agro-Economic Research Centre of the University of Madras (on what basis is not apparent), when converted to a constant base according to a variety of deflators, suggests that there has generally been a decline in real wages from 1951–2 to 1973–4. And though there appears to have been some increase in the average number of days worked, especially by male agricultural labourers, it is found that 'the earnings of agricultural labour . . . were way below what was necessary to be above the poverty line.' (1980, 389)

Kurien's interpretation of these findings depends crucially on the evidence from the census on the increasing proportion of agricultural labour in the rural labour force. The suggestion that there has been pressure on small farmers to leave their land and farming is only weakly supported by the finding that there has been a marginal increase in the percentage of households not operating land. The evidence on declining real wages in agriculture supports the suggestion of 'marginalization' in Kurien's interpretation. How robust are the data on which the interpretation is based? Are there other interpretations which would explain these 'facts' as well as the one that Kurien advances? To arrive at some answers to these questions we will look at the results of some 'micro-level' research. The purpose of the exercise, to repeat, is not to try to falsify Kurien's conclusions, but to examine the quality of the data on which they are based, and to find out to what extent the understanding of the key process of change in the rural economy of Tamil Nadu that he puts forward holds good at the micro-level. If it does not, we will have no grounds for saying that it is therefore 'wrong', but we may be able to suggest an alternative construction upon the 'facts'.

RESULTS OF 'MICRO' RESEARCH ON TAMIL NADU

The 'micro' research to be discussed here includes both anthropological studies (as defined above) and village surveys (which, as was pointed out, do not necessarily differ radically from 'macro' surveys in terms of their methodology). Reference to the map (Figure 1) shows that the existing village-level studies are unevenly distributed. Certainly the addition of the thirty-one village studies carried out in Tamil Nadu in connection with the 1961 census improves the coverage, including as they do six studies each for Salem and Tirunelveli and four for Madurai, districts which are otherwise hardly represented at all. But these were routinized studies of villages in hill areas, or with particularly large tribal populations, or with prominent craft industries. They are of uneven quality, and the compilers of the IDS Village Studies Bibliography considered the reliability of the data contained in them generally to be only 'fair'. They are of limited value for studies of economic change (see Guhan, 1985). The best, and the best-known studies (most of them 'anthropological') have been carried out in Chingleput (near Madras), in the Kaveri valley and delta (in Tiruchirapalli and Thanjavur districts), and in the eastern part of North Arcot, together with the 'Slater' villages in South Arcot (Iruvellpattu), Ramanathapuram (Vadamalaipuram) and Tirunelveli (Gangaikondan). These are villages which, together with Dusi in eastern North Arcot, and Palakurichi in East Thanjavur, were first studied by students of Professor Gilbert Slater of Madras University, in 1916; they were studied again in the 1930s by students of Thomas and Radhakrishnan; and they have been studied again by S. Guhán and some of his colleagues and associates at the Madras Institute of Development Studies, in 1982–3.

There is a remarkable dearth, certainly of reputed and widely available village studies for the whole of the western part of the state, including the important and distinctive Coimbatore district. Twelve of the fourteen villages in Coimbatore listed in the IDS Bibliography as having been studied were in fact included in a bench-mark survey undertaken by the Agricultural College in connection with an irrigation project. There is no good village monograph for Coimbatore dealing with economic and political issues. As it is, therefore, it is quite possible that the impressions that we have of agrarian change in Tamil Nadu from village-level research are biased towards areas of relatively well irrigated paddy agriculture (Chingleput, North Arcot, the Villupuram area of South Arcot, and the Kaveri valley and delta), and that areas of more uncertain irrigation and areas of dryland agriculture are rather under-represented (Vadamalaipuram in Ramanathapuram is the exception amongst the studies referred to). Certainly, this bias obtains in the village-level research on which the following discussion is based.

A further qualifying observation which must be made is that the interpretation of the results of different studies is complicated because of differences in the time periods covered. Kurien's 'macro' sources are for the period from 1950 to 1975, updated to 1981 for the crucial particular of the structure of the rural labour force by Subramaniam and Ramachandran; the Slater village studies refer to 1916, 1937 and 1982–3, with some material, usually, for the late 1950s or the 1960s as well; my own studies in North Arcot refer to the period 1973–84; and Gough's to the period 1953–76. These are the studies which will be referred to most extensively because they most lend themselves to discussion of trends of change.

Some of the results of my own studies in eastern North Arcot were referred to earlier, when it was shown that these 'anthropological' investigations indicate a lower incidence of agricultural wage labour in the labour force than survey investigations in the same villages (see Table II). Comparison of survey results for 1973–4 and 1983–4 suggests that there has

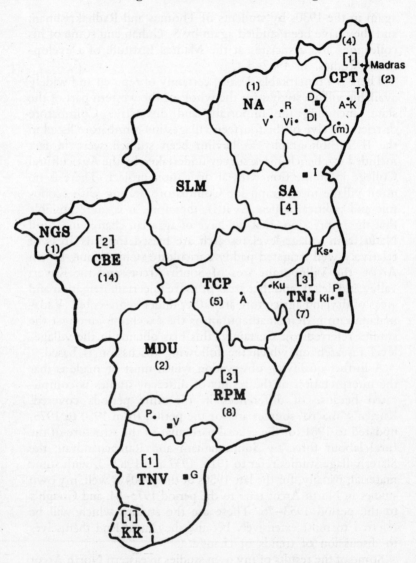

Figure 1. Location of Village Studies in Tamil Nadu
(After a listing by S. Guhan, Madras Institute of Development Studies)

figures in
[ ] = number of village surveys in district carried out by Agro-Economic
Research Centre

( ) = number of village surveys in a district carried out before 1975 according to the IDS Register

KEY

■ = 'Slater' village

CPT=Chingleput district
T=Thaiyur (Djurfeldt & Lindberg 1975)   (M)=village surveys
A-K=Asthapuram-Kanthapuram (Sivakumar 1978)   by Mencher 1978

NA=North Arcot district
V=Veerasambanur   (Chambers & Harriss. 1977;
R=Randam (Harriss 1982)   Harriss 1985)
Vi=Vinayakapuram
Dl=Duli
D=Dusi (Guhan & Bharathan 1984)

SA=South Arcot district
  I=Iruvellpattu (Guhan & Mencher 1983)

SLM=Salem district

CBE=Coimbatore district

MDU=Madurai district

TNV=Thirunelveli district
  G=Gangaikondan (Athreya 1985)

RPM=Ramanathapuram district
  V=Vadamalaipuram (Athreya 1984)
  P=Pooranur (Bradnock 1984)

TNJ=Thanjavur district
  Ks=Kshtrapalayam (Mayer 1984)
  Ku=Kumbapettai (Gough 1976, 1981)
  Ki=Kiruppur (Gough 1976, 1981)
  P=Palakurichi (Guhan 1983)

TCP=Thiruchirapalli district
  A=Appadurai
    + 4 studies by Japanese scholars in Lalgudi taluk

NGS=Nilgiris district

KK=Kanyakumari district

been a decline at the household level in primary dependence upon cultivation, and an increase in dependence upon agricultural labour, with little change in the incidence of dependence on other activities, recalling Kurien's first and major conclusion (see Table III). My findings on the primary sources of household income in four of the eleven villages in the survey samples, are compared with the Cambridge and IFPRI-TNAU survey results in Table IV. At both points in time, though markedly so

TABLE III

Percentage Households obtaining Primary Source of Income

	1974 Cambridge	1983 IFPRI
FAMILY FARM	49	40
AGRIC. LABOUR	35	42
ARTISAN	3	2
TRADE	2	1
PROFESSION	4	6
OTHERS	7	9

TABLE IV

Primary Source of Income, by Percentage of Households

	1973–4 JCH	Survey	1983–4 JCH	Survey
RANDAM				
FAMILY FARM	37	37	36	28
AGRIC. LABOUR	34	46	28	49
OTHER	29	17	36	24
VEERASAMBANUR				
FAMILY FARM	48	57	38	42
AGRIC. LABOUR	52	37	38	47
OTHER	–	6	29	11
VINAYAKAPURAM				
FAMILY FARM	60	59	38	31
AGRIC. LABOUR	35	29	18	53
OTHER	15	12	33	16
DULI				
FAMILY FARM	42	43	34	59
AGRIC. LABOUR	48	49	28	35
OTHER	10	8	38	6

in 1983–4, I have found less extensive dependence upon agricultural labour, and more dependence upon other non(cereal)-agricultural activities, though I have also found decreased dependence upon own cultivation (like the surveys, in three out of four villages). It is widely acknowledged, of course, that to attempt to classify households by 'primary source of income' is a proceeding which is likely to be subject to considerable amounts of error. What then of findings on the structure of the labour force in terms of principal occupation? The data of Table II are extended in Tables V and VI. My investigations lead me to conclude that in eastern North Arcot over the ten years from 1973–4 to 1983–4 the numbers of individuals depending primarily upon agriculture (as primary cultivators or as wage labourers) have remained roughly constant, and so have undergone relative decline. At the same

TABLE V (a)

Principal Occupations of Households in Randam (Principal Sources of Livelihood)

	1973	1983
CULTIVATION	102 (37%)	108 (36%)
AGRICULTURAL LABOUR	93 (34%)	84 (28%)
OTHER	80 (29%)	108 (36%)
TRADE	11	11
LIVESTOCK	6	9
ARTISAN/FUNCTIONARIES	12	18
TRANSPORT	2	2
SERVICE	36	45
DEPENDANTS	11	18
MONEY-LENDING	2	2
RENTS/INTEREST	–	3

Note: In this table the category 'Service' is meant in the conventional Indian usage, and refers to employment in government service or in private sector jobs which offer at least roughly comparable terms and conditions of work. It is not used in the sense of 'domestic service'.

TABLE V (b)

Labour Force in Random

	Men		Women	
	1973	*1984*	*1973*	*1984*
OWNER CULTIVATION	137 (38%)	109 (29%)	8	18
AGRICULTURAL LABOUR	107 (30%)	114 (30%)	136	158
OTHERS	112 (31%)	151 (40%)	14	25
TOTAL	356	374		
INCLUDING:				
SHEPHERDS	13	20		
TEACHERS	8	6		
WEAVERS	4	26*		
PADDY BUSINESS/				
RICE MILL	2	12		

* including side-workers (weavers' assistants)

time there has been a marked increase in the numbers of those primarily engaged in and dependent upon a range of other occupations. There does not appear to have been a shift from cultivation to agricultural wage labour, though the incidence of cultivators in the male labour force has certainly declined. My conclusion (see Harriss, 1989b) is that 'proletarianization' has been taking place, though this has not seen the creation of a larger (male) agricultural wage labouring class.

There are some interesting similarities in the findings of several of the Slater studies on trends in occupational/livelihood structure. Those for Palakurichi and for Gangaikondan certainly indicate an absolute and relative increase in the numbers of agricultural labourers, and a decline in the numbers of those whose primary occupation is own cultivation is almost universally reported. But there are also indications from all these studies of marked increases in numbers, depending on non-agricultural activities. Amongst the other village studies, Yanagisawa, writing about a village in the Kaveri valley (1983)

TABLE VI

Labour Force

(i) Men

(*Sample estimates*)	*Veerasambanur*		*Vinayakapuram*		*Duli*		*Dusi*	
	1973	1984	1973	1984	1973	1984	1973	1984
Primary occupation								
OWNER-CULTIVATION	27 (48%)	17 (38%)	29 (60%)	25 (49%)	20 (42%)	22 (34%)	32 (46%)	25 (30%)
AGRICULTURAL LABOUR	29 (52%)	15 (33%)	12 (25%)	9 (18%)	23 (48%)	18 (28%)	5 (7%)	5 (6%)
CATTLEHERD	–		1	–		4		
WEAVING		7 (16%)	–	9 (18%)	–	20 (31%)	17 (25%)	35 (42%)
WAGE EARNING		2 (4%)						4
SERVICE		1	3 (6%)	3	5	1		2
PETTY BUSINESS			3 (6%)	2			8 (12%)	7
PROFESSION				2		others 3	others 3	1
REMITTANCES		3		1				others 4
MONEYLENDING								
% OF MALE POP. IN LAB. FORCE	59	54	63	59	55	58	66	64

TABLE VI (Cont'd.)

(ii) Women

(Sample estimates)	Veerasambanur		Vinayakapuram		Duli		Dusi	
	1973	1984	1973	1984	1973	1984	1973	1984
Primary occupation								
OWNER-CULTIVATION	6 (18%)	22 (42%)	6 (25%)	19 (51%)	1	12 (35%)	20 (59%)	10 (21%)
AGRICULTURAL LABOUR	27 (82%)	27 (51%)	17 (71%)	13 (35%)	10 (91%)	16 (47%)	3 (9%)	12 (25%)
PETTY TRADE		1				5 (15%)	6 (18%)	18 (38%)
SERVICE (NOON MEALS SCHEME)				3		1		
DHOBI			1	1				
DOMESTIC SERVICE		1		1			others 5	8
WEAVING		1						
TAILOR		1						
% OF FEMALE POP IN LAB FORCE	34	51	29	47	18	43	27	37

TABLE VII

Harvesting and Threshing Wages Reported

| | 1973–4 | | 1983–4 | | |
	H(F)	T(M)	H(F)	T(M)	
KALP	3.5 mm	3.5 mm	3.5 mm	3.5 mm	no change
MEP	3.0 mm	4.5 mm	3.4 mm	4.5–6 mm	? increase
VAY	2.5 mm	5.0 mm	3.0 kg	6.0 kg	? no change
VEER	3.0 mm	6.0 mm	3.0 mm	6.0 mm	no change
VINAY	2.1 mm	2.3 mm	4.0 kg	6.0 mm	? increase
RAND	3.0 mm	6.0 mm	3.0 mm	6.0 mm	no change
AMUD	2.5 mm	3.5 mm	6.0 mm	8.0 mm	? increase
VENG	3.5 mm	3.0 mm	5.0 lit	6.0 lit	?
DULI	3.5 mm	1.0 mm	2.3 mm	6.0 mm	? increase
SIR	4.0 mm	4.0 mm	4.0 mm	4.0 mm	no change
VEGAM	4.0 mm	4.0 mm	?	?	?

Note: mm=one 'padi' or measure of paddy.

also reports an important expansion of non-agricultural employment, but Gough reports from her Thanjavur villages (one of them not far from Yanagisawa's) that the numbers of agricultural labourers have increased both absolutely and relatively, as in Palakurichi and Gangaikondan. She also notes that 'the figures suggest, although they do not prove, a decrease in the numbers and holdings of middle small owners, and an increase in the holdings and prosperity of at least some of the bigger landlords.' (1976, 14) What, more generally, of the direct evidence from village studies on trends in landholding, bearing in mind Kurien's suggestion from his study of the macro data that, in the 1960s and 1970s at least, there was 'a tendency for small farmers to leave land and farming and join the ranks of the rural proletariat'?

My own findings from a detailed investigation of the history of landholdings in Randam village, and amongst the households in my samples for another four villages—unlike Gough's suggestions for her Thanjavur villages—do not show up this tendency:

The distribution of ownership holdings (in circumstances where tenancy is of marginal significance) . . . shows little change between inheritance and the present and between 1973 and 1984, in Randam, Veerasambanur and Vinayakapuram, and it has become markedly more unequal only in Duli . . . In all the villages the number of 'gainers' of land since inheritance outweigh (though not always by much) the numbers of 'losers' of land . . . . It can be concluded . . . that except in the case of Duli there is no evidence for increased concentration of landholdings or for loss of land by the smallest landholders, but rather the reverse. (Harriss, 1989b)

Amongst the Slater villages, in Iruvellpattu Guhan and Mencher refer to the proliferation of small landholdings around one very big holding; in Palakurichi Guhan records a slight increase in the Gini coefficient between 1896 and 1983; in Vadamalaipuram, too, Athreya says that there has been a marginal increase in concentration of landholding between 1958 and 1983, as the average size of holdings in the upper-size classes has increased slightly and there has been a proliferation of holdings under five acres in extent; while both in Dusi and Gangaikondan decreased concentration over time is reported.

The evidence we have from village studies, therefore, presents a mixed picture, as one might expect. This is after noting the differences in methodology between the Slater studies and my own—the former resting on comparisons of aggregated data at different points in time, and the latter on a kind of 'dynamic' study of households' landholdings over time. It may be fair to conclude, however, that the overall indications of the village studies, and of the NSS data referred to by Kurien, are that there has not been a trend towards increased landlessness, and that the distribution of land ownership has been altered mainly by the proliferation of small holdings. Because such holdings do not supply the entire livelihood requirements of households owning them, this proliferation has not meant an expansion in the numbers of 'cultivators' (according to either 'principal source of income' or 'principal form of employment'), just as Kurien argued in his analysis of 'macro' sources.

The first element in Kurien's argument concerns occupational trends, and the second concerns trends in the distribution of landholdings and of assets. The third is about trends in real wages and levels of living. Kurien's conclusion is, most emphatically, that real wages declined over the period he was concerned with, and that though the number of days per annum of agricultural employment may have increased, especially for men, agricultural labourers' earnings were still way below the poverty line. Comparable findings come from the village studies of Iruvellpattu, Palakurichi and Vadamalaipuram; dissimilar ones come from Dusi and Gangaikondan, and from the North Arcot studies. In Iruvellpattu Guhan and Mencher observed no perceptible overall increase in real wages per diem, though they believe that the amount of employment available may have increased. Of Palakurichi Guhan says 'The minimal conclusion that emerges is that in the long span of more than four decades since ST's survey in 1937 real earnings of agricultural labour have not gone up, even if they have not declined.' (1983, 89) In Vadamalaipuram Athreya reports that agricultural wage rates have increased since 1958: 'a rise brought about by an increase in employment opportunities in manufacturing activity'. But he argues that the relative decline that has occurred in demand for male labour in agriculture means that the annual earnings of agricultural labour households have remained more or less constant. In Dusi Guhan and Bharathan show that real wage rates have increased slightly since 1937, except for ploughing (without cattle) and weeding, though only after a dip downwards in the late 1950s and early 1960s. They have no data on trends in the availability of employment, but are of the view that there has been a favourable shift in terms of the share of the product going to labour (1984, 67). For Gangaikondan Athreya reports that after taking a number of qualifications into account, 'real wage rates for males would show a substantial increase between 1958 and 1984 [though] by contrast, there has been only a rather modest rise in the daily wage rate for female casual labour.' (1958, 119) There has been an increase in the average number of days of employment, so that he concludes unequivocally: 'Annual real earnings of agricultural labourers from hiring out—both in agriculture and outside—have thus increased between 1958 and 1984.' My own data for villages in eastern North Arcot show a clear increase in the real wage rates for men and women, except in one village (Veerasambanur), where agriculture has stagnated and where real wages appear to have declined. Generally the evidence for eastern North Arcot suggests that demand for agricultural labour has increased, that there has been a tightening of the labour market and an increase in real incomes of agricultural labour. But of course the contrast between these findings for the 1970s and the early 1980s in Gangaikondan, Dusi and North Arcot, and the indications of the Annual Wage Rate Series data referred to by Kurien, may well be due to the differences in the time period covered by the different studies.

COMPARISON OF THE RESULTS OF 'MACRO' AND 'MICRO' RESEARCH

Crucially important 'facts' in Kurien's account of agrarian change in Tamil Nadu are those on the changing structure of the labour force (declining importance of cultivation, increasing importance of agricultural wage labour); those on the distribution of land ownership and of land operation (decline in the incidence of absolute landlessness, with proliferation of very small holdings; slight decrease in the incidence of land operation); and those on wage rate and levels of living (decline in real wages; agricultural labourers' incomes are generally below the poverty line). What do the 'micro' studies (of both 'anthropological' and village survey type) suggest about the *quality* of these 'facts'?

With regard to the structure of the labour force it is possible to find clear correspondences between the findings of 'macro' and 'micro' research. There is widespread evidence from village studies of decline in the relative importance of cultivation, though the evidence on the incidence of agricultural wage labour is more varied. Where it is possible directly to compare the findings of survey research on the structure of the labour force with those from anthropological investigation (in the North Arcot studies) it appears that the former method tends to overemphasize the importance of agricultural labour and probably to underestimate the extent of diversification and of employment in non-agricultural activities. It is likely that the 'macro' sources used by Kurien (notably the census) have a similar bias. The finding that there has been 'pressure on small farmers to leave their land and to become agricultural labourers', based principally on the indications of the census, may rest therefore on a misapprehension of the extent of diversification and of non-agricultural employment. It might be countered that this does not at all alter the main thrust of Kurien's argument: the census probably records as a shift to agricultural wage labour what is in fact a shift to more diversified economic activity; but this more diversified economic activity (including considerable occupational multiplicity, which makes it so difficult to allocate individuals and households to discrete labour force categories) is characteristic of peasantry in the course of proletarianization—which is the core of Kurien's argument about what has been going on in Tamil Nadu. The difficulty with this defence of the 'facts' and the interpretation of them offered by Kurien is that he clearly suggests that the kind of proletarianization that has taken place is associated with declining real wages and with increased poverty. Thus he is suggesting that, in so far as the observation of 'increased incidence of agricultural wage labour' is actually a proxy for 'increasingly diversified employment,' the activities in which people are now engaging are of lower productivity than those they were involved in before. And the problem with this is that so little is known—not just about the actual patterns of employment in rural Tamil Nadu but also about the productivity of different activities. There is some evidence in the North Arcot studies that the productivity of much non-agricultural activity is higher than that of agricultural labour or marginal. But the whole subject has been insufficiently explored (and, as I shall discuss at some length later on, the favourite research instruments of the 'survey' or the 'village study' are blunt instruments in this area of enquiry).

The second set of facts concerns landholding and land operation, and here we find that the results of the micro studies and the indication of the sources used by Kurien correspond with each other quite closely. Contrary to a still popularly held view, there is no clear evidence either that the incidence of absolute landlessness has increased or that the concentration of land ownership has increased. Rather, there are strong indications of proliferation of very small holdings. Kurien's emphasis on 'the tendency of small farmers to leave land and farming' seems somewhat misplaced in view of the evidence he himself cites on decreased landlessness. The conclusion from micro studies in North Arcot and elsewhere—that the tendency has rather been one of proletarianization without depeasantization—can just as well be inferred from Kurien's macro data.

With regard to trends in real wages paid to agricultural labourers, and trends in their real incomes, divergent impressions are obtained depending, it seems, on precisely where one looks, and over what period. In the absence of information on the sources and mode of collection of the Agro-Economic Research Centre's Annual Wage Rate Series used by Kurien, it is difficult to know how much these data can be relied on. The clear indications of micro-level research on rural labour markets and wage rates are that these markets are parcellized and that there are often marked differences in wage rates even between villages that are close together (see for example Harriss, 1989a). In these circumstances it is extremely difficult to derive an aggregated, 'average' picture which is at all reliable (see Appadurai in this volume on the problems of aggregation).

Comparison of the findings of macro and micro research on agrarian change in Tamil Nadu does not show up very major differences as to the essential 'facts'. It does suggest a need to qualify these facts, however, and the possibility that a different construction can be placed upon them from that proposed by Kurien. His interpretation is that there is a hidden process of change in which proletarianization is taking place but in the absence of structural transformation. The result, it was suggested, might be described as one of pauperization and 'marginalization': when some small landowners are ceasing to be cultivators and are becoming agricultural labourers, when there are declining real wages in agriculture, and when there is widespread and massive poverty amongst agricultural labourers. We have seen that the evidence for the first element in this interpretation, and possibly for the second too, is questionable. It appears possible that Kurien's interpretation was influenced by the general model of agrarian transformation as necessarily involving 'differentiation' and 'polarization' of peasant households, which, in circumstances of late industrialization and limited overall structural transformation, may well mean pauperization and marginalization within the rural economy. Contemporary agrarian studies are not very different from the historical studies of which Bayly says 'in the absence of . . . data a consensus has been built up on the basis of random insights.'

Kurien's interpretation of processes of agrarian change in Tamil Nadu rests on quite a weak empirical base and it perhaps gains credibility from the way it recalls the orthodox Leninist model.

The evidence that Kurien refers to can just as plausibly be interpreted as showing—like many of the village studies, incidentally—that there has been a process of proletarianization without depeasantization, and that the rural economy has become much more diversified. What the effects of these tendencies has been on incomes and levels of livelihood is uncertain at an aggregated level, but undoubtedly varied locally and regionally. It is probably more important for research to try to establish in what conditions rural labour markets have been tightened and real wages pushed up, than to attempt to establish aggregated measures. One last general observation in this connection. The impression given in Kurien's interpretation that the prevalent process is one of pauperization and marginalization is supported by some of the data he cites, especially on wage and income trends. But recent debates on the measurement of poverty (see for example Lipton's review, 1983) teach us to be a little sceptical about the poverty-line argument. My own field experience is consistent with the findings of Caldwell and his associates in part of southern Karnataka, which have shown that conditions are conducive to fertility decline (Caldwell *et al.*, 1985). Caldwell argues, on the basis of long-term and exceptionally thorough research, that the possibilities of finding rewarding urban employment are sufficiently good, in the Karnataka villages he studied, as to have given people a strong incentive to educate their children, both male and female, in order to improve their chances of finding urban work or an urban spouse, and that this in turn has contributed a powerful incentive to limitation of fertility. There are indications—from comparison of the 1971 and 1981 censuses; and in the evidence from village studies on the take up of family planning methods over the last decade—that this virtuous spiral may be in operation in parts of Tamil Nadu like eastern North Arcot. Obviously, much more research is needed on this issue, but there are here some further grounds for at least questioning the validity of Kurien's general interpretation of economic trends in rural Tamil Nadu.

CONCLUSIONS: IMPLICATIONS FOR AGRARIAN RESEARCH
METHODOLOGY

In the main body of this essay I have sought to illustrate some of
the problems involved in understanding what is happening in
the rural economy of Tamil Nadu (and they are unlikely to be
peculiar to the Tamil Nadu case). There are problems in
ascertaining the 'facts'; there are also problems in aggregating
and disaggregating in such a way as to avoid misleading
generalized 'averages' on the one hand, and fragmented local
knowledge on the other; and there are problems of interpretation. The upshot of the discussion is not to advocate more micro
research and to inveigh against the survey methodology of
much 'macro' research (which has been carried out recently
with verve and force by Chambers, 1983; and by Hill, 1984,
1986). Rather, I am led to cry, like Mercutio, 'A plague o' both
your houses!' for the fruitful development of agrarian research
in South Asia seems to me to depend on getting away from the
orthodoxies of both the 'agro-economic survey' on the one
hand, and 'village studies' on the other.

The extent to which these two approaches have been
conventionalized and ritualized is remarkable. For example,
large numbers of village studies have been done, and quite a large
number of villages (like the 'Slater' villages in Tamil Nadu) have
been studied at several points in time. But the only kind of
analysis which has been undertaken has involved static, aggregated comparisons of data sets from different points in time.
There has been no attempt until very recently to undertake
'dynamic studies' of households over time that are at all
comparable with those developed by the Russians in the late
nineteenth century. They undertook a form of panel research in
which the characteristics of individual households were studied
at different points in time. It was on the basis of such research
that some Russian economists questioned the view that there
was a secular trend of differentiation by showing how the
patterns which were then being interpreted as indicating such a
trend could result from movements of households between 'class
positions', as they went through the developmental cycle. No
attempt has been made, when Indian villages have been
restudied, to trace household mobility patterns, as might be

done by means of transition matrices, simple cross tabulations of households according to landholdings at a point of time in the past and at the present (see Cain, 1981; and Harriss, 1989b). Cain has developed a method for studying household mobility from single point data as well, by asking questions which trace the history of household land ownership (or, it could be, sources of livelihood) since the time the household's head inherited land. On the basis of these data he draws up matrices which show the extent of mobility that has occurred. Comparison of aggregated landholdings data from different points in time would not permit the drawing of comparable conclusions about, for example, the extent to which smaller landholders at inheritance may have gained, and larger landholders lost land. The results of this study have called seriously into question widely accepted notions about trends of change in rural India, as well as providing the foundation for an important argument about the risk environments of different groups of households and their implications for fertility decisions. Another recent study which breaks the mould is that of van Schendel, who has written a subtle history of rural Bangladesh based on a procedure more like that of the early Russian studies, comparing data from different points in time to trace the fortunes of households (van Schendel, 1981). This approach could be used in the analysis of village survey data held in the records of the Agro-Economic Research Centres in India; and such analysis would probably be very informative about trends on agrarian change.

In a similar way, for all the numbers of local village studies for India, very little research at all has been done on household budgets and labour allocation of the kind carried out by White in Java (1976). On the basis of intensive and immensely time-consuming research on labour allocation, White called into question the then conventional wisdom on the character of the employment problem in rural Java. It had been held that the employment problem was one of the limited duration of work, but White showed that people are in fact rather fully employed in terms of the duration of work, and that the problem is rather one of the very low productivity of so much work that is done. His findings depended upon intensive investigation of labour allocation and incomes, involving 60 visits to each of 20 households throughout one year, and a smaller number of visits to another 84 households. Intensive investigation of this kind could not possibly be matched in a conventional agro-economic survey, nor in a more or less 'standard' village study of the type characteristic of much rural research in India (and which is often taken to be what 'micro-level' research is). Such intensive studies as White's are required in order to understand more adequately the structure of rural employment in a region like that of Tamil Nadu, to resolve problems like that which arises from Kurien's reliance on census data for a major element in his interpretation, and, crucially I believe, to determine the productivity of different types of activity and thus to evaluate the effects on livelihoods of the diversification which seems to be taking place in the rural economy. The importance of this sort of research is illustrated in recent debates on agrarian change in Indonesia. The results of White's research (and of the comparable studies carried out by Hart, 1978) have been interpreted as showing that work in paddy agriculture in Java constitutes a kind of 'formal sector' of relatively privileged employment within the rural economy (see World Bank [Little and Majumdar]. 1985). More recent village studies (see Collier *et al.*, 1982) suggest, however, that by the beginning of the 1980s significant diversification of the rural economy had taken place in Java, and that this was associated with some tightening of rural labour markets and upward movements in real wages. A debate has thus been joined on the implications of the diversification of rural economic activity for livelihoods (see the optimistic assessment of World Bank, 1980, and the more pessimistic one of World Bank, 1985; and also Jones, 1984). The resolution of this debate—which has strong parallels in Tamil Nadu, as I have argued above—really requires further micro-level research on labour markets, and on household budgets and labour allocation on the lines of White's original work.

It is the theme of other recent research, such as that reported and discussed by Lipton (1983), that understanding of the process of poverty and under-nutrition may call for much finer analysis than has been carried out hitherto. It is probably not very helpful for analytical and practical purposes to describe '40 per cent or more' of the population as being 'below the poverty line'. Lipton has put forward an argument for distinguishing between people within the broad category of 'the poor'.

Analysing differential vulnerability to different kinds of hazard and stress probably calls for more detailed and thorough time and budget studies than have been carried out hitherto, either in large-scale surveys, or in what has passed for 'micro' research. Such research may also involve the deconstruction of the household, too readily taken as the fundamental unit of analysis in agrarian research. The desirability of taking into account intra-household relations has come increasingly to be recognized (see Redclift, 1985, for a general argument; and B. Harriss, 1986, for a discussion in relation to South Asia).

I will give one more example of a mode of investigation which does not fit into the category of the orthodox 'micro-level' village study. The importance of farmers' knowledge of the agricultural environment, and of perceptions of hazard, have also come to be more widely recognized. Adequate study of them cannot rest on the kind of 'opinion surveys' which have sometimes been carried out as part of conventional village studies. Such surveys are notoriously liable to bias, partly because the design of the questionnaire itself imposes a structure on responses. It is necessary to explore much more refined methodologies for the elucidation of peoples' constructs and theories—the modes of thought in terms of which they make judgements and form their opinions. One way of eliciting people's personal constructs and ways of classifying is through the use of the repertory grid method. Richards explains:

The basic procedure . . . is that of the triads test in which respondents are presented with elements—mostly concrete objects such as weeds, pests, rice varieties or grain legume seeds—in sets of threes and asked to discriminate by pairing two on the basis of similarity and isolating the third on the basis of difference. Respondents are then asked to explain the 'construct' underlying their discrimination . . . the test is repeated until combinations amongst a given set of objects are exhausted and a complete classification of the object under scrutiny personal to the respondent is created. This is the repertory grid which forms the basis for subsequent analysis . . . (Richards, 1979; more generally on the subject of 'farmers' knowledge' see Richards 1985; and on personal construct theory see Kelly, 1955).

The process of eliciting people's constructs in this way sets up a dialogue between investigator and respondent. The purpose is not simply to find out *what* the respondent knows (which is done, often badly, in opinion type questionnaires), but to *analyse* what s/he knows and to elucidate the process by which s/he comes to know what s/he knows.

Part of the burden of these remarks is, if not to argue against, at least to utter a note of caution about the genre of village studies which treat 'villages' as self-evident, clearly bounded entities, which are intended to be comprehensive, 'fact-finding' exercises, and lack a defined analytical purpose. Village studies of this type may yield results which are of value—and of course they may be a way to being surprised—but the devotion of research effort and resources to them diverts attention and resources both from lower levels for empirical investigation, such as the household, and rather higher ones. Amongst the latter is the level of inter-village comparison. Studies in single villages may have considerable merits, but it is difficult for a single researcher undertaking such a study to draw out what is peculiar about the village. Equally, the significance of systematic differences between villages, such as those in some of Ashok Rudra's research (e.g. Rudra, 1984), is easily obscured in survey research in which a small number of households is studied in each of several villages. It is possible that greater knowledge of and understanding of differences between villages within fairly small regions will yield results in terms of knowledge about the processes operating within the rural economy as a whole, different from and complementary to those arising from very detailed micro-level research and from the macro survey method. An example important for Tamil Nadu was referred to earlier: understanding the differences between villages and regions where some tightening of the rural labour market has occurred and those where it has not.

Reflection on a Conversation: I share in the consensus obtaining between most of the participants in the conversations of this volume, concerning the desirability of integrating different approaches so that the complementarities between 'macro' and 'micro' scales of investigation, and between economic and anthropological/sociological analysis may be utilized more effectively. We are, I think, implicitly united in rejection of some of Polly Hill's extreme pessimism about the results of anything other than 'anthropological' investigation (Hill, 1986). We share optimism about the possibilities for improving measurement and refining and enlarging interpretation by recognizing and deliberately building upon complementarities. It is also generally held that there is a need for more research which is, in a sense, *between* (and, I would add, *below*) the levels of the conventional approaches which have ruled hitherto in South Asia. I have explained my reasons for thinking this, and so have others (Rudra, in particular). An important part of the argument refers to the significance of understanding variations rather than of deriving aggregated measures. This must often involve concern for the 'relational' rather than the 'distributional' aspects of social phenomena to which Appadurai gives much emphasis.

The most challenging arguments advanced in our conversations are those put by Appadurai concerning the constitution of the 'macro-level'. He concludes with the powerful remark that 'Until we develop ways of looking at relational processes at the micro-level, and do so in a way that refines aggregation by improving the framework of macro-sociological theory, efforts to measure rural economic change will remain either trivial (because of their non-representativeness) or sterile (because they do not illuminate relationships between actors/social units).' This seems to me to be too pessimistic a judgement and one which may be counter-productive because it seems to imply that there is a mountain to be climbed before we can begin our journey. There are at least some ways of '. . . looking at relational processes at the micro-level' which include study of the 'entitlement events' to which Appadurai refers. Some anthropological investigation does this. It is really the foundation of the approach, described as 'situational analysis', developed by the 'Manchester School' (see van Velsen, 1967). The approach was developed as part of a deliberate critique of the structural-functionalism which had dominated anthropology, and it involved study of strategic interactions and of the construction and deconstruction of 'society' in their outcomes. There is work in this vein relating to Indian rural society, including older work like some of that of F. G. Bailey (see for example his 'The Peasant View of the Bad Life', 1966) and more recent studies of the interactions of bureaucrats and rural people (e.g. Gebert, 1987). While I agree with Appadurai that there is much to be done in 'improving the framework of macro-sociological theory', I believe that the effort has at least begun. The problem is part of the general one of the dearth of anthropological/sociological analysis of the rural economy and of economic life in India more generally.

REFERENCES

Athreya, V. B., 'Vadamalaipuram: a resurvey', Working Paper No. 50, Madras Institute of Development Studies, August 1984.

Athreya, V. B., 'Gangaikondan 1916–1984: Change and Stability', Working Paper No. 56, Madras Institute of Development Studies, June 1985.

Bailey, F. G., 'The Peasant View of the Bad Life', *Advancement of Science*, Dec. 1966.

Bayly, C., 'Indian Merchants in a Traditional Setting: Benares 1780–1830', in C. Dewey and A. G. Hopkins, eds., *The Imperial Impact*. London, Athlone Press 1978.

Bradnock, R. W., 'Agricultural Development in Tamil Nadu', in T. Bayliss-Smith and S. Wanmali, *Understanding Green Revolutions*, Cambridge: CUP, 1984.

Breman, J., *Of Peasants, Migrants and Paupers: Rural Labour Circulation and Capitalist Production in West India*. Delhi etc.: Oxford Univ. Press 1985.

Cain, M., 'Risk and Insurance: Perspectives on Fertility and Agrarian Change in India and Bangladesh', Population and Development Review 7, 3, pp. 435–74 1981.

Caldwell, J. et al., 'The Causes of Demographic Change in Rural South India: A Micro Approach', Population and Development Review, 11, pp. 689–727 1985.

Chambers, R., *Rural Development: putting the last first*. London, Longman 1983.

Collier, W. et al., 'Acceleration of Rural Development in Java', Bulletin of Indonesian Economic Studies, 18, 3 1982.

Djurfeldt, B., and S. Lindberg, *Behind Poverty: Social Formation in a Tamil Village*. London, Curzon Press, 1975.

Etienne, G., *India's Changing Rural Scene 1963–1979*, Delhi: Oxford University Press 1982.

Farmer, B. H., ed., *Green Revolution? Technology and Change in Rice-growing Areas of Tamil Nadu and Sri Lanka.* London, Macmillan 1977.

Gebert, R., 'Exchange and Environment: Local Officials and Poverty Alleviation Policy in South India', Unpublished PhD dissertation, Australion National University 1987.

Geertz, C., 'Culture and Social Change: The Indonesian Case', *Man* (NS), 19, pp. 511–32 1983.

Gough, K., 'Changing Agrarian Relations in Thanjavur 1952–1976', Kerala Sociological Review (quotation from mimeographed version) 1976.

Guhan, S., 'Palakurichi: a resurvey', Working paper No. 42, Madras Institute of Development Studies, November 1983.

Guhan, S., 'Thirty-one Villages of Tamil Nadu: The 1961 Census monographs'. Digest Series, No. 4, Madras Institute of Development Studies 1985.

Guhan, S. and Mencher, J., 'Iruvellpattu Revisited', *Economic and Political Weekly*, 4 and 11 June 1983.

Guhan S. and Bharathan, K., 'Dusi: a resurvey', Working Paper No. 52, Madras Institute of Development Studies, December 1984.

Harriss, B., 'The Intra-Household Allocation of Hunger in South Asia' (mimeo) 1986.

Harriss, J., review of G. Etienne, *India's Changing Rural Scene,* in Journal of Development Studies, 21, pp. 148–9 1984.

Harriss, J., 'Population, Employment and Wages: A Comparative Study of North Arcot Villages 1973–1983', in Hazell and Ramaswamy, eds. 1989a.

Harriss, J., 'What happened to the green revolution in North Arcot? Economic trends, household mobility, and the politics of an 'awkward class', in Hazell and Ramaswamy, eds. 1989b.

Hart, G. *'Labour Allocation Strategies in Rural Javanese Households'*. Ph.D. dissertation. Cornell University 1978.

Hazell, P. and Ramaswamy, C., eds., forthcoming, *The Green*

Revolution Revisited. Baltimore: Johns Hopkins University Press 1989.

Hill, P., 'The Poor Quality of Official Socio-Economic Statistics Relating to the Rural Tropical World: With Special Reference to South India'. *Modern Asian Studies*, 18, 3, pp. 491–514 1984.

Hill, P., *Development Economics on Trial: The Anthropological Case for a Prosecution.* Cambridge, Cambridge University Press 1986.

Jones, G. W., 'Links between urbanisation and sectoral shifts in Employment in Java', *Bulletin of Indonesian Economic Studies*, 20, 3 1984.

Kelly, G. A., *The Psychology of Personal Constructs.* New York, Norton 1955.

Kurien, C. T., 'Dynamics of Rural Transformation: A Case Study of Tamil Nadu', *Economic and Political Weekly*, Annual Number 1980.

Lipton, M., 'Poverty, Hunger and Undernutrition', Working Paper prepared for the World Bank, mimeo, IDS, Sussex 1983.

Mayer, P., 'Is There Urban Bias in the Green Revolution', *Peasant Studies*; Vol. 11 no. 4, 1984.

Redclift, N., 'The Contested Domain: Gender, Accumulation and the Labour Process', in N. Redclift and E. Mingione, eds., *Beyond Employment: Household, Gender and Subsistence.* Oxford, Blackwell 1985.

Richards, P., 'Community Environmental Knowledge and African Rural Development', *IDS Bulletin*, 10, 2, pp. 28–36 1979.

Richards, P., *Indigenous Agricultural Revolution.* London, Hutchinson 1985.

Rudra, A., 'Local Power and Farm Level Decision Making', in M. Desai *et al.*, eds., *Agrarian Power and Agricultural Productivity in South Asia.* Delhi etc., Oxford University Press 1984.

Sivakumar, S. S., 'Aspects of Agrarian Economy in Tamil Nadu', in *EPW*, May 1978, in 3 parts.

Subramaniam, S. and Ramachandran, V. K., 'Agricultural Labourers in the Working Population of Tamil Nadu', *Bulletin*, Madras Institute of Development Studies 1982.

Schendel van, W., *Peasant Mobility: The Odds of Life in Rural Bangladesh*. Van Gorcum 1981.

van Velsen, J., 'Situational analysis and the extended case method' in A. L. Epstein, ed., *The Craft of Social Anthropology*. London, Tavistock 1967.

White, B., 'Population, Involution and Employment in Rural Java', Development and Change, 7, pp. 267–90 1976.

Yanagisawa, H., *Socio-Cultural Change in Villages in Tiruchirapalli District, Tamil Nadu, India, Part 2: Modern Period No. 2*. Institute for the Study of Languages and Cultures of Asia and Africa, Tokyo 1983.

World Bank, *Indonesia: Employment and Income Distribution in Indonesia*, Washington DC, World Bank 1980.

World Bank, *Indonesia: Wages and Employment*. Washington DC, World Bank 1985.

Chapter 7: Social Science Research on Rural Change: Some Gaps*

N. S. JODHA

1. INTRODUCTION

One feature of contemporary field-oriented social science research is the frequently noticed contradictions and inconsistencies between the results obtained by macro-level and micro-level studies—between the observed or experienced realities and the picture of realities generated by field research, and between observed new developments and the complex changes to be captured by standard and simplistic methods. Hence, inconsistencies between results from different field studies can be largely attributed to methodology. This essay discusses the methodological aspects of rural economics and suggests the need for supplementing standard techniques with methodological approaches appropriate to the field. A case study covering two villages in Rajasthan is presented to illustrate different results on the incidence of poverty when this is assessed through two different approaches.

2. THE METHODOLOGICAL GAPS

The methodological deficiencies within field studies in social science are often associated with: (i) the concepts and categories used for the identification of rural realities; (ii) the yardsticks and norms employed for the assessment or measurement of rural

* I wish to thank R. A. E. Muller, Robert Chambers, Jere Behrman, T. S. Walker, Pranab Bardhan and G.P. Temple for their valuable comments and suggestions on an earlier draft.

realities; and (iii) the 'communication gaps' between researcher and respondent while using (i) and (ii).

2.1 Restrictive Categories and Standardized Yardsticks

The concepts and categories used to identify and classify rural realities are often too restrictive to encompass the details of petty but collectively significant components of rural characterization. Appendix A presents a few examples. These examples indicate the possibility of disregarding variables and their interactions, while using the formal/standard concepts for identification of different facets of rural household economy.

What applies to the choice of concepts and categories also applies to the choice of norms and yardsticks. The limited coverage of rural realities, owing to the use of restrictive categories, is further reduced by using standard yardsticks to measure them. The factors that do not lend themselves to easy assessment/measurement through these yardsticks are often bypassed while measuring and quantifying different variables.

These limitations are now increasingly recognized and the need for supplementing the formal concepts and norms by qualitative approaches is emphasized (see Streeten 1974, McCloskey 1983, Sen 1983, Chambers 1986).

2.2 Communications Gaps

Realizing the gap between results reported through formal field studies and reality, researches have attempted to dilute or widen the standard categories and yardsticks. Despite this, inconsistencies between results from different field studies persist. They exist because of several factors, which we may call 'communication gaps'. 'These gaps take place in three forms: (i) Differences in the connotation of the same concepts as they are understood by the respondent and researcher. For instance, the connotation of 'man–day' or 'man–hour' of labour input as understood, estimated, and reported by a 'not so time-conscious' farmer may be different from the investigator's understanding; (ii) Qualitative differences in the yardsticks and norms used by researcher and respondent for the measurement of variables. For instance, a farmer reports use of farmyard manure in terms of cart-loads, the researcher attempts to understand and record it in terms of quintals. Establishing quantitative equivalence between such categories is often difficult;[1] (iii) Differences in the degree of precision/vagueness attached to the quantitative information by the respondent while giving the response, and by the investigator while recording it. For instance, a farmer often reports quantitative information in terms of range of units or hyphenated terms (e.g. 10–12 man-days spent on weeding a plot), while the investigator seeks and, using his best judgement, records it in precise terms. The analyst often goes a step further and subjects these data to sophisticated quantitative techniques which are sensitive to variations as small as a fraction of an hour.

Appendix B illustrates some possible 'communication gaps'. Their extent depends on the difference in the background and working environment of the respondent and the researcher, the relative degree of seriousness with which investigations are taken up by the two, and the ability of the investigator to establish precise equivalence between the respondent's report and the researcher's intended or actual record.

Depending on the degree of communication gap, the results of different field studies of the same phenomenon in the same area/community may differ. Other things being equal, the possibility of such gaps being wider is greater in the macro-level studies than those in micro-level studies. There are greater opportunities for participant observation as well as prolonged and more intimate contact between the respondent and researcher that help narrow down communication gaps.[2]

---

[1] In ICRISAT's village-level studies, the measurement problems have been handled by physical weighing or measuring of the quantities reported in volumes. Such conversions were done on a random basis to evolve equivalence between two categories. See Binswanger and Jodha (1977).

[2] Various types of measurement errors emanating from the aforementioned factors will influence the results, depending on the type of analysis. For instance, if a variable is measured with a random error, that will not affect the estimate of its mean and regression estimate if it is the dependent variable in a multivariate regression. But it will still bias towards zero its coefficient if it is used as a right-side variable in a regression. On the other hand, systematic measurement error may cause more or less problems, depending on the mode of analysis and the nature of the error. Systematic

It is not difficult to imagine the distortions (under-reporting/
over-reporting) generated by these gaps in values of different
variables recorded through household surveys. Table I illustrates the point on the basis of data culled from different studies
with which I have been associated. The data reported in Table I
relate to cases where the extensive approach to data gathering
was supplemented by subsequent detailed purpose-specific and
intensive investigation, following the first-stage screening of
data. Although the number of observations in most cases is
small, they do help illustrate the point.

Important implications of methodological gaps include the
generation of inconsistencies in the results from different studies
on the same subject and the possibility of misleading the whole
approach of future research as well as future policies relating to
specific subjects.

One way to reduce these gaps is to supplement the
researchers' approach by the respondents' approach of looking
towards the issues being studied. One may profitably look at
categories and norms used by the respondent for identification
and assessment of variables affecting him or her.

In the following section this approach has been attempted.
For the purpose of illustration we have taken one of the most
debated themes of the day, namely the change in incidence of
poverty in rural areas.

3. THE APPROACH AND DATA

3.1 The Study Area and Reference Period

To study changes in the incidence of poverty we have data for
two periods of time covering a sample of farmers from two
villages in the arid zone of western Rajasthan.[3] There are several

---

measurement error will bias the mean but may not bias the regression. It
may be added that systematic mismeasurement over time should not lead
to the obfuscation of changes in the variable that is being mismeasured. If
mismeasurement errors themselves do not change over time, valid
conclusions on dynamics can still be drawn.

[3] The sampling procedure used for the study was as follows:
During the bench-mark (1963–6) a sample of 200 households, from a

TABLE I

Differences in the Values of Selected Variables according to the Method of Data Gathering

Variable	No. and type of observation	Unit of measurement	Value as per the choice of methods (b)		Difference in values		Reasons for difference: items bypassed by (A) and captured by (B)
			Method (A)	Method (B)	absolute $A-B$	$\dfrac{A-B}{A} \times 100$	
Average income	78 house-holds (hh) (4 villages)	Rs/hh	6814	7564	− 750	− 11.0%	Income from casual, routine activities based on common property resources. (Jodha 1986).
Gross returns	19 hh 23 plots, (1 village)	Rs/ha	291	334	− 43	− 14.8%	Casual harvest of minor crops for self-provisioning, etc. (Jodha et al. 1977).
Per worker/day engagement in farm activities	12 hh 44 workers (2 villages)	hours/day	6.75	9.58	− 2.53	− 41.9%	Petty and routine farm activities (Jodha et al. 1977)
Value of food consumption	32 hh (4 villages)	Rs/person (for 3 week one in each season)	68	79	− 11	− 16.2%	Food items from common property resources/petty self-provisioning arrangements (Jodha 1986).

Item	Sample	Unit	A	B	Difference	%	Reasons
Use level of tractor	12 Tractors (2 villages)	hours/week	73	105	− 32	− 43.8%	Most part of Tractor hiring (Jodha 1974).
Extent of land tenancy	Total leased in/out land. 86hh (6 villages)	ha 86hh	67	120	− 53	− 79.1%	Tenancy status of plots initially concealed (Jodha 1977).
Cost of food borrowed during drought year	26 hh (2 villages)	Rs/hh	648	822	−174	26.9%	Costs due to interlocked factor markets (Jodha 1978).
Capital investment	78 farms hh	Rs/hh	382	471	− 81	− 21.27	Accretionary process of capital formation (Jodha 1967).
Cost of credit from institutions	23 borrowers (5 villages)	Cost as % of principal	9%	22%	− 13% − 144%		Cost of borrowing beyond interest rate. (AERC 1971).

(a) Based on data/information for selected cases, from the studies referred in the last column.

(b) Method 'A' indicates the conventional extensive approach to data gathering through one or two short surveys using structured questionnaires. Method B involves prolonged and intensive interviews and in most cases participant observations, besides what is indicated under A.

(c) These reasons can be related to items mentioned under appendixes A and B.

criteria—for example changes in household income, consumption levels, extent of employment, etc., used by social scientists to assess changes in poverty levels. We have data on net household or per capita income, collected by using conventional concepts and yardsticks to measure income. Additionally, we have included the categories or concepts which farmers/villagers themselves use for assessing changes in their economic status. These indicators of their economic status or poverty levels not only help in assessment of change, but also facilitate the understanding of the process of change. They tend to capture the existing situation as it operates, rather than capture its formally quantifiable proxies. Through use of these norms or indicators it is easier to reduce communication gaps and capture the past, despite long periods of recall. Their major limitation is that they involve a more 'investigation-intensive' approach to field research because they require researchers to approach the respondents' level of thinking and the issues studied. They put greater emphasis on participant observation.

The choice of these 'unconventional' indicators of change in the present study emerged from anecdotal information collected during resurveying the villages studied in 1978. They were initially studied through a prolonged stay there of over twenty days in every month for three years, ending 1965–6. The anecdotes suggested the possibility of substantial change in the economic status of households considered poor during 1963–6. These anecdotes were used for developing specific questions and

population of 628 households in two villages, was selected through a simple random sampling method with a provision of replacement. During the resurvey a sub-sample of 100 households from the old sample was selected, again using a random sampling procedure with a provision for replacement. The sub-sample included a number of households which had split into two or more households since the bench-mark period. We reconstructed such households by collecting data from all components of the split households and pooling them for analysis. However, at the time of analysis several data gaps were noticed in the case of five households, and we could not fully reconstitute them. Consequently, they were dropped from the analysis. Thus the effective sample for the present study is 95 households. The essay compares their situation at two points of time. The values of some attributes of the total sample (200 households) of bench-mark survey are also presented in Table II.

a list of variables which, in the village context, were considered the real indicators of change in people's economic status over time. These indicators guided the participant observation as well as the collection of quantitative information from ninety-five selected households. The households belonged to two villages, one each in Nagaur and Jodhpur districts of Rajasthan. They constituted a part of a larger sample of households studied in 1963–6. Information about and from these ninety-five households was collected in instalments during 1977–8, 1982–3, and 1983–4, during fieldwork for other projects.[4] Additionally, details about the whole village situation were collected. Broad information on major changes (since 1963–6) observed in the villages studied was also gathered from *chokala* (clusters of neighbouring villages). The information indicated that the villages studied were not atypical in terms of these changes. The sub-sample of ninety-five households consisted of farm households only. It included thirty-five small and marginal farm households, i.e. which owned less than 4.5 hectares of arid land.

3.2 Farmers' Perception of Change

Income data of the sample households were collected using the standard concepts employed by farm management studies in India. Net income data covered the following sources: crop production, animal husbandry, labour/bullock hire, remittances, rental, petty trading, and property income. Net income figures were arrived at by deducting paid out and imputed costs of all inputs from gross income. Being so standardized and so often used, these concepts hardly need further elaboration. However, it may be added that the main purpose of collecting income information during the base period was to relate it to the process of capital formation by the sample households. The income data during the second period were collected to ascertain

[4] Data were collected during 1963–6 as a part of the fieldwork for my Ph.D thesis, 'Capital Formation in Arid Agriculture' (Jodha 1967) and land transformation studies of the Central Arid Zone Research Institute (CAZRI). The data for subsequent periods were gathered while collecting information for ICRISAT's research projects of Farmers' Group Action for Watershed Based Resource Development in 1977–8, and Role of Common Property Resources in Farming Systems in 1982–4 (Jodha 1986).

the extent of contribution of common property resources (pasture, forests, etc.) towards household income.

The terms in which villagers narrated change in their own economic status are unconventional and require explanation. They are classified under the following five major groups:
  (i) reduced reliance of the poor on traditional patrons, landlords, and resourceful people for sustenance, employment, and income;
 (ii) reduced dependence on low pay-off jobs/options;
(iii) improved mobility and liquidity position;
(iv) shifts in consumption patterns/practices;
 (v) acquisition of consumer durables.

Information on most of these items was available from benchmark data on resource endowment, production, marketing, and consumption activities of the sample households. For the resurvey period, it was purposely collected to see the change.

The indicators of change perceived by the villagers can be grouped under categories which are more familiar to economists and used in their professional communication. They are:

(a) Indicators of enlarging opportunity sets or an increasing number of choices (e.g. in the matter of employment, borrowing, marketing, etc.);

(b) Indicators of consumption activities with high income elasticities (e.g. travel, slack season purchases, length of maternity feeding of women, etc.);

(c) Indicators of investment in lumpy consumer durables (e.g. pucca structures of houses, compounds to houses, etc.).

4. CHANGES IN THE INCIDENCE OF POVERTY

The incidence of poverty in the ongoing debate on the subject in India is judged with reference to the poverty line and the changes over time in the proportions of the population below the poverty line. Though conceived in terms of per capita consumption expenditure the poverty line is indicated by a figure of monthly per capita income, such as Rs 15 for rural areas at 1960–1 prices according to Dandekar and Rath (1971), and Rs 65 at 1977–8 prices according to the Indian Planning Commission (1981). Per capita annual income of Rs 180 (at 1964–6 prices) may be considered a poverty line comparable to the one suggested by Dandekar and Rath (1971). The proportion of sample households in the villages studied falling below this income level during the two periods is indicated in Table II.[5] However, our further analysis follows a different approach. As a first step we compare for each household the annual per capita income (i.e. constant at 1964–6 prices) during the two periods (1964–6 and 1982–4). The proportion of households showing more than a 5 per cent decline in their per capita annual income is considered an indicator of the increased incidence of poverty. The increased incidence of poverty thus revealed is compared with changes in the economic status of the people, revealed by qualitative indicators of change as perceived by the villagers.

4.1 Per Capita Income

The analysis of the income data (Table II) showed that the average per capita annual income of the sample households was Rs 162 during 1964–6. This increased to Rs 1050 at current prices during 1982–4. However, when the income was deflated and expressed in terms of constant prices (1964–6 prices), the figure came down to Rs 175. To arrive at average annual income figures for the base period, the year 1963–4 was not included because it was a severe drought year. The household-by-household comparision of per capita income during the two periods (including by pooling the data of households which had split since the benchmark period), indicated that for 38 per cent

[5] In terms of rainfall and crops 1963–64 was a complete drought year. As per the *Annawari* system of crop assessment 1964–65 had bumper crops, while 1965–66 had average crops. The year 1982–83 had above average crops while crops were below average during 1983–84. On an average cropwise the period 1964–66 was slightly better than 1982–84. This influenced the income positions of the sample households to some extent. Of 95 sample households, 35 had less per capita income during 1982–84 compared to 1964–66. A part of it could be due to life cycle related factors such as increased number of members especially dependents in the households. However, due to a variety of factors 22 of the 35 households had income below poverty line during 1982–84. This included 7 households who were already below poverty line and 15 households who were above it during 1964–66. There were 11 households who moved above poverty line during the same period.

TABLE II

Details of Income Position of Sample Households at two points of time

(per capita annual net income in Rs)[a]

Details	Average situation during		
	1964–6[b]	1982–84	
		At current prices	At constant prices[c]
Average per capita annual income (Rs)	162 (168)[d]	1050	175
Contribution of different sources of income (%)			
– crop farming	48 (49)	43	–
– animal husbandry	17 (12)	23	–
– labour/bullock hire	14 (13)	11	–
– others (rent, remittance etc.)	21 (26)	23	–
Proportion of households with per capita annual income (at constant prices)[c]			
– less than Rs 180 (i.e. poverty line) (%)	17 (18)	–	23
– showing increase of more than 5% over the period (%)	–	–	47
– showing decline of more than 5% over the period (%)	–	–	38
– showing positive or negative change upto 5% over the period (constant income) (%)	–	–	15

[a] Data relate to 95 sample households from two villages, one each from Jodhpur and Nagaur districts in Rajasthan.
[b] 1963–4 being a severe drought year, its income figures are not considered.
[c] At 1964–6 prices.
[d] Figures in parentheses indicate the situation with reference to the total sample of 200 households during the benchmark.

of the households the per capita annual income had declined by more than 5 per cent of the base period income. For 47 per cent of the households, income increased by more than 5 per cent. The remaining households, where per capita annual income changed only within ($\mp$)5 per cent, have been treated as the cases where per capita incomes remained constant 'during the reference periods.

According to these figures, 38 per cent of the sample households have become poorer during 1982–4 compared to twenty years ago. If one goes by the poverty line, i.e. per capita income of Rs 180 per year, the proportion of households below it has increased from 17 per cent in 1964–6 to 23 per cent during 1982–4. But the latter does not include all the households that constituted the group under the poverty line during the base period. In other words, some households that were below the poverty line in 1964–6 have risen above it during 1982–4.[6]

4.2 Qualitative Indicators

If one goes by the qualitative indicators of poverty or the absence of it, as mentioned earlier, the very opposite picture seems to appear. Tables III to VII illustrate the phenomenon. These tables give details of only those thirty-five (out of ninety-five) households whose per capita annual income has declined by more than 5 per cent during the period under review. Furthermore, these tables present the extent of change in terms of proportion of households whose situation (as per the indicators mentioned) has changed during 1982–4 compared to the base period.

[6] It may be noted that the issue of the poverty line is not central to our discussion. This has been presented more as an additional piece of information, assuming that, if the poverty line as defined is relevant, proportions of households fall on both sides of it at two points of time. In the text more information on the shift of the households is indicated. If the level of the poverty line in the specific context is changed, the above-mentioned proportion will change. However, our substantive argument is that all approaches, including the poverty line (expressed in income terms), pick up specific information at some points of time rather than over a period of time, and they are not sensitive to qualitative indicators of change over time (see section 5 on reconciliation).

TABLE III

Indicators of Declining Indispensability of Patrons' (rich people's) Support/Mercy/Patronage for Employment, Income and Sustenance of the Poor Households[a]

Indicators	% of households during	
	1963–6	1982–4
Households with one/more members working as attached/semi-attached labour	37	7
Households residing on patron's land/yard	31	0
Households resorting to off-season borrowing of foodgrain from patrons	77	26
Households taking seed-loan from patrons	34	9
Households marketing farm produce only through patrons	86	23
Households taking loan from others besides patrons	13	47

[a] Details in this and the following 4 tables relate only to 35 households whose per capita annual income (at constant prices) had declined during 1982–4 compared to 1964–6.

Table III indicates the extent of decline in the reliance on patronage and the support of the rich (patrons) for the employment and sustenance of poor households, i.e. the households that have become poorer since 1964–6 (Table II). Some of the indicators, such as the practice of attached labour, seed-loans in kind (at an exorbitant interest rate), the marketing of produce only through patrons, sole dependence on patrons for credit, and residence on patron's land necessitating supply of unpaid and unaccounted labour services to the patrons—all have inherent in them an element of exploitation on *vis-à-vis* the poor. The poor person's ability to dispense with these practices is the surest indicator of his improved economic status. Despite several socio-economic reform measures, such as laws against bonded labour, the poor continue to accept these exploitative arrangements by their patrons. They tend to give up these arrangements only when they become economically independent.[7]

The inferior or low pay-off jobs (including food gathering from fast declining common property resources) are usually taken up by the poor in the villages (Jodha 1986). The recourse to such jobs declines as one improves his or her economic condition. Table IV indicates that the group of households that have became poorer in 1982–4, as per the formal income criteria, had relied more on these inferior options during the base period when they were relatively rich. Now, despite an increase in their poverty (i.e. reduced per capita income) their preference for inferior jobs had declined, as indicated by the proportion of households in the relevant categories under Table IV.

TABLE IV

Indicators of Reduced Dependence on Low Pay-off (inferior) Jobs in the case of Poor Households

Indicators	% of households during	
	1963–6	1982–4
Households engaged in[a]		
– food gathering	100	20
– fuel gathering	100	63
– fodder gathering	100	23
Households having members engaged in part-time petty jobs[b]	100	23
Households with members seasonally out-migrating for jobs	34	11
Households withdrawing their children from school during crop season for work help, earning, etc.	17	6

[a] Only items like wild fruits during summer season, and fuel/fodder during the post-harvest period, are considered. In these cases supply is not a constraint to reduce people's dependence on them.
[b] Jobs like helping in fencing, etc. for getting one meal as wage.

[7] Reduced reliance on the patronage of the rich and on inferior options such as Common Property Resource (CPR) activities could be both

TABLE V

Indicators of Improved Mobility and Liquidity Position of Poor Households

Indicators	% of households during	
	1963–6	1982–4
Households selling over 80% of their marketed produce during post-harvest period	100	46
Households retaining upto 25% of surplus for sale upto next rain	0	6
Households purchasing key provisions in bulk	0	6
Households relying on day-to-day petty purchases of key provisions[a]	100	51
Households making cash purchases during slack season, festivals, etc.	6	51
Households possessing ready cash upto Rs 200 or more at home during slack season	0	26
Households with members who travel by paid transport more than twice a year outside the district	17	78

[a] Provisions like chillies, onions, gur, oil, etc.

supply-determined and demand-determined options. However, in our study we have included only demand-induced cases. For instance, the patrons now given up by the poor households were still (at the time of resurvey) in the same business of offering facilities like site for living, crisis period food and money supply, etc. However, they didn't have many of the relevant customers to work as attached workers. The poor who left their patrons now have their own house site and untied facilities of credit, marketing; etc. from others, including from co-operatives. The factionalism of the rural rich, indirectly favouring the poor on the one hand, and some public programmes on the other, seem to have helped the poor in getting rid of exploitative patronage.

In the case of dependence on CPRs, only those activities have been considered where supply was not a constraining factor. They included collection of wild fruits (*ker, sangari,* etc.) during the summer season, and fuel/fodder accumulation during the period soon after the harvest of crops.

Several indicators in ·Table V reveal that the general liquidity of the group of households that has become poorer is better now (i.e. in 1982–4) than it was during the base period, when, income-wise, this group was relatively rich. The ability of these households to make purchases of provisions in bulk by paying for it in a single instalment, to make cash purchases during the summer-season festivals, and to keep significant amounts of cash in hand during the slack season, are definite signs of improvement—notwithstanding the decline in their formally recorded income position.[8]

The consumption pattern, particularly in terms of inclusion of items which poor people rarely use, is another indicator of substantial change in the economic condition of these people. Now there is a much higher proportion within the group of households (Table VI) that frequently consumes better-quality food items,[9] offers a better maternity diet to women for a longer period, and within which women and children regularly wear shoes. The only area where the situation seems to have deteriorated is within the proportion of households regularly using milk and milk products. This is, in fact, a side-effect of improved milk marketing facilities in the villages. The sale of milk has helped raise the share of livestock income in total income (Table II), but has also reduced the opportunities for self-consumption of milk and milk products.[10]

[8] The very first anecdote which provoked me to undertake this investigation related to the liquidity position of the rural poor. During my 1978 revisit to one of the villages, I was talking to a villager whose room I had rented during my early (1963–6) stay in the village. A woman labourer arrived there to collect her wages for the work she did for my ex-landlord. To avoid her, he pleaded non-availability of change and called her two days later. The woman promptly untied a knot in her *lugari* (sari), took out change and said: 'you need change for how much—Rs 100? Rs 50?' Contrast this with the situation during 1963–6, when, if by mistake I failed to carry change, there was nobody in the village who could offer me change for Rs 100; I had to visit the neighbouring town to get change.

[9] Of the 35 households, more than 20 used to offer tea made with jaggery during my frequent visits to their houses for data during 1963–6. During revisits I found all of them using sugar instead of jaggery for the same purpose.

[10] The cash nexus induces farmers to part with practically all their milk supplies, leaving little milk for self-provisioning or for sharing (butter-

TABLE VI

Indicators of Shifts in the Consumption Pattern of Poor Households

Indicators	% of households during	
	1963–6	1982–4
Households occasionally consuming green vegetables during non-crop season	0	100
Households consuming curries, mainly made from cereals[a]	100	14
Households using milk and milk products regularly	34	6
Households consuming sugar regularly	0	20
Households consuming rice on non-festive occasions also	0	14
Households with adults skipping the third meal of the day during the summer (scarcity period)	86	20
Households where women and children wear shoes regularly	0	86
Households where maternity feeding to women is provided upto a month or more	6	23

[a] As per the local saying, one who cannot afford vegetables, etc. eats cereals with the help of poor-quality curry made only of cereals.

The situation with regard to changes in the possession of consumer durables seems more impressive (Table VII). Pucca structures of houses, the provision of doors and gates, compound walls, separate quarters for humans and livestock in the house, and better facilities for women are important indicators of a positive change in the economic status of people. The higher proportion of the households possessing these items in 1982–4 as compared to the base period indicates a substantial improvement in their economic position.

---

milk, etc.) with others in the villages. Cases were observed where households producing as much as 10 l. of milk a day brought milk from the tea shop to prepare tea for visitors (including myself).

TABLE VII

Indicators of Change in the Asset Position of Poor Households

Indicators	% of households during	
	1963–6	1982–4
Households having houses with:		
– fully pucca structure	0	14
– partly pucca structure	9	52
– only katcha structure	91	34
– gate with doors	6	43
– compound wall/fence	13	52
– separate provision of stay for humans and animals	6	52
– private place (bathroom, etc.) for women	0	23
Households possessing:		
– quilts of cotton	6	20
– quilts of old rags	94	80
– radio	0	7
– bicycle	0	3

The detailed explanation of these changes falls outside the scope of this essay. However, it should be mentioned that a combination of factors has led to the improved condition of the households in the villages studied. The occurrence of these factors, observed in several villages of the districts of Nagaur, Jodhpur, Pali, and Sikar in western Rajasthan, would suggest that the changes reflected in the villages studied may extend to wider areas of the region.

The possible factors that are responsible for the improved economic conditions of sample households include the following:

i. A continuous spell of good rain years from 1974 to 1978.

ii. The possibility of double-cropping in sandy loam soils without change in rainfall or irrigation due to *raya* (a minor oilseed) crop for the post-rainy season (brought by seasonal migrants to Punjab in the early 1970s) and its spread in the dry region without any research and extension effort. The net returns from this crop are higher than the main rainy season crops, e.g. pearl millet.

iii. The coverage of a larger area by the moisture conserving practice of bunding, which, in association with timely ploughing through tractors, helped in the adoption of a hybrid pearl millet like BJ4.

iv. The facility of milk marketing, which generated a regular cash income and also induced changes in the composition of animal holding, discouraging the ownership of unproductive animals.

v. The reducêd incidence of guineaworm among adult workers in recent years, which often incapacitates them during the crop season. This happened on account of the Drought Prone Area Programme (DPAP) provision of piped groundwater supply for drinking, which replaced the traditional practice of using pond water.

vi. Off-season employment under the rural works programme (DPAP) and regular off-farm jobs for some people.

vii. Institutional reforms that have helped people get land, including house-sites, and reduced indebtedness.

viii. Gains to the poor as a by-product of factionalism among the rural rich, where each faction tried to woo the poor for their support.

5. TOWARDS RECONCILIATION

The first inference from the perusal of information under Table II on the one hand, and Tables III to VII on the other, is that the extent of increased incidence of poverty reflected by Table II is not borne out by the qualitative indicators of change under the remaining tables.

Part of the explanation could be that we have considered all households—whose per capita annual income has declined by more than 5 per cent of base period income—as having become poorer over time. They may include some households who were rich enough, and where a fall of 5 per cent in income did not make them much poorer. However, the data for households grouped according to level of decline in income were also examined. The emerging number of observations in each group become too small to be meaningfully reported. Yet the inferences from retabulation, which could help to satisfy the above objection, may be mentioned:

(a) The proportion of households showing qualitative improvement in economic conditions as per the above indicators was not very different in the case of sub-groups of high and low income households, which suffered a decline in their per capita annual income, as per Table II.

(b) Even the 23 per cent of sample households that were below the poverty line (i.e. with a per capita annual income of Rs 180 at constant prices, Table II) had a fairly large proportion of households that showed an improvement in their economic status as per the qualitative indicators discussed above.

(c) There was a small number of households in the group that neither faced decline in their per capita annual income nor slipped below the poverty line, and yet did not show an improvement in terms of qualitative indicators.

Thus the main explanation may lie in the use of specific approaches to assess and record economic change affecting rural households. Furthermore, change in economic status revealed by qualitative indicators is an outcome of gradual change over a period of time. A difference of per capita net income at two points of time may not capture this change. The measurement of income at one point in time captures only the current transitory component of income. The permanent components (accumulated transitory components) of income in the past are not captured. This reinforces the need for revising the research approach to understand the dynamics of rural change, and to cover permanent components of income besides the transitory components, each of which may not move in the same direction.

The reported case study is too small in its coverage to encourage any generalization of results. However, this does indicate the need for complementing formal concepts and norms by more informal categories and methods to capture a greater extent of reality through social science research in the field. It also underscores the importance of participant observations and indepth micro-level investigations in field studies.

Intensive and qualitative information gathering may prove costly. Hence, this approach can be used for generating relevant indicators (proxies) that can form part of large-scale, formal data-gathering projects. Furthermore, the insights received through such intensive investigations can help in the better interpretation of results from extensive studies.

A factor which can enhance the complementarity of the macro-level and highly quantitative studies on the one hand, and intensive and micro-level research on the other, is close links between principal researchers and the field.

This case study indicates the need for a fresh look at the conceptualizations underlying the measurement of the level and change in rural poverty. The complementary use of quantitative and qualitative concepts can help improve our understanding of the dynamics of poverty.

To the extent that the incidence of poverty can be partly inferred from the observance of poverty indicators, the next problem relates to the possibility of measurement of these indicators for comparative studies. To the extent that a part of the indicators of change discussed here may be area- or community-specific, their use for inter-community comparisons will be limited. Thought may be given to evolution of some indices on the pattern of the currently debated 'Quality of Life Index', as against gross domestic product, etc., as a better indicator of a nation's economic well being.

APPENDIX A

Examples of Concepts/Categories and Yardsticks/Norms used by Social Science Researchers to identify and measure Variables comprising Rural Realities and Facets of Reality likely to be bypassed by them

Concepts and norms	Aspects covered	Facets bypassed
Household income	Cash and kind inflows (including imputed values of major non-traded items)	Ignores time context and transaction partner context of income-generating activity; disregards flow of low

Concepts and norms	Aspects covered	Facets bypassed
		value self-provisioning activities with significant collective contribution to sustenance of the people
Farm production	Production from all farm enterprises	Series of intermediate activities (often considered as consumption activities), which facilitate the final output from farm enterprises in self-provisioning societies
Food consumption basket	Volume and quality of formally recorded food items	Ignores seasonally varying streams of self-provisioning items/services
Household resource endowment	Only privately owned land, labour and capital resources	Ignores households collective access to common property resources; access to power and influence too
Factor/product market	Competitive, impersonal interactive process or framework	Ignores distortions, imperfections etc. due to factors like influence, power, affinities and inequities
Farm size grouping	Based on owned or operated land-holdings (often standardized for productivity and irrigation)	Ignores totality of asset position including household's access to common property resources, its work force which determines households' ultimate potential to harness land resources and environment for sustenance

APPENDIX A (*Contd.*)

Concepts and norms	Aspects covered	Facets bypassed
Labour input	Labour as standard unit expressed in terms of man-hours or man-days etc. (Differentiation based on age and sex not-withstanding)	Disregards heterogeneity of labour of same age/sex in terms of differences in stamina and productivity; ignores differences in intensity of effort of a self-employed worker and hired worker. (Inappropriate imputation of value of the labour of self-employed worker is done on the basis of wage rate of hired or attached labourer)
Capital formation	Acquisition of assets	Ignores accretionary process, and petty accretions which are important collectively
Depreciation of assets	Book-keeping value based reduction in the worth of the asset	Ignores continued usability and recyclability
Efficiency/ productivity norm	Quantity and value of final produce of an activity (based on market criteria)	Ignores totality of the operation of the system directed to satisfaction of multiple objectives rather than single criterion

APPENDIX B

Examples of 'Communication Gaps' (under three categories)

(1) Possible differences in connotation of same concept as understood by respondent and researcher

| Concept | Connotation as per: | |
	Researcher	Respondent
Food consumption	Total food	Major food items excluding petty self-provisioning
Produce	Total	Final produce excluding items harvested during the intra-season period
Man-day	Formal work hour 8–10 hours, etc.	Total work time often more than 8–10 hours
Hired labour	Hired + exchanged	Only hired
Unemployment	Involuntary unemployment	Disguised unemployment treated as full unemployment

(2) Possible gaps in yardsticks guiding respondent's quantitative responses and researcher's recording of responses which may make it difficult to establish perfect equivalence between the reported and recorded quantities

Item	Researcher	Respondent
Length/area	Modern units (metre, hectares, inches, etc.)	Traditional—foot-lengths, steps, arm-lengths, fingerwidths
Weight/volumes	Modern measures such as kilograms, quintals, litres, etc.	Cart-loads, bagfuls, volume based measures (barrels etc.)
Production	Modern measures— quintals, etc.	Self-sufficiency periods of subsistence-requirement—e.g. total

APPENDIX B (*Contd.*)

Item	Researcher	Respondent
		production equal to 6 months of requirements, etc.
Time	Precise—days, hour, etc.	Vague—in terms of proportion of a day or a week, etc., i.e. half-a-day, 3/4 of a day, etc.

(3) Degree of precision/vagueness associated with responses as they are given and recorded

Item	Recording by researchers	Reporting by respondent
Labour input	Exact days/hours	Ranged units, e.g. 5–7 hours, 10–12 days, etc.
Grain yield	Exact quantities in modern measures/units (quintals/kg, etc.)	Range: e.g. 5–6 bags or 50–55 quintals, etc.
Input use/output sold	Exact quantities	Range in terms of proportion 1/3 to 2/3 of bag, etc.

REFERENCES

AERC, *Some Aspects of Long-term Cooperative Agricultural Finance*. Agro-Economic Research Centre, Vallabh Vidyanagar, Gujarat, 1971.

Binswanger, H. P., and Jodha, N. S., '*Manual of instructions for economic investigators in ICRISAT's village-level studies*', volume II, ICRISAT, Economics Program, Village Level Studies Series, Patencheru, A.P., India, 1978.

Chambers, R., *Poverty in India: concepts, research and reality—an exploration*. Institute of Development Studies, University of Sussex, Brighton, U.K., 1986.

Dandekar, V., and Rath, N., 'Poverty in India: dimensions and trends'. *Economic and Political Weekly*, 6(1), 1971.

Jodha, N. S., 'Capital formation in arid agriculture: A study of resource conservation and reclamation measures applied to arid agriculture'. Unpublished Ph.D. thesis. Jodhpur, Rajasthan: University of Jodhpur, 1967.

Jodha, N. S., 'A Case of the Process of Tractorisation'. *EPW*, 9 (52): A111–A118, 1974.

Jodha, N. S., 'Effectiveness of farmers' adjustment to risk'. *Economic and Political Weekly*, 13(25):A49–A62, 1977.

Jodha, N. S., 'Common property resources and rural poor in dry regions of India'. *Economic and Political Weekly*, 21(27): 1169–1181, 1986.

Jodha, N. S., Ashokan, M., and Ryan, J. G., 'Village Study Methodology and Resource Endowments of the Selected Villages'. Economic Programme Occasional Paper No 16, ICRISAT, Patancheru, AP, India, 1977.

McCloskey, D. M., 'The rhetoric of economics'. *Journal of Economic Literature*, vol. xxi: 481–517, 1983.

Planning Commission, *Sixth Five-Year Plan 1980–85*. New Delhi, Government of India, 1981.

Sen, A. K., *Choice, welfare and measurement*. Oxford, Blackwell, 1983.

Streeten, P. P., 'Social science research on development: Some problems in the use of transfer of an intellectual technology'. *Journal of Economic Literature*, pp. 1290–1300, 1974.

Chapter 8: An Approach Towards Integrating Large- and Small-Scale Surveys*

SURESH D. TENDULKAR

1. A POSSIBLE METHOD OF INTEGRATING
LARGE- AND SMALL-SCALE SURVEYS

The results of socio-economic large-scale surveys (LSS for short) reflect the quantifiable end-results of the aggregation across households, or individuals, of the characteristics being studied—such as the rate of unemployment, the level of per capita total expenditure, the rate of migration, the incidence of morbidity, and so on. The quantifiable characteristics being studied at the level of each individual unit of observation (household or individual) are the end result of certain economic, social and demographic processes at work. These processes involve interactions within and between households, as also between the households and/or individuals and institutional arrangements in the society in which they live. Consequently, in analysing, interpreting and explaining the results of LSS, it is frequently desirable to have certain supplementary micro-level information which, most often, cannot be collected through LSS because of the constraints under which LSS operate. (The nature of these constraints is discussed in Section 2.) The

* I am indebted to Mr. S. M. Vidwans of the Bureau of Economics and Statistics, Maharashtra, for making available the tabulated results of the survey on social consumption and to Dr. B. S. Minhas, Chairman, National Sample Survey Organization for the permission to use the results for illustration in Section 4 of this paper. They are not responsible for the views and interpretations presented in this paper.

micro-level small-scale surveys (SSS for short) of various types can supply supplementary information and enable us to interpret and explain the macro-level reality reflected in LSS. The need for supplementary micro-level information arises because the same observable end-result can emerge, on a priori ground, from alternative causal forces. The micro-level SSS can provide us with a basis for choosing one set of explanatory factors *vis-à-vis* others. On this basis meaningful policy can emerge.

Similarly, the macro-level perspective provided by LSS can be used to assess the possible generalizability and representativeness of the micro-level observations emerging from different types of SSS (discussed in Section 3) and casual empiricism. There can thus be a fruitful two-way interaction between LSS and SSS. Some illustrations may help in amplifying these points.

In the statistics of reported incidences of diseases, one finds that the reported rate of incidence is higher in Kerala, for example, than in Bihar. This result could hypothetically be because the hygienic and sanitary environment makes populations more disease-prone in Kerala than in Bihar. Alternatively, it could be because the more readily available medical facilities (especially diagnostic) in Kerala may lead to a higher *reporting* of disease there than in Bihar. In resolving these questions, one needs supplementary information on the hygienic and sanitary environment, the nature of available medical facilities, the quality and nature of access to the health delivery system, and so on. SSS at micro-level can throw light on these aspects. Similar problems may exist with reference to the infant mortality rates across states.

One frequently finds the diffusion of certain technologies—chemical-biological technology under the Green Revolution, for example—to be greater in certain states/regions than in others. A satisfactory explanation requires information, among other things, about the following: size distribution of assets (in particular operational holdings) which may be available from LSS, the minimum viable farm size, the availability of infrastructural facilities, including the availability and efficiency of and access to irrigation, input delivery systems and output marketing systems, the working of the credit disbursing institutions, and so on. Only SSS can throw meaningful light on all these aspects (expect possibly the size distribution of assets).

Also worth mentioning is an illustration of the macro-level perspective tempering the generalizability of field-level observation. Lakhs of agricultural labourers are reported to be migrating seasonally to Punjab in response to the labour scarcity that develops there during the peak harvesting season. A recent survey in Punjab found 2.86 lakhs and 5.86 lakhs of migrant workers employed during the lean season and the peak season, respectively, in 1983–4. The numbers are indeed large and impressive, but they cannot be expected to change the overall employment picture of the 300 million-plus labour force in India.

2. LARGE-SCALE SURVEYS: CONSTRAINTS AND LIMITATIONS

Generally, there is inadequate appreciation of the constraints operating on LSS, leading to unreasonable expectations from this method of enquiry.

LSS can be on a census, or on a sample basis. Given the budget constraint, a sample survey is expected to ensure better quality information than a census survey, both by using relatively more trained investigators and by spending a longer time on each unit of observation. The cost is in terms of introducing a sampling error in the estimate obtained.

In the subsequent discussion, LSS are taken to indicate nationwide large-scale surveys of the National Sample Survey (NSS) type. The focus is mainly on socio-economic enquiries.

LSS are typically conducted by hired investigators who are not specialized in the subjects of sample enquiries but who may have been trained in survey techniques, or have acquired skills in survey techniques (if the turnover among them is not high). They do not stay where the respondents live, nor do they know the respondents. They spend only a limited time with each respondent in order to fill the schedule of information to be collected in a given enquiry. The information is collected mostly through the recall method and the role of direct observation is minimized. Often, direct observation is not used at all because of time constraints.

These investigator characteristics make possible 'neutral'

observation and the reporting of only those characteristics which are directly and easily observable and recallable. This may be useful under several circumstances requiring 'objective' assessment, but may turn out to be a handicap under several other circumstances.

Within the constraints imposed by the investigator characteristics, the quality of data collected by the investigator is determined mainly by the following factors:

  (i) the format, sequence, wording and length of the schedule or questionnaire;

 (ii) the workload of the investigator, his motivation and skills acquired on the job;

(iii) the accuracy of recall and its transmission to the schedule;

(ɪv) the responsiveness of respondents— co-operative, neutral, hostile.

It needs to be emphasized that, in the Indian context, information is collected from only one member of the household—usually the head of the household—regarding the collective characteristics of the household (such as land owned, household size, and its age-sex composition), as also about the individual members of the household as regards their gainful activities. Frequently, other members of the household join in supplying the information which may provide a possible check on recall by the head of the household.

It should be obvious that whatever is bought or sold in the market is relatively more reliably recallable than whatever is not. Similarly, it is more difficult to elicit reliable information on whatever goes on within the four walls of the household than outside. These limitations on what can be feasibly collected from LSS follow from their investigator characteristics.

At the aggregate level, the extent to which, and the success with which, LSS can manage to reliably capture the macro-level reality is determined by the conceptual framework of measurement that is adopted, easy observability/measurability and recallability of the items of information being collected, the investigator biases (leading to non-sampling errors), and the sampling design and its implementation in the field (leading to sampling errors). Their results reflect an aggregation of measurable and recallable responses which are end-results of the operation at the micro-level of economic, social and demographic processes.

The major advantage of LSS is that the estimates yielded by them are expected to be representative of the universe being covered through such surveys. This is because of their extensive coverage in terms of both the number of households covered and the character of information that is collected. This is what we may call the representativeness in the statistical or sampling sense. The National Sample Surveys guarantee representativeness in the sampling sense at the all-India level and at the level of the states. The sampling errors increase progressively as we try to disaggregate below the state level to the region/block/village level.

It is necessary, however, to bring into the picture another dimension of the concept of representativeness in the sense of broad homogeneity with respect to the characteristics being studied and their implication for aggregation. In a country of continental dimensions such as India, there exist wide regional variations, so that homogeneity or, more strictly, aggregability of the characteristic being observed, is likely to be greater at the disaggregate level. For example, although one gets a representative estimate, in a statistical or sampling sense, of the rate of unemployment at the all-India level (separately for rural/urban, age, and sex) it represents an aggregation of diverse labour-market situations which may not be conceptually aggregable. Similarly, household-specific per capita total expenditures, reflecting levels of living, can be aggregated only for those households that are located in a homogeneous socio-economic environment and face, more or less, the same set of prices. The point is not to minimize variability or eliminate it altogether through disaggregation, but to ensure 'homogeneity' of the overall environment in which aggregation of responses may turn out to be more meaningful for explanation and interpretation. This is not to deny the role of all-India estimates as broad, descriptive indicators of the performance of the economic system. But if one wishes to look behind the aggregated estimates for explanation, the need for disaggregation should be obvious not only for explanation but also interpretation. However, as indicated earlier, sampling errors of the disaggregated estimates from LSS may turn out to be unacceptably large.

3. SMALL-SCALE SURVEYS: LIMITATIONS AND POSSIBILITIES

It is possible to distinguish at least three major types of small-scale surveys (SSS).

The first type of SSS replicate more or less the same methodology as LSS but concentrate on a limited geographical area/section of the population. This reduces the sampling error by having a larger sample than is possible under the nationwide surveys. They can also ensure homogeneity of the environment and make possible more meaningful aggregation, thereby yielding some clues about the more intelligent interpretation and possible explanation of the end-result emerging from the survey. This type of survey is also used as a pilot for introducing new concepts/schedules/items of information, or for launching new enquiries under LSS. The comparability of this type of SSS with LSS depends on the comparability in conceptual framework, sampling design, and the quality of investigators.

The second type of SSS is conducted on a much smaller scale than the first type but with a radically different methodology. This type is usually conducted by specialized experts themselves, or in collaboration with carefully chosen, well-motivated investigators. They adopt the participant-observation method, using mostly unstructured schedules/questionaires. The representativeness, in a statistical sense, of the comparable quantifiable information collected through such surveys, i.e. comparable to that collected through LSS, is doubtful. However, direct observation (rather than recall), the specialized character of the investigators and the use of the participant-observation method make possible a more reliable macro-level response on matters collectable as well as non-collectable through LSS. This type of SSS is potentially capable of throwing light on phenomena which are not necessarily quantifiable but which impinge on the working of the economic, social and demographic processes at the micro-level. As observed at the beginning, it is these processes which give rise to the quantifiable end-result reflected in LSS, and any qualitative information about these processes would help us interpret, analyse and explain the results of LSS. Clearly we need a cross-section of such studies from different parts of the country on matters such as appear in the following illustrative list.

    (i) The working of the local-level economic (such as a co-operative), social (such as the caste system), political (such as panchayati raj) institutions with reference to the methods of conflict-resolution evolved and used, the access of these to different sections of the population, the bias in their working in relation to different classes, and so on.

    (ii) Quality of and efficiency in the health, education and productive input delivery systems.

    (iii) The character of social stratification and its effects on participation in economic activity, access to economic and social institutions, and on economic and social mobility.

    (iv) The role of economic and non-economic factors in intra-household activities such as work allocation and work sharing, as well as food and income distribution.

    (v) The socio-economic character of the block and village development administration, their attitudes towards different social classes, the range of activities they are expected to perform, their workload, as well as relative priorities amongst different activities.

This list is admittedly subjective and illustrative. It has been drawn up with an eye on certain major themes of development, such as the diffusion of new technology, social classwise distribution of the benefits of economic growth, the availability and quality of basic needs, the implementation of anti-poverty programmes, and the intra-household exploitation of women and children.

Finally, the third type of SSS consists of a wide cross-section of fieldwork-based observations carried out by specialized and perceptive observers without any structured schedule or questionnaire, but depending much more on eyes, ears and legs. This type of SSS has been made respectable in economics by Thorner and Ladejinsky, the most adept practitioners of this type of SSS. While focusing on economic problems, their observations trespass into social, human and institutional spheres and enrich our knowledge of several micro-level processes and behavioural responses. While their observations reflected certain aspects of a strictly micro-level reality, an aggregation of such observations relating to a diversity of micro-level situations has certainly improved our understanding of the dynamics of technological change in agriculture. A very loud note of caution needs to be sounded about this type of SSS. The perceptive character of the observer, his capacity to sift typical from atypical observations and to decipher underlying specificities and commonalities amongst the diverse set of observations—all these are crucial enough in these types of surveys to make them an art which cannot be practised by everybody. There exists a strong possibility of being overwhelmed by those aspects of the micro-level reality which are not representative of the macro-level reality. If one wants to arrive at a meaningful macro-level aggregation from the macro-level situations from these sorts of surveys, it is extremely important to have firmly in mind a macro-level perspective provided by the quantitative orders of magnitudes emerging from LSS. The usefulness of the third type of SSS lies—as in the second type—in throwing light on the variety of micro-level processes at work and in helping us understand the role of these processes in bringing about the macro-level quantifiable results for LSS.

4. AN ILLUSTRATION

In this section is illustrated the approach suggested in Section 1 with reference to school education facilities, as revealed by the large-scale survey of social consumption in Maharashtra. The focus is on (i) quantifiable regularities emerging from the survey; (ii) making explicit the judgements required to interpret these regularities in an economically meaningful fashion; and (iii) emphasizing the inherent limitations of large-scale surveys and thereby pointing to the need for small-scale micro-level surveys.

The survey of social consumption under consideration was conducted as part of the socio-economic enquiries carried out by the National Sample Survey Organization (NSSO) between July 1980 and June 1981. The survey had two samples: the Central Sample canvassed by NSSO, and the State Sample on a matching basis canvassed by the state government. The results given below relate to the state sample alone, consisting of 3513 rural and 3350 urban households.

To fix a broad perspective on the state of Maharashtra, we should note that it is one of the most industrially developed states, with a 35 per cent urban population out of a total population of 62.78 million in 1981. Its per capita state domestic product was nearly 38 per cent higher than the all-India average for the year 1980–1. However, the productivity per hectare as well as the productivity per worker in crop production were below the national average in the early eighties. We may, therefore, expect the urban population to be economically better placed and rural population to be correspondingly worse placed than the all-India average.

Households are ranked according to the increasing size of monthly per capita expenditure (or MPCE for short). The households so ranked are then grouped into k MPCE class-intervals (denoted as 1, 2, . . . , j, . . . , k).[1] The implicit premise underlying this grouping is that any characteristic relating to households that is being studied—namely, here, that relating to school education—would have a monotonic relationship with the economic processes whose end-results are the levels of living as reflected in the ranking variable MPCE.

When the monotonic relationship is obtained, it is necessary to examine the inter-fractile group differences in magnitude of the characteristic under consideration. For this purpose, the following procedure is adopted: We first locate that MPCE class-interval, say j, in which the mean value of the characteristic is located. We then aggregate MPCE class-intervals from 1 to j to constitute what we call the bottom fractile group. The aggregated MPCE class-intervals from (j + 1) to k then constitute what we call the top fractile group. A comparison of the fractile group-specific weighted average values of the characteristic would indicate the extent of differentiation across the two broad fractile groups in respect of the characteristic being

[1] It is important to note that the absolute value of MPCE in the survey was collected from a one-shot question with minimal probing regarding its accuracy or consistency. Earlier experiments in NSSO indicated that the *ranking* of households according to the size of *MPCE* did not differ significantly whether one used (a) MPCE collected from a detailed enquiry on consumer expenditure, or (b) MPCE collected from a one-shot question. The latter namely (b), is, therefore, taken to be adequate for the broad fractile groups considered in this section.

studied. In case there is no differentiation, the obvious inference is that factors other than (broadly) economic (strictly, other than those related to levels of living) are at work. These may refer to demographic and/or social processes. On a priori grounds it may be possible to suggest certain hypotheses for the differentiation or its absence across the broad fractile groups. Verification of these hypotheses would require micro-level small-scale surveys of the second or the third type discussed in the last section. In the tables that follow, we indicate (i) the percentage of the total population in each fractile group, and (ii) the percentage of the quantifiable characteristic or the percentage of the target-group to which the characteristic relates.

In the case of school education, the survey focuses on the following broad quantifiable characteristics, namely (a) the percentage of *never*-enrolled children; (b) the percentage of *ever*-enrolled children—a complement of (a); (c) the percentage of *currently*-enrolled children during the period of the survey; and (d) the percentage drop-out which is the difference in the percentage under (b) and (c).

Two age groups are distinguished, namely 5 to 9 years for primary education and 10 to 14 years for secondary education. Each of these age groups is further distinguished according to sex (males-females) and according to location (rural-urban). While sex and location dimensions are known to be crucial for a variety of socio-economic enquiries, the focus on school education made it necessary to distinguish the two target age groups mentioned above.

Table I presents the summary information relating to the participation in education and drop-outs among children aged 5–9 years. The following empirical regularities emerge.

1. The characteristics under consideration, namely the percentage of children never-enrolled, ever-enrolled and currently-enrolled exhibited a monotonic relationship with MPCE.

2. The percentage of never-enrolled children was distinctly higher for rural children than for their urban counterparts, and for female children than for male children.

3. The inter-fractile group differentiation in respect of the percentage of never-enrolled children was the least (i.e. 7 percentage points) for rural male children, whereas it exceeded 20 percentage points for rural female as well as urban male and female children.'

TABLE I

Participation in Education and Drop-Outs: Maharashtra (1980–1); Children aged 5–9 years

Ser. No.	Location of population	Fractile group of population (%)		Target age group	% of target age group in fractile group	Percentage of target age group in the fractile group that is			
						never-enrolled	ever-enrolled	currently-enrolled	drop-out
(1)	(2)	(3)		(4)	(5)	(6)	(7)	(8)	(9)
1.1	Rural	Bottom	59.07	Males	60.56	45.76	54.24	51.53	2.71
1.2	Rural	Top	40.93	5–9	39.24	38.18	61.84	60.21	1.63
1.3	Rural	All groups	100.00	Years	100.00	42.76	57.24	54.95	2.29
2.1	Rural	Bottom	86.64	Females	88.70	56.69	43.31	40.31	3.00
2.2	Rural	Top	13.36	5–9	11.30	28.55	71.45	68.36	3.09
2.3	Rural	All groups	100.00	years	100.00	53.51	46.49	43.48	3.01

2.1a	Rural	Bottom	59.07	Females 5–9 years	63.79	58.16	41.84	38.57	3.27
2.2a	Rural	Top	13.36		36.21	45.32	54.68	52.12	2.56
3.1	Urban	Bottom	47.47	Males 5–9 years	51.53	33.70	66.30	63.88	2.42
3.2	Urban	Top	52.53		48.47	11.81	88.19	87.72	0.47
3.3	Urban	All groups		years	100.00	23.09	76.91	75.43	1.48
4.1	Urban	Bottom	47.47	Females 5–9 years	48.67	39.11	60.89	58.80	2.09
4.2	Urban	Top	52.53		51.33	13.67	86.73	84.76	1.97
4.3	Urban	All groups		years	100.00	26.05	73.95	72.13	1.82

Notes: 1. The number of sample households is 3513 (rural) and 3350 (urban).

2. For rural males and females in the 5–9 years age group, the MPCE class-interval containing the average level of the characteristics in columns (6) to (8) was found to be different. In lines 2.1a and 2.2a we provide the comparable figures for females 5–9 years as in lines 1.1 and 1.2 for males 5–9 years. For urban males and females in 5–9 years, the MPCE class-interval containing the average level of the characteristics turned out to be the same.

4. The inter-fractile group differences in the percentage of children dropped out were negligible for female children—rural and urban. For male children the drop-out percentage fell as one moved from the bottom to the top fractile group.

5. In a supplementary table giving reasons for non-enrolment by never-enrolled children (the classification of reasons is given in the Appendix), we find that non-availability of a school was given as a reason in the case of a very small percentage of children. 'Too young to go to the school' was reported to be an overwhelming reason across rural-urban location, across sex, and across the fractile groups.

What do we conclude from the foregoing quantitative findings? First, the non-availability of physical facilities for schooling in the age group 5–9 years was not responsible for the non-enrolment of children in this age group. The major reported reason—too young to go to the school—appeared to be important more for female children than male˙ children, more for rural children than urban children, and more for the bottom fractile group than the top one. Whether this was due to differences in perception regarding the need for schooling or whether it was a response to the inadequate, low-quality and possibly non-relevant schooling facilities is a question which cannot be answered by large-scale sample surveys. The invariance of the drop-out rates across the fractile groups for rural as well as urban female children indicates that non-economic factors may be responsible for this phenomenon once school entry occurs.

Table II presents summary information relating to the participation in education and drop-outs among children aged 10–14 years of age. The following regularities stand out.

1. The characteristics being studied exhibit a monotonic relationship for all the target age groups but this seems to be very weak for rural females in this age group.

2. The percentage of never-enrolled children is considerably higher for rural than for urban children, and for female children than for males. This is similar to the finding for the age group 5–9 years.

3. The inter-fractile group differentiation was the least for rural female children (4 percentage points) and the highest for urban female children (20 percentage points). It was less than 10

TABLE II

Participation in Education and Drop-Outs: Maharashtra (1980–1); Children aged 10–14 years

Ser. No.	Location of population	Fractile group of population (%)		Target age group	% of target age group in fractile group	Percentage of target age group in the fractile group that is			
						never-enrolled	ever-enrolled	currently-enrolled	drop-out
(1)	(2)	(3)		(4)	(5)	(6)	(7)	(8)	(9)
1.1	Rural	Bottom	59.07	Males	59.41	22.11	77.89	60.11	17.78
1.2	Rural	Top	40.93	10–14	40.59	12.65	83.65	73.73	13.62
1.3	Rural	All groups		Years	100.00	18.27	81.73	65.64	16.09
2.1	Rural	Bottom	59.07	Females	60.15	35.90	64.10	39.52	24.58
2.2	Rural	Top	40.93	10–14	39.85	39.99	60.01	52.30	7.71
2.3	Rural	All groups		Years	100.00	37.53	62.47	44.61	17.86

TABLE II (Contd.)

(1)	(2)	(3)	(4)	(5)	(6)	(7)	(8)	(9)
3.1	Urban	Bottom 41.91	Males	43.69	9.59	90.41	75.85	14.56
3.2	Urban	Top 58.09	10–14	56.31	2.05	97.95	91.67	6.28
3.3	Urban	All groups	Years	100.00	5.34	94.66	84.76	9.90
4.1	Urban	Bottom 41.91	Females	44.16	23.26	76.74	66.34	10.40
4.2	Urban	Top 58.09	10–14	55.84	3.23	96.77	88.40	8.33
4.3	Urban	All groups	Years	100.00	12.07	87.93	78.66	9.27

Notes: 1. The number of sample households is 3513 (rural) and 3350 (urban).

2. Notice that in the age group (10–14) years, the cohort refers to those who were in (10–14) years during the survey period. Those *ever-enrolled* given in column (7) may have been enrolled for the first time when they had been in age group (5–9) years or in (10–14) years. Those enrolled for the first time while in (10–14) years age group may not necessarily be in secondary school. Similarly, those currently-enrolled need not all be in secondary school. Some of the drop-outs in column (9) may have dropped out before entering the (10–14) years age group. Consequently, the drop-outs in column (9) have to be interpreted as drop-outs from the schooling system as a whole, and *not* drop-outs exclusively from secondary schools. In the text, we refer to the drop-outs in the *age group* rather than those from secondary schools. Similarly, those currently enrolled in column (8) are to be interpreted as retained in the schooling system as a whole during the survey period.

percentage points for both rural and urban male children.

4. The percentage of children that dropped out of the schooling system varied between 10 per cent (rural males) and 18 per cent (rural females) for rural children and was around 9 per cent for urban children.

5. The inter-fractile group differences in the percentage of children dropped out was the least for urban females (2 percentage points) and rural males (4 percentage points) and the highest for rural female children (nearly 17 percentage points).

6. 'Non-availability of schooling facility' was again a very unimportant reason for non-enrolment. 'Not interested in schooling' was the major reason, followed by certain economic compulsions for both non-enrolment and drop-out. There was no specific pattern across sex or location or MPEC groups.

The inferences we draw from the foregoing quantitative regularities for children in the 10–14 years age group can now be noted. The non-availability of schooling facilities was not responsible for non-enrolment. Though the proportions of never-enrolled are considerably smaller for this age group than was the case for the younger group, the drop-out problem for this age group is considerably more acute—relatively much more for rural children than urban ones. The inter-fractile group differences in the drop-out are the sharpest (more than 16 percentage points) for rural female children and the least (2 percentage points) for urban female children. The reasons for and the magnitude of both the non-enrolment and the drop-out strongly suggest the hypothesis of an excess supply of educational services given the opportunity cost of education, and the non-relevance as well as the inadequacies in the availability of education facilities. The results also indicate that economic factors are responsible for the differential inter-fractile group drop-out rates. What they do not explain are the extreme order of differentials for rural and urban female children, for which small-scale micro surveys are clearly required.

What are the policy implications of this analysis? A negative implication is obviously that the expansion of educational facilities in their existing form is *not* required, given the overall situation of excess supply. However, if one wants to pose the question of what needs to be done to increase the enrolment rate and reduce the drop-out rate, the broad quantitative findings are inadequate. What is needed for this purpose is a micro-level survey which investigates the causes of low enrolment rate or a high drop-out rate in a specific area.

5. CONCLUDING OBSERVATIONS

This essay has suggested a possible method of integrating the results of the macro- and micro-level surveys (Section 1). In the light of this method, we examined the constraints and limitations operating on LSS (Section 2), followed by the limitations and possibilities of SSS (Section 3). Briefly, the message that is intended to be transmitted is that, in the context of any given economic or social problem, reality is too complex to be comprehended by either LSS by themselves, or SSS by themselves. Both throw light on different aspects of reality. If one appreciates clearly the constraints and limitations operating on each, it is not difficult to integrate them so as to intelligently interpret, analyse and explain complex reality. The conceptualization of reality on this basis could form a proper basis for meaningful theorizing. Section 4 provided an illustration of the approach suggested in this essay, with reference to schooling facilities for children in age groups 0–4 and 5–14 years.

APPENDIX: EDUCATIONAL NON-ENROLMENT AND DROP-OUT

The reasons for non-enrolment as well as drop-out are distinguished in the survey as follows:

1. Too young to go to school
2. Schooling facility not available in the neighbourhood
3. Not interested in education/further studies
4. For participating in household economic activity
5. For other economic reasons
6. Busy attending domestic chores
7. For failure
8. Other reasons
9. Not recorded

Reason no. 2, i.e. schooling facility not available, may be taken to indicate the constraint from the supply side given the perceived quality as well as adequacy of the facility, the relevance or otherwise of the syllabus, as also the formal method of teaching as an accepted form of educational technology.

The remaining reasons (except no. 9) reflect the perceptions of the respondents regarding the demand for educational services. Reasons 1 and 3 can be taken to reflect the perceived non-relevance of the available educational facilities. Reasons 4 and 5 are indicative of the non-zero opportunity cost of education. Reason 6 can also be included in this category as domestic chores, in turn, may be taken to release other members of the household for economically gainful activities. The interpretation of nos. 7 and 8 is not clear. These also turn out to be quantitatively not significant at all.

Chapter 9: Field Survey Methods

ASHOK RUDRA

1. INTRODUCTION

1.1 This essay is about methods of field investigation in the social sciences, in particular economics. Empirical research calls for the use of data, and for many problems the existing data collected by various agencies are not sufficient: the researcher requires to gather fresh data from the field to meet his own purposes. We shall keep in mind such data as have to be collected from/individuals or households. The statistical part of most empirical research papers by even competent social scientists reveal a lamentable lack of knowledge about the appropriate tools to be used. Mostly, the methods used are extremely elementary; if linear regression represents the height of sophistication at the analysis stage, at the data-collection stage random sampling, at the most stratified, represents the pinnacle of expertise. When use is made of more sophisticated techniques, they are more often than not ones that are not best suited for the problem at hand. We shall suggest several techniques which have the virtue of simplifying procedure and decreasing the workload while not reducing effectiveness. We shall confine ourselves here to methods of data collection, leaving out problems of data analysis.

1.2 We shall not be primarily concerned with the data presented by the census authority, the National Sample Survey, the Reserve Bank of India, the Central Statistical Organisation, etc. Our focus will be on methods that are used or may be used to give better results by individual researchers or small research units. However, in discussing the latter we shall occasionally make, for purposes of comparison or criticism, references to the methods used by these vast national-scale organizations.

2. SAMPLING VERSUS COMPLETE ENUMERATION

2.1 The first decision that a research investigator has to take is about the choice between the above two alternative methods of field investigation. The actual choice made is quite often a function of the discipline to which the researcher belongs. Thus, social anthropologists usually accept, almost as a matter of faith, the approach which covers every individual or household of the community selected for study. We shall leave social anthropology out of our discussion precisely because it seems to rule out, by decree as it were, all approaches other than the one called participation-observation. (While sticking rigidly to this doctrine, most eminent social anthropologists, at least in our country, seem paradoxically to spend most of their lives in urban environments, far away from the communities which they might have studied by the participation-observation method at some time or the other in their younger days.) We shall be concerned with the relative merits and flaws of the two approaches in subjects like economics, demography, sociology, political science, etc.

2.2 We state squarely that our preference lies with the sampling approach. The advantages of the sampling approach are obvious and well known. Given a total number of units to be investigated, the sampling approach allows inferences to be drawn for a much bigger population, the magnifier being given by the inverse of the sampling fraction. If one starts with a given population, then the workload can be reduced by taking a sample rather than completely enumerating the population. This allows much better control over the information collection process and therefore much greater chances of reducing different kinds of non-sampling errors. Of course this has to be balanced against the fact that the sampling process would necessarily give rise to sampling errors. In most problems that social scientists other than social anthropologists have to tackle, it is the experience of researchers that on balance it is better to deal with sampling errors, which are scientifically controllable, than different kinds of non-sampling errors predominant in the complete enumeration approach.

2.3 If, despite these well-known advantages of the sampling approach, some social scientists prefer to take the complete enumeration approach, it is done in the name of the holistic character of the population under study, which rules out studying it on a fractional basis. For example, the Agro-Economic Research Centres in the country carried out over many years a large number of what were called Complete Village Surveys, and in many cases the same villages were subjected to Repeat Surveys. As a matter of fact there is in the country quite a large collection of such complete village surveys. In taking the complete enumeration approach rather than the sampling approach the argument presumably was that each village constituted an organic whole, and that this holistic character of the village economy could not possibly be captured by any sampling method. The fact remains that these complete village survey reports have proved to be of very little use to researchers and other users of information about our village economies. As is well known, research in the country has made much more use of the data presented in the Farm Management Survey reports which are collected by the sampling approach. This is a sure indication that nothing much was gained, and much effort lost, in covering all the households of the village.

2.4 As a matter of fact, it appears to us that the village as an organic whole is just empty talk insofar as sampling design is concerned. Nobody has yet theoretically demonstrated the advantages of including in a sample all the households of a village because of organic linkages between them. There are indeed plenty of linkages, but the specific ones of interest to researchers may be captured by drawing a properly designed cluster-sample. Thus, if one is interested in tenancy, one can draw a random sample of tenants; then consider all the landlords connected with them by lease agreements; then add all the other tenants of these landlords; and so on. One can do such clusterings with labourers and their employers, debtors and their creditors, sellers of products and their purchasers, etc. It is therefore our judgement that complete enumeration is never really called for. Sampling with clustering, stratification, and other such devices always give better results.

3. RANDOM VERSUS PURPOSIVE SAMPLING

3.1 Once again the choice between these two approaches is, quite often, not determined by any theoretical considerations but is predetermined by the researcher's discipline. Sociologists and social anthropologists seem to prefer purposive sampling whereas economists seem to be inclined towards random sampling. The choice ought, however, to be based on the research purpose one has in mind. Random sampling is called for when one is interested in making estimates valid for a population from which the sample is drawn. Purposive sampling cannot possibly yield any theoretically defensible estimates. But quantitative estimates for a community as a whole may not be the only or even the most important purpose for which a research project is undertaken. In many projects the researcher is interested in studying very closely and intimately the working of a social phenomenon. Such a purpose cannot be served through a vast field survey. The deeper one wants to probe the intricacies of a phenomenon, the smaller has to be the size of the sample. And not only the size: the sample has to be rich in information relating to the phenomenon. Further, the respondents have to be such as are willing to co-operate with investigators. A random sample can hardly satisfy all these conditions. The researcher may therefore purposely choose a sample so as to fulfil all these conditions.

3.2 Given that a purposive sample cannot yield estimates for a larger population, one may wonder at the value of a study based on such a sample. There are two answers to this. The first is that while such a sample cannot yield valid quantitative estimates, the qualitative information it supplies may have relevance much beyond the sample and, to some extent, for the entire population. To what extent is precisely the thing that cannot be known or reliably stated. But that it is considerable can be asserted on the basis of one of the fundamental premises of science, namely that of the Uniformity of Nature. The physical sciences are based on this important assumption—that different parts of the universe are not subject to different laws. Of course in the social sciences there are no laws which reproduce complete uniformities. Different situations have different combinations of the general and the particular. It is the general part that any researcher aims at. The purposive sample does throw light on this general part, but to an extent that is unknown.

3.3 In the field of economics, the two approaches of random sampling and purposive sampling can be complementary rather than rivals. Thus, an intensive research based on a purposive sample can be the basis for formulating hypotheses which can then be verified for their general validity with the help of random sampling. On its part, a random sample can suggest ideas which call for such deeper probing as can be carried out only with the help of a purposive sample.

3.4 We can illustrate the interdependence of these two kinds of sampling from our own experience. In collaboration with Pranab Bardhan, I carried out a large-scale survey into such interlinked agrarian phenomena as labour relations, tenancy relations, credit relations, etc. in 1976, and then in 1979 conducted another large-scale survey on labour relations alone, both using the random sampling approach. (The results of these are presented in the references appended at the end of this essay.) These surveys, while yielding a rich harvest of quantitative estimates, also raised many questions and indicated the existence of a number of dark corners. In the light of the above, I decided to conduct intensive enquiries on the basis of two clusters of purposively selected villages. Among other considerations in purposively selecting the samples, one was the proximity of the villages. I favoured those that I could myself visit and make enquiries in as often as necessary. The results presented in Rudra (1982) threw light on a number of dark areas within our knowledge, but, much more importantly, led to the discovery of certain problems the existence of which was not only not known to the author but was also unrecognized in the literature. The problem was of course studied thoroughly on the basis of the purposive sample itself. But it also pushed us both to undertake yet another large-scale survey, based on the random sampling principle, to verify whether the phenomenon that interested us was a peculiarity of the purposively selected villages or something that could claim wider validity. The results of this last mentioned survey have been presented in Bardhan and Rudra (1986).

4. SAMPLE SIZE

4.1 It is a very common misconception among those who use the survey method, but who do not have a good grounding in statistical theory of sampling, that the larger the sampling fraction the better. This is totally wrong. As is well known, the efficiency of a sampling scheme depends on the combination of the sample size and the population variance. The size of the population, and therefore the sampling fraction, does not matter at all. This is clearly seen in the simplest case of a simple random sampling in the formula

$$V(\bar{x}) = \frac{\sigma^2}{\eta}$$

where σ is the population standard deviation, $\bar{x}$ the sample mean, and n the sample size. As one may see, the expression does not involve the population size. Imagine an extreme situation where $\sigma = 0$. In that case, a sample size of $\eta = 1$ would give complete information about the population, and it would be quite redundant to take even a second observation.

4.2 The simple argument given above has significance for the designing of a survey which seems not to have been widely recognized. The significance lies in the fact that if one can either stratify the population (or draw a multi-stage sample) such that each stratum (or each last stage sample) is very nearly homogeneous, then a sample of very small size, even of size 1 or 2 from each stratum (or each last stage sample), should be sufficient.

4.3 We have actually made use of this result in the following way. It is an interesting fact of our agrarian society that there are certain things which are uniform within village society, whereas they vary quite largely even among neighbouring villages. Thus, the daily wage-rate of casual labourers is usually the same in a village. The sharing arrangement in crop sharing tenancy usually takes a single or at most two or three configurations in any one village. The marketing channels, the existence or otherwise of village moneylenders, the nature and extent of irrigation facilities, etc., are really information pertaining to the village and therefore do not vary from respondent to respondent. To enquire into such matters it is utterly wasteful from every point of view to take a large number of respondents from each village. Given a total sample size, the best strategy is to take a maximum number of villages and a minimum number of respondents within each village.

4.4 We give a concrete illustration of this approach from our own experience. In the surveys jointly conducted by Pranab Bardhan and myself (Bardhan and Rudra, 1978 & 1980), we chose from each village only a few respondents for each branch of enquiry. Thus, to enquire into employer-employee relations we sometimes took no more than four respondents, two casual labourers and two farm servants. To enquire into leasing arrangements we often took no more then two tenants. We are quite convinced that if instead of two we took twenty, we would not have got better results. We took two and not just one in order to avoid the risk of idiosyncratic persons getting selected as respondents. The second respondent acts as a check. To ensure further check, we verified the responses obtained with other randomly selected villagers of unspecified number who might have gathered, say, in a tea shop. It goes without saying that on the rare occasion when the responses from the respondents are at variance with each other, one has to take the trouble of a more thorough investigation. The advantage of our approach is that such further thorough investigations are required to be carried out only in exceptional cases.

5. RANDOMIZATION METHODS

5.1 We do not want to go over all the different methods of random sampling, with different efficiencies associated with them for different kinds of populations. Any textbook of sampling theory presents detailed discussions about such methods as multi-stage sampling, sampling with probability proportional to size, systematic sampling, circular systematic sampling, etc.

5.2 We, however, want to discuss certain short-cut methods that we have used for simplifying the work of selecting a random sample in the ultimate stage. To be concrete, let us consider the ultimate stage of a village or stratum within a village. For instance, suppose we want to select a number of casual labourers from a village. The usual procedure would be first to make a complete list of all the households, with a mention of each household occupation; then to define a stratum consisting only of casual labourer households; then to draw a sample, simple random or of some other type, with the help of random numbers. Now we have, in many of our field investigations, eliminated the entire laborious and time-consuming work of listing households. The principle that we have made use of is that of randomizing the population and then drawing an arbitrary sample. Randomizing the population does not involve listing the population. It can be achieved by adopting a selection procedure such that the sample consists of the first few members of the population which has been arranged in a random permutation. In selecting labourers or tenants we followed the rule of not entering the village proper, but instead walking across fields and talking to labourers or tenants, who were either engaged in work or travelling to or from the place of work. This procedure was followed not only for simplifying the randomization procedure but also to minimize respondent biases discussed in greater detail in the next section.

6. RESPONDENT BIAS

6.1 Respondent bias affects all investigations which involve the interview method, but it is all the more important when the questions concern the economic condition of the respondent. It seems to be a common characteristic of members of economically developed societies to be secretive to different degrees about their economic condition, in particular about such matters as income, savings and wealth. It is well known that the investigation method has not succeeded in India in yielding estimates of aggregate personal income, personal savings or personal wealth.

6.2 Apart from deliberately falsified replies, one has also to reckon with the problem of memory lapse. The respondent may genuinely fail to remember the answers to certain questions. There may be certain other matters about which the respondent may not be in the habit of memorizing details, so that the question of forgetting does not arise. Yet another kind of respondent bias arises out of the respondent being impatient, uncooperative or even hostile towards the investigator.

6.3 It is therefore necessary to take resort to various devices to minimize these respondent biases. Obviously, different kinds of measures have to be taken to tackle wilful falsification, memory lapse and respondent hostility. We shall discuss some of the methods that we have used, and obtained promising results.

6.4 As to deliberate suppression or falsification of information, it is as well to recognize that different categories of respondents have got different sensibilities. Thus, the very poor seem to have little tendency to falsify information relating to their income or wealth. The propensity to hide information seems to operate weakly with those who have very little to hide. The problem with such people is more to do with their not keeping track of their meagre economic transactions. Better-off people are typically reluctant to divulge their income, savings or wealth, but they may have less problem remembering their transactions.

To take a very different kind of enquiry, women of the poorer and less-educated sections might be reluctant to talk about their family planning practices, whereas women in educated and economically better-off families might have much less inhibition about such matters, especially if the investigators are female. It is clear, therefore, that one has to be very inventive and adopt different measures for different kinds of respondents with regard to different types of questions.

6.5 We have said that the very poor usually do not tend to falsify information relating to their economic conditions. However, one faces a different problem with them. If they are replying to questions in the presence of richer members of village society, especially those who are their employers, landlords or moneylenders, they usually feel compelled to give answers which the other parties present would expect them to give. The 'important' people of village society tend systematically to overstate the wage rate and understate the interest rate on loan. In general, they try to make out that their own conditions are worse and the conditions of the poor better than is true. They not only present such an account when interviewed themselves, they also exert moral pressure on poor respondents to answer along such lines when interviewed in their presence. They also try their best to impose their presence when the poor are interviewed. For this reason we found it expedient not to talk to labourers and other poor people inside the village, but to catch hold of them while they were working on fields or outside the village.

6.6 When interviewing economically better-off people we found it best not to ask questions relating to a range of items such as the amount of land owned or possessed, gross production, output of individual crops, income from different sources, savings, etc. This does not mean that we did not want to form an idea on these aspects of the respondents. We were quite successful in extracting information relating to these points by various indirect means, i.e. with the help of certain questions not directly related to the magnitudes we were after. For instance, a fairly good idea about the amount of land and total production can be obtained by using the following information which farmers are not usually reluctant to divulge: (a) number of man-days employed for different agricultural operations; (b) number of man-days used for threshing of paddy or other crops; (c) number of bullock-days used for ploughing; (d) yield per acre of different crops on farmers' plots, etc. These involve certain technical norms which the villagers themselves willingly supply. Not knowing the use to which they might be put, they do not try to distort them. Using such information, one can form more than one estimate of the same magnitude, and it is safe to assume that the true value would lie within the range.

6.7 Using such stratagems, one may be able to form fairly reliable estimates about certain magnitudes directly involved in production. It is, however, as well to recognize that it is impossible to form even indirect estimates of certain other items. Tangible assets other than land can be easily estimated, being open to direct observation, but intangible assets like money—in cash or in the form of outstanding loans or bank deposits or gold and jewellery—can hardly be estimated by any means. Benami land in the same village can in principle be discovered by cross-examining other villagers. But it is next to impossible for a researcher to estimate how much benami land might be possessed in other villages. Our experience suggests that it is best to leave these questions alone; any attempts, direct or indirect, to estimate them only result in antagonizing the respondent. Given that capital formation in concrete form can be reasonably estimated, we have found it is possible to form a fairly good idea about the economic conditions of even the better-off villagers.

6.8 We have till now discussed items of information which respondents might deliberately want to hide. There are, however, other items which get distorted without deliberate intent on the part of the respondent. As to memory lapse, it is a problem connected with the reference period and the frequency of questioning. This is dealt with later. We are left with the problem of respondent bias, which is due neither to deliberate falsification nor to memory lapse. As mentioned before, the problem arises with items to which the respondent does not pay attention. One has to try to approximate these magnitudes with the help of such associated information to which the respondent does pay attention. We may illustrate the problem and the solution by referring to the National Sample Survey approach to consumption expenditure.

6.9 If a person is asked how much s/he has spent by way of consumption during a reference period, one could get answers that are subject to wild margins of error. The problem of not keeping accounts would get compounded by the respondent or by the investigator not being clear as to what the constituents of consumption expenditure are. The NSS solution has been to ask questions about individual items in all their minute specificity. The idea is that the respondent might, with effort, recall these details and then the job of estimating the total consumption expenditure might be left to the analysis stage.

6.10 A comparable example is the following: a small producer of foodgrains may not have a precise idea of how much he has produced. Farmers, in West Bengal, at least, are not given to the habit of measuring their produce. As such, any figure he might give about how much he has produced might be quite unreliable, even though he may not want to give a false account. On the other hand, he would usually have a fairly good idea of how much foodgrain he consumes per day. With the help of that data and supplementary data about sales and purchases of grain, use of grains for seeds, etc., one may be able to arrive at a fairly reliable estimate of his produce.

7. TIME REFERENCE AND FREQUENCY OF INTERVIEWS

7.1 In the common run of economic enquiries one usually visits and interviews a respondent only once and poses questions for a given reference period, which, instead of being a fixed interval of calendar time, is sometimes made rolling: e.g. the week or the month preceding the day of the interview. For consumption and employment surveys by the National Sample Survey, one has adopted such rolling periods. There has been a great deal of discussion about the optimum length of the reference period. It is easy to understand that one has to strike a balance between two opposite effects. The longer the period, the greater problem of memory lapse. But the shorter the period, the greater the chance of some infrequent event not taking place at all during that period. It is because of this latter that it has been observed, quite correctly, that the estimates of the number of the employed and the unemployed in the National Sample Survey depend on the arbitrarily chosen reference period. (A person is regarded as employed if he says he has worked during a minimum number of days during the reference period).

7.2 There are, however, certain types of problems, the investigation of which calls for repeated visits to the same respondent. The Farm Management Surveys sponsored by the Ministry of Agriculture required a daily collection of information from a selected sample of farmers. This information relates to activities connected with farming, such as operations carried out in the field, employment of labourers, use of inputs, harvest of products, sales, purchases, etc. In this particular case, a daily visit is neither necessary nor possible. It is not possible because the same investigator cannot possibly collect all these different sorts of information from all the households allotted to him in the course of the same day. It is not necessary because the kinds of information involved are not forgotten so quickly by the respondents. When I directed the Farm Management Survey for the Hoogly district during the years 1969 to 1973, I took the liberty of providing an interval of ten days between two successive visits to the same farmer. As ten households were allotted to each investigator, this constituted a reasonable time pattern.

7.3 Similarly, we found a weekly visit quite adequate for our purposes when we wanted to study the time pattern of sales of paddy as well as a few other important farm decisions with respect to a selected number of big farmers. (The results of this particular study are presented in Rudra, 1983.) It would be impossible for any farmer to recall how much paddy he sold on a particular day when a particular price was in effect, three months after the event. But there cannot be any difficulty with memory if the time lag is only seven days. On the other hand, a daily visit cannot but be regarded as a bit of a nuisance by the respondent. This factor, the not causing of too much irritation to the respondent, has also to be given its due importance.

7.4 Nevertheless, despite all these negative reasons—namely the reaction of the respondent and the physical strain of the investigator—a daily visit, with the logical corollary of the reference period being a single day, is unavoidable for certain kinds of enquiries. We have followed this time pattern in an enquiry that we conducted in collaboration with some scientists of the Indian Statistical Institute into the cash receipts, cash disbursements and food consumption of very poor households. The enquiry was prompted by the consideration that large-scale surveys like the National Sample Survey probably fail to properly account for the consumption of all food items consumed by very poor households. Such households meet a part of their food requirements by means other than purchase from shops. Such means are: scavenging upon nature, receiving food items as a part of wages, receiving them as gifts, etc. Even the items purchased are mostly procured from the shop on a daily basis. Given such a procurement pattern, it was thought that questions relating to a period of a whole month or even a whole week would not elicit reliable replies. It goes without saying that for such an investigation, involving daily visits, a sample to be covered by a single investigator has to be pretty small, the questions to be asked have to be simple and few in number, and the respondents have to be selected purposively to ensure co-operation with the investigator.

8. SCRUTINY AND FEEDBACK

8.1 Responses brought back by field investigators require to be thoroughly scrutinized before being processed. This is necessary to check and eliminate different errors in the returns. Some of them may be the result of sheer carelessness on the part of the investigator or, worse, pure invention by him. Another part may reflect the different respondent biases that we have discussed before; yet another part may be contributed to by investigator biases of different kinds.

8.2 Problems of carelessness as well as deliberate falsification by field investigators are rather serious in our country in any survey in which a large number of investigators are employed. It is deplorable that the level of the work ethic in our country is generally very low. Shirking duty is the rule rather than the exception. In such an environment it is almost the rule that field investigators minimize their work by conducting interviews hurriedly and casually, or do not even take the trouble of visiting the respondent, filling up returns with invented entries. Large-scale surveys usually employ supervisors to check the work of investigators. This, however, ensures nothing, for supervisors may also shirk their work just as much as investigators, independently or collusively.

8.3 The problem can be eliminated only when the survey is conducted on such a limited scale that one can do with the services of only a few field investigators. They may be selected to be, or trained up to be, involved in the problem itself, and thus have a moral commitment to the project as much as the principal researcher himself. On such considerations, in our own practice, we have never worked with more than four field investigators at a time. We have never made use of supervisors. Supervision implies distrust, and distrust can never stimulate a worker to work to the best of his ability. It is clear that we take a rather pessimistic view of large-scale surveys that employ investigators in hundreds or thousands.

8.4 While we believe in avoiding supervision, scrutiny is of paramount importance not only for locating errors, inconsistencies, gaps in information, etc., but also for detecting deliberate falsifications. This latter purpose can be achieved better if one frames the questionnaire in such a fashion that the same information is aimed at indirectly in several questions. It may be so done that neither the investigator nor the respondent would suspect the trap that is laid for capturing falsified or invented answers.

8.5 To have the full benefit of scrutiny, its results have to be fed back to the investigators for obtaining rectification. This, however, becomes unfeasible in all surveys where the practice, all too common, is to take up the returns for scrutiny and processing after a long time lapse from the date of the interview. The quality of data collection can be improved enormously if the scrutiny is carried out simultaneously with field investigation, with a minimum time lag. In the intensive survey carried out by me, the results of which have been presented in Rudra (1982), I followed the practice of the field investigator submitting his returns once every week, and being fed back the results of scrutiny in the very next week. In the surveys that I carried out in collaboration with Pranab Bardhan, this interval had to be made a month (but no more) in view of the fact that the investigators had to travel to different, far-away districts.

9. QUESTIONNAIRE DESIGN

9.1 Many a research investigator tends to load the questionnaire with as many questions as possible, with the idea that all of them are somehow or other relevant for the problem under examination. The philosophy here obviously is, 'the more the better'. We, however, subscribe to the opposite philosophy, namely, 'the less the better'. We believe that to obtain information pertaining to a problem the questions should be as narrowly focused on the problem as possible.

9.2 One finds, very commonly, a very large number of questions which obviously the researcher thought necessary but which, on examination, can be shown to be redundant. The best way of judging redundancy is to compare the items included in the questionnaire with the items which occur in the final tables. It is seen in most cases that a large number of items included in the questionnaire do not find any place in final tables. As a matter of fact, many of the items in the questionnaire are such that they cannot possibly be included in any tabulation scheme. This happens because at the time of framing the questionnaire the researcher only looks at the questions from the point of view of their relevance for an individual respondent; he does not ask himself how the information will be aggregated over the different respondents.

9.3 A good rule for framing a questionnaire is to start at the other end, i.e. the tables. One may write down a number of 'dummy tables', i.e. tables with no entries but with all other specifications representing the kind of results one would like to present. One may then work back to the questions that require to be answered if the dummy tables are to be filled up with actual entries. If this procedure is strictly followed, one would arrive at a questionnaire shorn of all redundancies.

9.4 To give an example that may appear somewhat extreme to many a researcher, in the survey conducted by us we desisted from asking questions about the family composition of our sample households. All standard questionnaires began with a block listing the household members by name, indicating their age, sex, marital status, and relation with the head of the household. We were interested in different aspects of production relations and not in demographic particulars, or the average consumption level, or the intra-family distribution of consumption. As such, we did not have any difficulty completing our analysis with no information on these points. Nor have we seen many studies by other researchers where the understanding of production conditions has been enriched by information collected on demographic particulars.

9.5 The case for a narrow focusing of questions is further strengthened by a consideration from Sampling Theory. As is well known, a multi-purpose survey does not permit the solution of the problem of optimum sample design in terms of stratification, scheme of staging, etc. This is because the optimality of sample design has been tackled in the Theory of Sampling only for one variable at a time. When different variables are highly correlated, it may be expected that the same sample design may be nearly optimum for all of them. This will, of course, not be true when the variables are not closely correlated. As a result, the sample design of a survey with multiple focus has usually a sampling design which is an efficient for each focus.

10. STRATIFICATION

10.1 As is well known, stratification is resorted to for reducing sampling errors associated with estimates. We shall neither mention here the standard textbook results relating to Stratification Gains nor discuss the different bases on which stratification may be carried out in different socio-economic surveys. We shall discuss a single point, namely a particular kind of stratification that is made necessary by the very nature of much economic data, and the problems which arise when not taking resort to that kind of stratification—the importance of this has not been recognized in the literature.

10.2 The nature of the data in question is the highly skewed character of the distributions of a number of economic variables associated with the income of households. As is well known, income and assets of any kind are distributed most unevenly. A very small proportion of people are distributed extensively over a very long range of incomes. There are many variables associated with income earners that take zero value up to quite a high income level, and only then start to take positive values. All the items of luxury consumption belong to this category. So do such things as personal savings, land owned, etc. If the distribution of income itself be of the log normal shape with acute positive skewness, the distribution of these associated variables are J-shaped, with a high concentration at the variable value zero.

10.3 It is a matter of experience that sample surveys fail to yield any reliable estimates of these variables with J-shaped distributions. The NSS data provide reasonably reliable estimates for most items of mass consumption. They, however, fail to yield any acceptable estimates of items belonging to the consumption pattern of the rich. One cannot think of estimating the number of owned televisions or motorcars from NSS data, even though all these items are included in the NSS questionnaire schedule. Table I illustrates the problem for a few selected items. As one may see, the estimates of a number of durable consumer goods based on the NSS under-estimate the figures based on production statistics by extremely large factors.

10.4 There are, however, statisticians who obstinately hold on to the idea that there are no reasons why in principle the NSS data should fail to provide reliable estimates of even these items. To satisfy these critics we undertook, jointly with a collaborator, a rigorous analysis of the problem, the results of which are presented in Roychowdhuri and Rudra (1988).

10.5 We present below the salient points of our findings in the paper cited above:

(a) If a population of observations that cannot take negative values be such that the proportion of members with a variable value greater then zero is p and if the p be so small that $np \leq 0.65$ where n is the sample size, then for such a sample the probability is greater than half that the sample will include no observations with a non-zero variable value. That is, the probability is greater than half that the sample estimate of the aggregate value of a variable would be zero when it is small in the population. By similar reasoning the probability will also be high that the sample estimates would be lower than the true population value.

(b) In the same set-up as above, the expected number of observations in the sample taking positive values would usually be so small that the error of the estimate of the aggregate in which we are interested would be very large.

These two points taken together mean that the estimates of aggregates of items associated with the rich would be underestimates and subject to wide dispersion.

10.6 Two other interesting results are worth mentioning.

(a) The error of estimation will be significantly reduced if the population is divided into two strata, the first consisting of all observations with variable value zero and the second consisting of that part of the population with non-zero variable values and drawing the entire sample from the second part. (An example: to estimate the average size of land owned it is more efficient to draw a sample from among those who have got some land, leaving out all the totally landless).

(b) The errors of estimation may be even further reduced if that part of the population that takes non-zero variable values be divided into a number of strata, each corresponding to a fractile group of the variable in question. The optimum allocation of the sample among these strata would require a monotonically increasing sequence of sub-sample sizes. That is, if n be the total sample size, and $n_i(y)$ be the optimum allocation of sample observations to the ith stratum corresponding to the ith fractile based on the variable y, then $n_i(y) \leqslant n_j(y)$ if $i \leqslant J$.

10.7 Given that we are never interested in a single variable y but a number of variables y, z, u, v, etc., the optimum allocations, $n_i(y)$, $n_j(z)$ etc. would be different. All the same, if the population is divided into a number of fractile groups on the basis of a variable like per capita income or any other proxy variable x for the level of living, the estimates of the aggregates of all variables y, z, etc. positively correlated with x would be very much more efficient than if no such stratification was adopted.

10.8 The conclusion we draw is as follows: Given the highly skewed nature of the distribution of per capita income and all variables positively associated with it, any sample design that does not stratify the population according to per capita income or some proxy for it would yield estimates that would, with a

TABLE I

Underestimation of Luxury Items by the National Sample Survey

Item	Purchase per household according to NSS (28th round)	Production per household according to official statistics	Ratio of col. 3 to col. 2
(1)	(2)	(3)	(4)
1. MOTOR CARS	0.00006	0.0004	6.67
2. TYRES/TUBES	0.01	0.5	50.00
3. BICYCLES	0.006	0.024	4.00
4. ELECTRIC FANS	0.008	0.02	2.50
5. RADIOS	0.008	0.01	1.25

Note: The NSS gives estimates for the items above in value only. The quantity figures have been arrived at by using very approximate price figures. The figures from official sources represent production which is not all available for consumption purposes because of uses outside households, including addition to stocks and foreign trade.

high probability, be lower than the true values. On the other hand these errors may be easily lessened by adopting a proper stratification scheme. As for the National Sample Survey, we would strongly recommend that such a stratification be adopted for the population of the village selected in the last stage of the multi-stage sampling scheme. If this is carried out, not only luxury consumer goods but all such assets, e.g. land owned and possessed, farm machinery, personal savings, personal wealth, etc., would in principle become included in what may be estimable by the National Sample Survey.

REFERENCES

Bardhan, P. and Rudra, A., 'Interlinkage of Land, Labour and Credit Relations: An Analysis of Village Survey Data in East India', *Economic and Political Weekly*, vol. 13, Annual No., Feb. 1978.

———, 'Terms and Conditions of Sharecropping Contracts: An Analysis of Village Survey Data in India', *Journal of Development Studies*, vol. 16, April 1980.

———, 'Types of Labour Attachment in Agriculture: Results of a Survey in West Bengal 1979', *Economic and Political Weekly*, vol. 15, 30 August 1980.

———, 'Labour Employment and Wages in Agriculture: Results of a Survey in West Bengal Villages in 1979', *Economic and Political Weekly*, vol. 15, 8–15 November 1980.

———, 'Labour Mobility and the Boundaries of the Village Moral Economy,' *The Journal of Peasant Studies*, vol. 13, no. 3, April 1986.

Roychowdhuri, R. and Rudra, A., 'A Case for Oversampling the Rich in Statistical Investigations', *EPW*, 5 March 1988.

Rudra, A. 'Extra-economic Constraints on Agricultural Labour: Results of an Intensive Survey in some Villages near Santiniketan, West Bengal,' Asian Employent Programme Working Paper, Bangkok: ILO-ARTEP, August 1982.

———, 'Non-Maximizing Behaviour of Farmers,' *Economic and Political Weekly*, vol. 18, 1 October, 26 November and 17 December 1983.

Chapter 10: On Studying Socio-Economic Change in Rural India

T. N. SRINIVASAN

At the very outset let me state my convictions: first, without measurement any pretence at scientific analysis is impossible; second, even to know what to measure, let alone how to measure, a theoretical framework is necessary; and third, measurement or data collection has to be carefully designed, whether it relates to the design of scientific experiments or to studies of socio-economic change. It is very unlikely that the sharpness and sophistication of tools of analysis by themselves can completely compensate for the deficiencies of design in data collection, although, contrary to common belief, crudeness of data will require sophisticated rather than simple tools of analysis to derive valid inferences from them. The contributions to this volume only strengthen these beliefs.

The initial motivations for the Bangalore workshop out of which this volume has emerged were apparently two: (i) A perceived contradiction between the 'findings' from large–scale surveys of no significant improvement in the 'conditions of villagers' and the hopeful picture of improvements as seen from village studies; (ii) An assertion attributed to anthropologists that 'the large-scale data systems cannot capture many of the nuances of village life and the process of its socio-economic transformations, for which one needs the richly detailed participant observations of the ethnographers'; and another assertion, this time attributed to statisticians, that 'the small-scale purposive nature of many of the anthropologists' units of study (invalidates) wider generalization.'

The assertion that village studies are not representative just because of their small number can be misleading. As long as the rules of random sample selection are observed, what matters are (i) the *absolute* size of the sample and not its magnitude relative to the size of the population; and (ii) variation in the population of the characteristic one is estimating. As such, studies of a *few* villages could be adequate if either the population is relatively homogeneous or if the desired degree of precision is not too high. Thus, it is not a question of *large-scale surveys* versus *small-scale village studies* as long as the villages are chosen with a suitable sampling design.

It is also the case that purposive selection per se need not invalidate some forms of inference. To take a mundane example, if the relationship between expenditure on food and total household consumption expenditure can be assumed to be the same for all households in a village, it is not necessary to choose a 'representative' sample of all the households to estimate the relationship. All that is necessary is sufficient variation in total expenditure among the chosen households. R. A. Fisher's concept of randomization in the design of experiments was also meant as a device to obtain valid inferences, even though experimental subjects may not have been randomly chosen. Even if valid general inferences are precluded by the purposive selection, it is still likely that they can generate a number of hypotheses that can be tested with a better designed survey. In this sense almost all village studies are likely to be useful.

A second obvious point is this: if in a village study one covers *all* households in the chosen village and in a large-scale survey only a few households are sampled from each chosen village, whether a given level of precision is achieved for a given cost by a village survey or by a large-scale survey depends on the relative magnitudes of inter-village and intra-village variation in the characteristic under study. To take an extreme example, if *all households* within each village have the same value for the characteristic while two households from any two different villages differ, there is no point in studying all households within each village—a sample of one household will do!

Some arguments against surveys appear to be irrelevant. For example, the argument that the survey method is incapable of capturing the subtle nuances of village life and changes in them is without merit. If there is any 'nuance' that is objective in concept—so that all reasonably well-trained observers will arrive at the same description of it when they study a village—then in principle a sample survey investigator with adequate training can capture it in a survey. That such training may be time consuming, costly and will require a fairly highly educated investigator, possibly with a degree in anthropology, are not arguments against the survey as a *method*. The linguistic and terminological problems discussed by Appadurai (Chapter 11) can arise, in principle, both in the surveys and in the intensive village studies. Their severity can be considerably reduced, though not eliminated altogether, by choosing investigators who understand the version of the local language spoken by most of the respondents, and acquainting them with the intended meaning of the contents of the questionnaire to be administered. While it is true, as Appadurai argues, that respondents when asked about absolute magnitudes such as the size of their harvest often think in terms of comparative ranking, with some imagination a questionnaire can be designed that extracts a reasonable approximation of the underlying absolute magnitudes through a *series* of questions making the respondent engage in a *number* of comparative statements. If the description of nuances can vary with the observer in a conceptual sense, then there is no scientific point in attempting to describe them anyway. Conceptual subjectivity is to be distinguished sharply from the standard survey problem of 'investigator bias' For example, in crop-cutting experiments for crop yields, one investigator may have a tendency to include every plant that is just on the boundary of the sample cut, while another may exclude all of them. In this case the problem is not with the concept of a crop-cut but with the investigator training.

The quantitative *versus* qualitative argument is again a phony one. If by qualitative one simply means an ordinal measure of ranking of a characteristic rather than a cardinal one, it is *still* quantitative. Most often some mode of scaling is employed in psychological enquiries where the problems of qualitative characteristics are particularly severe. In any case, if the focus of enquiry is an analysis of *change*, then some way of quantifying the qualitative becomes almost inevitable.

The age-old problem of non-sampling errors has once again

been raised. In the workshop, someone quoted Stone and Campbell (1984) as saying, 'In our view, the role of non-sampling error is underestimated in Third World surveys because of the assumption that Western survey research methods can be indiscriminately adopted everywhere with the same assumed "insignificant" level of unmeasurable data validity.' For anyone familiar with the development of the sample-survey literature, to be told that survey research method is Western is laughable. After all, Professor Mahalanobis of India, a pioneer in the development of sample surveys, was the one who introduced the so-called 'inter-penetrating sub-sample' method by which each of the several independently chosen representative samples are canvassed by different teams of investigators, so that a comparison between estimates obtained from each of the samples is a measure in both the sampling and non-sampling errors. The National Sample Survey (NSS) of India regularly publishes estimates based on sub-samples.

Several problems have been raised about concepts and definitions in schedules of enquiry used in surveys, problems of communicating what the researchers had in mind to the respondent, and of translating the responses into entries in the schedule, etc. First of all, none of these is peculiar to the survey method, though their seriousness may be greater in its use. Second, any careful user of the survey method would first go through a 'pilot survey' in which alternative concepts, methods, schedules, etc. are tried out before choosing the appropriate method and schedule for the large-scale survey. While it is true that this will perhaps lead to a 'least common denominator' schedule and not take into account 'the sociological peculiarities of given communities', any good survey schedule will also leave room for individual investigators to record any problems with the use of the schedule in their context. Some survey organizers may encourage investigators to keep field notes of their observations that they may consider relevant from the broader objective of the survey. In any case, the problems with the definition of a 'worker', 'employment', 'unemployment', etc. are not peculiar to surveys of rural households in developing countries. The British official survey definition of unemployment is not the same as that used by Americans in their surveys. Whether or not to include the so called discouraged worker in the labour force is another issue that arises. Once the definition used is clear, one can attempt in the analysis of the data to allow for (to the extent feasible) any peculiarities in the application of the definition in specific contexts.

In some of the comments about the survey method using schedules or questionnaires there seems to be an inadequate appreciation, if not outright confusion, about the distinction between *'bias'* and *errors of measurement*. No instrument of measurement, even mechanical and electronic, is free of errors of measurement (if for no other reason than that all instruments provide *discrete* measurements of continuous variables, and as such rounding errors are inevitable!). But *errors* will be of either sign, and averaging of values from a sufficient number of independent observations will reduce the measurement errors to a negligible level. *Biases*, as contrasted with errors, are distortions in one direction in all observations and no amount of averaging will reduce bias to a negligible level if it is serious.

The problem of bias can indeed be serious in using a questionnaire as an instrument of enquiry in a number of contexts. For example, whenever the question relates to some aspect of a patron-client relationship, patrons may have an interest in systematically overstating (or understating) the value of a characteristic involved in the relationship, while their clients may have a bias in the opposite direction in their responses. Once again a knowledgeable survey researcher will be aware of this problem. At best s/he can attempt to estimate the extent of bias if the analytical framework enables her or him to predict the extent of bias as a function of other characteristics of the respondent. At worst, the responses of patrons and clients can be averaged *separately* and the 'true' average value of the characteristic will lie between the two if the underlying model is correct.

There is also the even more serious problem of evaluating relationships as such, as contrasted with some characteristics of relationships. This problem is raised by both Appadurai and Jodha herein. They argue that traditional surveys are not well-equipped to collect data that are 'relational' and, even if designed specifically to collect such data, 'cast light—on net *outcomes* of social processes . . . ', and do not capture 'the *relational* dimension of the processes which lead to these outcomes' (Appadurai). Jodha makes a related point: in villages studied by him the extent of rural poverty as measured by the proportion of households having incomes below a poverty threshold increased from 17% to 23% between 1964–66 and 1982–84. Yet he says the extent of increased incidence is not borne by the qualitative indicators of change. The qualitative indicators (or more precisely, quantitative indicators of qualitative *attributes* of households) included indicators of dependency on a patron's support, of dependence on 'inferior' jobs, of mobility across space, financial liquidity, etc. As is well known, income is difficult enough to define conceptually. It is even more difficult, if not impossible, to measure it accurately however it is defined. Still, Jodha's problem cannot be attributed only to such measurement errors in incomes.

At a somewhat superficial level, the problem of understanding the structure of social processes appears similar to the well known and analysed one of inference relating to a *dynamic* and *on-going* process from repeated cross-sections. But at a deeper level, the problem is that by definition *relations* involve more than one individual or household at the same time and place, as well as across time and space. The characteristics of a relationship and, above all, the value placed on its abrogation or its continuance, may be specific not only to the parties involved in the relationship but to the general socio-economic-political context in which the relationship is situated. If this were not the case and an 'objective market value' (positive or negative) can be imputed to a relationship (i.e. how much is the continuance of a relationship worth to each party), then the relationships in which a household is involved can be enumerated and their imputed values could be incorporated in computing its net wealth, as one would do with any of its tangible assets or liabilities. Unfortunately, the possibility of market value imputation is rare. For example, if a tenant attaches different values to a loan from his landlord as compared to one received from a bank, even though the amount of the loan and its other observed terms are identical, it must be because of some unobserved (and perhaps unobservable) differences in other, often, though not always, vague characteristics, in the relationship between the parties in the two loan contracts. Also, the landlord and the tenant may not view the loan transaction identically. The notions of 'power', 'patronage', 'dependency', etc., come readily to mind in this context. In some bilateral relationships, power and dependence may be symmetric, as in the notorious example in the power of mutual assured destruction (MAD), and in others it may be entirely one-sided in the extreme.

Of course, the apparatus of dynamic game theory and the associated concepts of strategies, threats, credibility, pay-offs, valuations, information available to participants, and equilibria would seem relevant in formalizing the intricate web of relationships. However, even if one ignores the numerous solution concepts and possible equilibria and lack of robustness of the propositions that such a theory yields, it is clear that even the most sophisticated of game theoretic formulations are likely to be inadequate, even simplistic, as abstractions of the myriad interrelationships at social, cultural, religious, economic and political levels that exist even in a relatively less developed and slowly changing village community. In any case, neither the survey method nor an intensive village study can ever put together *all* the needed data on the relevant participants in on-going relationships even to attempt to model them as a game. This means that, in practice, while recognizing the importance of such relationships, one can at best hope to obtain information on and characterize, that too partially, no more than a subset of them by either approach. Any pretence that participant observation can do more is just that— pretence—and no more.

Appadurai also believes that 'the deeper issue is *epistemological*, and involves debates about the social scientist (and the effects of his or her methods on the objects of study), a problem which should not appear trivial to anyone familiar with the Heisenberg problem of observer-effect on experiments', and that

the major questions are whether problems of social life (and standard of living) can be reduced largely to their quantitative dimensions (and still remain significant); whether the difficulties of grasping even these quantitative dimensions can be further reduced to the technical issues of 'bias', 'error' and 'sampling', as defined and perceived through the lens of statistics; and whether the problems of how rural people talk and think can be divorced from the fact that serious differences of world-view and terminology separate them from the social scientists who study them.

Let me set aside the issue of whether Appadurai's interpretation of the Heisenberg principle of uncertainty, and his reference to debates among philosophers of science, are correct nor do I wish to quibble with him about what is 'knowable' since I believe, with the Hindu philosophers, that true knowledge lies in knowing what one does not know and cannot even know! These are not central to my argument. My point is simple: any debate about methods of studying rural change can be joined only if there is a common understanding among the participants at a *conceptual level* of what is to be studied. If the term 'qualitative' as applied to a factor simply cloaks the conceptual fuzziness as to what that factor means, there is no point in attempting to assess how it has changed! And a sharp distinction must be drawn between fuzziness at the conceptual level and approximations as well as errors in measurement of a well-defined concept, a distinction that Appadurai seems to ignore. If the gaps between the language, terminology, thought processes, and the world-view of rural people are so different from those of the social scientists as to be indeed insurmountable, neither the survey method nor the participant observation can ever generate knowledge about rural folk.

Returing to the *relational dimension*, the surveys of Rudra and Bardhan (1983) are examples of the partial approach. Another is a collaborative study by the Agro-Economic Research Centre at Andhra University, the Indian Institute of Management at Ahmedabad, and the World Bank in which Clive Bell and I were involved (Bell and Srinivasan, 1984). The survey collected information on a set of characteristics of a relationship from both parties to the relationship (e.g. landlord-tenant, employer-employee, borrower-lender). It showed that responses by the two parties did not always match and in some cases one of the parties did not even acknowledge the existence of the relationship!

Another area where biases are likely to be serious relates to morbidity studies. Obviously, a response to the question 'were you ill at any time during the last week, month (or whatever is the reference period) and if so what was the nature, seriousness and length of each episode of illness', will depend on the respondent's perceptions of illness. In a socio-economic context where the poor or women or some other groups do not perceive or are socially conditioned not to admit an illness unless it is sufficiently serious, while the rich tend to be hypochondriacs, one cannot use morbidity rates, as estimated from such responses, as estimates of the underlying 'true' morbidity rates that frequent clinical examination of the respondents would have revealed. Of course, the availability of treatment facilities may itself induce admission of illnesses that would have been ignored by the respondents had the facilities not been available.

One could list other familiar areas of potentially serious bias, such as in response to questions involving recall (we are all familiar with the alleged tendency to telescope events, of selectively shutting out some events, etc., etc.), and the way a question is posed. These problems plague both village studies and surveys, perhaps the latter more seriously. The phrasing of a question can influence the answer. Of course, any sensitive researcher would be aware of the likely perception problems and would try to deal with it by asking essentially the same question in different ways without appearing to do so. Incidentally, this has some relation to the issue of the length of questionnaires. Sometimes by asking separately about components of a total and the total itself, one builds in internal consistency checks about responses even though one may not be interested in the individual components themselves. This naturally will lengthen the questionnaire.

To sum up, there is nothing inherent in the *survey method* that precludes it from generating the same information as a village study based on participation observation. However, it would involve the use of well-trained investigators, carefully designed and tested (in a pilot survey) schedules of enquiry, an analytical frame that allows for the biases in responses that cannot be eliminated, etc. And above all, it will be costly. While some analytical construct or framework, implicit or explicit, necessarily influences all empirical studies even of a descriptive kind, it is essential in surveys or studies of socio-economic changes in villages. The notion that one can just barge into a village and 'observe', without some prior theorizing about the nature of the socio-political-economic relations to guide the observation, is untenable. After all, one has to have at least some notion as to what to observe and why, if the scarce investigative resources are not to be wasted.

The design of a survey can usefully include not only responses to a household questionnaire but also a collection of relevant information on the village as a whole, made by a sensitive investigator and supplemented by free-form (i.e. not bound by questionnaires) interviews over an extended period of time with individuals purposively selected by the investigator after s/he has been 'accepted' in the village. This is an attempt to incorporate the best from both modes of study. I have already mentioned the surveys by Rudra and Bardhan (1983) and the collaborative study in which I was involved as examples of such attempts. It goes without saying that an ideally designed and executed survey with similarly conducted village study would show no difference in findings. However, in the real world neither is ideally done, and whether one is better than the other has to be decided on a case-by-case basis.

The alleged contradiction between the findings of large-scale surveys and studies separated in time of the same villages can be explained in part using the theory of sampling. Consider two alternative data collection methods: surveying an independently selected set of households at two points in time, i.e. the so-called independent cross-sections method as in the Indian National Sample Survey (NSS), or re-interviewing the same set of households at both points in time as in the panel method. It can be shown that if there is a positive serial correlation within households in the characteristics in which we are interested, then the most accurate *estimates of change* from a given sample size are obtained by using the panel method. As Ashenfelter, Deaton and Solon (1986) argue, the issues are fairly obvious.

For one individual respondent, or for the pairing of a respondent and an interviewer, two kinds of errors can be usefully distinguished: those that are essentially random, and will be independent over time, and those that are persistent. . . the total response error will then be the sum of both types. The random errors will have identical implications for cross-section and panel estimates of change. However, the panel data do better with the persistent errors since differencing for individuals will tend to remove at least part of the error and thus give a more precise estimate of the true change in means. It is only in the event of *negative* serial correlation in reporting errors that the estimate of change from the independent cross-sections would be more precise'

Clearly random errors of measurement are of the first kind, and biases are of the second kind. There is a presumption on the basis of this discussion that large-scale independent cross-sections such as the NSS surveys may not show any significant change, while village studies that approximate panel data do. Ashenfelter *et al.* also discuss the virtues of a rotating panel which combines independent cross-section and panel features by retaining only a part of one period's sample households for the next. If one is interested not merely in the change in mean between periods but also in the means of each period, a rotating panel trades off some loss of precision in estimating the change for gain in precision in estimating means.

I cannot resist adding another personal note. When I was on the governing council of the NSS the decision to move to a quinquennial canvassing from the until-then annual canvassing of consumer expenditure survey (on which most analyses of poverty change were based) was taken. If my memory does not fail me, I argued without success then for canvassing a smaller rotating panel of households annually along with the large quinquennial survey. I still believe that the dropping of annual surveys altogether, rather than a reduction in their size, was an unwise decision. I understand that it has now been rescinded and relatively small annual surveys of consumer expenditure are being restored.

The fact that large-scale surveys are usually multi-purpose surveys necessarily forces some trade-offs on them which village studies do not have to face to the same degree. Again, a small-sized annual rotating panel between large-scale surveys at widely separated points in time can help mitigate the impact of these trade-offs. Yet another trade-off that is apparently wrongly exercised in India and elsewhere is between resources devoted to data collection *versus* those devoted to the timely coding, taping, cleaning, tabulation and analysis. There is no point in spending a lot of resources in collecting data that are never cleaned and tabulated. What is worse, it could have been anticipated that they would never be cleaned even before any data were collected! In India, vested interests have managed to retard the movement towards computerized editing, cleaning and tabulation. It is one thing to sing the virtues of village studies, but it is entirely another to turn processing of survey data into a village or cottage industry under the protective umbrella of the government.

REFERENCES

Ashenfelter, O., Deaton, A. and Solon, G., 'Collecting Panel Data in Developing Countries: Does it Make Sense?' Working Paper No. 23, Living Standard Measurement Study, World Bank, Washington, D. C. 1986.

Bell, C. and T. N. Srinivasan, 'The Salient Features of the Areas Under Study, Market Structures and Public Policies', Working Paper No. 2, RPO, 671–89, Development Research Department, World Bank, Washington, D.C. 1984.

Rudra, A. and P. K. Bardhan, *Agrarian Relations in West Bengal: Results of Two Surveys* (Bombay, Somaniya Publishers) 1983.

Stone, L. and J. G. Campbell, 'The Use and Misuse of Surveys in International Development: An Experiment from Nepal', *Human Organization* Spring 1984.

Chapter 11: Small-Scale Techniques and Large-Scale Objectives*

ARJUN APPADURAI

My objective in writing this essay is *not* to offer any new wisdom on the thorny problems of comparing and integrating the methods and results of work done on rural economic change at the macro and micro levels. My purposes are: (1) to raise a set of conceptual issues (many of them familiar to students of rural economic change in India); (2) to place them in an anthropological perspective; (3) to reflect on my own efforts to integrate qualitative and numerical work at the village level; (4) to suggest some hypotheses about the divergence between results at the two levels; (5) to propose a specific strategy for improved dialogue between analysts working at disparate levels; (6) to

* The fieldwork on which this essay is based was conducted with financial support from the Social Science Research Council, the National Science Foundation and the American Institute for Indian Studies. The essay was prepared with financial support from the University of Pennsylvania and the Center for Advanced Study in the Behavioral Sciences, Stanford (through grant BNS-8011494 from the National Science Foundation). In the early stages of conceptualizing the essay I had useful discussions with Ellen Comisso, Paul DiMaggio, Stephen Fienberg, Ulf Hannerz and Karl Shell, though none of them is responsible for the views expressed here. An earlier version of this paper was presented at a conference on 'Rural Economic Change in South Asia' sponsored by the Joint Committee on South Asia of the American Council of Learned Societies and the Social Science Research Council, in Bangalore (India) on 5–8 August 1986. I am grateful to all the participants at the Conference for their comments and suggestions, and especially to Pranab Bardhan, the organizer and editor of this volume. Amartya Sen generously commented on an earlier draft and helped me to sharpen several key points.

provide an analysis of the reasons why such dialogue faces certain major obstacles.

A word about my own qualifications: I have worked as an anthropologist at the village level in Maharashtra, and, though I am not entirely innumerate, I am largely a passive consumer of aggregate, numerical analyses of rural India. However, I am committed to criticism and improvement of approaches at *all* levels.

SOME TERMINOLOGICAL CLARIFICATIONS

The terms 'micro' and 'macro' have a technical meaning in neo-classical economics, but there is apparently no simple or straightforward agreement as to what exactly that meaning is, even among economists. What is clear is that the loose sense in which the softer social sciences use these terms (to mean something like large- *versus* small-scale) is confusing (and therefore unacceptable) to most economists, whose use of the terms does not necessarily have anything to do with scale. If, for purposes of clarity, we drop the terms 'micro' and 'macro', we are left with three pairs of terms that seem to cluster together in certain standard ways in discussions of the methodology of the study of rural economic change. They are: (1) small- *versus* large-scale; (2) qualitative *versus* quantitative; and (3) aggregative *versus* non-aggregative. Put crudely, village studies by anthropologists tend to be small-scale, qualitative and non-aggregative; village studies by economists and agronomists (such as those conducted by ICRISAT and the Agro-Economic Research Centres) tend to be small- or medium-scale, quantitative and aggregative; and large-scale studies (such as those of the NSS) tend to be large-scale, quantitative and aggregative.

Though there are exceptions to this general characterization, it seems fair to say that not much systematic thought has been given in studies of rural economic change in India (or elsewhere) to how we might break this conventional lumping of small-scale, non-aggregative and qualitative approaches on the one hand, and large-scale, aggregative and quantitative approaches on the other. In the final section of this essay I shall propose a relatively new strategy. But first we need to cover some more familiar ground.

MUTUAL CRITICISMS

There is no need to go over in detail the criticisms made by practitioners at large- and small-scales of each others' methods and interpretations. Criticism of the deficiencies of large-scale survey research has a long history (see, for example, Gibson and Hawkins 1968; Leach 1967; Srinivas 1979; Zeller and Carmines 1980) and in recent times there have been several discussions of the problems of exporting Western survey techniques to the Third World (Hursh-Cesar and Roy 1976; Mitchell 1965). A recent essay by Stone and Campbell (1984) summarizes many of these problems and proposes an interesting strategy for using these approaches in a complementary manner. Criticisms of village-level anthropological work by those working at larger scales and with quantitative techniques are less frequently published, but are no less harsh. On the one side, there are accusations of losing cultural salience, processual links and relational information. On the other side, there is the problem of non-quantifiability, indefinite representativeness, and limited comparability. Less noted is the fact that village-level anthropological work frequently does not overlap in *content* with the concerns of the large-scale surveys. In general, until recently, anthropological work at the village level in India did not focus on problems of agricultural life, economic opportunities and standards of living.

But there have recently been a variety of signs of efforts to link village studies with studies undertaken at larger scales. These include the VLS (Village-Level Studies) undertaken by ICRI-SAT since 1976; the work of the Agro-Economic Research Centres in India; the work in Bengal of Rudra and Bardhan, and of CRESSIDA; the work of some individual scholars (Etienne 1982; Mencher 1978; Harris 1982; Hill 1982), and the work of scholars associated with B. H. Farmer in Sri Lanka and South India (Farmer 1977; Bayliss-Smith and Wanmali 1984). The purposes of these individuals and institutions vary greatly and it is only in some of these cases that the use of village-level data to make larger-scale arguments is a central objective. In the discussion that follows, I have been influenced by data and techniques contained in these studies, but I shall not cite them extensively.

In order for there to be any worthwhile co-operation between analysts working at the village level and those working at larger scales, village-level studies, especially those conducted by anthropologists, must focus, at least in part, on rural economic life. One very detailed blueprint for what exactly this means is contained in the *Manual of Instructions for Economic Investigators in ICRISAT's Village Level Studies* (Binswanger and Jodha 1978), though aspects of the underlying approach of this manual could be subject to the criticisms recently made by J. Harriss (1983) of the village studies of the Agro-Economic Research Centre in Visva Bharti, West Bengal. For those particularly interested in contractual aspects of rural agricultural life, an excellent model is to be found in Rudra and Bardhan (1983). What needs to be emphasized is that these are models for capturing data concerning certain relationships. But a general model of Indian villages *as* economies and of agriculture regarded as a social form is only gradually beginning to emerge (Bliss and Stern 1982; Harriss 1982, 1983; Desai, Rudolph and Rudra 1985), though there have been important earlier steps in this direction (Beteille 1974; Breman 1974; Epstein 1962, 1973; Mencher 1978). Thus, the analysis of rural economy by anthropologists is not just a matter of looking at the right things, but also of evolving an appropriate theory of the village as an agrarian economy. It is worth noting, in this context, a series of recent arguments to the effect that although Indian villages are not autonomous as in the nineteenth-century administrative myth, they are nevertheless coherent, significant and fairly well-bound locations for social and economic processes (Harriss 1983; Rudra 1984; Schlesinger 1981). But this sort of coherence does not necessarily support the sort of 'holism' traditionally guiding the work of anthropologists (see the last section of this essay). Thus, the fear that anthropologists were confined to an arbitrary and meaningless locus of human activity—the village—seems to have been premature.

There is an inverse problem at the level of the large-scale survey. On the whole (and here the National Survey Sample is the outstanding example), the statistical sophistication of these studies is not matched by the richness or sophistication of the macro-sociological theory underlying the statistical work. Nor is this simply the charge of what to do about 'non-sampling' error, something of which statisticians involved with large-scale survey work, especially in India, are very aware, and others frequently remind them. The problem is more basic.

DEFICIENCIES IN LARGE–SCALE STUDIES

To my knowledge, there has been no explicit discussion of the *macro-sociological* foundations that underlie the economics, which in turn underpins the statistical techniques on which these surveys are based. That is, what is the model of social *structure*, of social *relations*, and of social *processes* that justifies *what* is being measured and how it is being measured, in these surveys? The partial exception to this involves the very lively debates surrounding poverty and income-distribution (Dandekar 1981; Sen 1981; Srinivasan and Bardhan 1974; Sukhatme 1981) but even these debates have been more precisely terminological and methodological, rather than theoretical.

Let me suggest two major inadequacies in the sociological basis of most large-scale survey work in India. In common with most large-scale surveys whose minimal unit is the 'household' or the family, Indian surveys assume that these units are *formally independent* loci of action and of choice, even if they differ in various endowments (such as income, family size, etc.). But a large amount of sociological and anthropological work in India (and not all of it 'Marxist') shows that unequal and reciprocal relations *between* households are central to the 'choices' made by actors and to their reasons for these choices. These highly localized structural relationships between households are not merely masked by the techniques of most large-scale surveys but are virtually incompatible with their basic sociological assumptions. Indeed, to the degree that the entire country is regarded as an *aggregation* of households, the large-scale surveys (however statistically sophisticated) will inevitably end up with data that is *distributional* rather than *relational*.

Since the contrast between distributional and relational data (and models) is the key to the proposal with which I shall conclude this essay, let me briefly discuss its implications. All aggregate data-gathering techniques associated with neo-classical economic assumptions regard the critical data regarding standard of living as contained in *measurable distributions* of goods, usually at the household level. Although there are a few exceptions to this approach, the only major alternative approach to it is found in the political-economy tradition, particularly in its Marxist variant. Though Marxian economists have concentrated on *relations* between groups (usually classes), rather than simply on distributions of goods and services, they have not been able to translate this sociological critique into a methodological alternative to current methods and models for the aggregation of data concerning standard of living. In general, they use data generated by standard statistical methods in order to conduct debates with neo-classical economists about the interpretation of these data. Thus the relational bias of Marxism, with which I am fully in sympathy, does not provide a real alternative to the problem of effective aggregation without the sacrifice of the relational perspective.

The recent survey research by Bardhan and Rudra at the intermediate levels of rural society in Bengal constitutes a promising start for breaking through the impressions that relational approaches and aggregate analyses are mutually exclusive. Yet though their approach, especially in regard to tenancy and labour, is admirably relational, it too remains confined to *outcomes* of social processes, rather than to the structure of those processes themselves. When I discuss my own approach to 'entitlement-events', in a later section of this essay, this observation will be clarified.

The challenge is not just to capture social relations at the large scale through surveys conducted at smaller levels (a problem which is hardly simple in itself). Nor is it only a matter of having a more articulate (and thus debatable) general social theory at the locus of the design of the large-scale surveys, though this too would be helpful. The problem, at least in regard to rural economic change in India, is how to build a model of *standard of living*, which is not a mechanical aggregation of easily quantifiable bundles of goods and services (quantities of food, medicine, education, shelter, sanitation, etc.)

This is not the place for a full-scale review of the extensive literature on the 'standard of living', its measurement and operationalization. But a few points are worth making. Few will deny that to the degree that measures of standards of living are studied in the aggregate, they tend to lose the critical qualitative dimension which must belong to any robust conception of the standard of living. Components of this qualitative dimension include: the perception of security in livelihood, the sense of freedom from harassment and abuse at home and at work, the feeling of dignity in day-to-day transactions, the belief in the reliability of officialdom, the expectation (or lack of it) that life will improve for one's offspring, and so forth. The fact that these are matters that are not easy to operationalize for the purposes of large-scale survey work does not make them sentimental issues, irrelevant to the understanding of rural economy. It does mean, however, that our macro-sociological theory must take into account 'well-being' as well as welfare'; (here I borrow the contrast from Das and Nicholas 1985) 'subjective' as well as 'objective' criteria of well-being'; and emotional and ideological states as much as bundles of commodities. To use another set of terms which I have paired in another context, it is essential not simply to look at 'entitlement' (Sen 1981) but also at enfranchisement' (Appadurai 1984a).

The second inadequacy in current macro-sociological theory regarding rural economic change involves a problem created at the intersection of *scale and aggregation*. There is no single term or concept which captures this particular problem, but important aspects of it have been dealt with by Elster (1979), Hirsch (1976) and Schelling (1978). In its simplest form, the problem is that the aggregate outcome of a series of identical (from the micro point of view) actions may be a macro-pattern which frustrates 'micro-motives'. There are many examples of such 'ironies of aggregation'[1] and their analysis brings together problems of scale, interaction and 'centricity' (Hannerz 1979) in social life.

In order to clarify my view of such ironies of aggregation, to which I shall return in a later section of this essay, let me draw on an example, based on my field experience in Maharashtra. In many parts of Maharashtra, as well as in other areas of scarce or unreliable water supply, open-surface (dug) wells are a critical component of agricultural technology. In Maharashtra, in the

---

[1] I owe this evocative phrase to Ulf Hannerz.

last few decades, many small farmers have taken to devoting small portions of their holdings to commercial crops. In many cases, they do so by investing in electric (or diesel) pumps, in order to draw water more efficiently on to their plots. The objective, for most farmers, in investing in commercial agriculture, even with tiny plots, uncertain labour and fluctuating prices, is two-fold: (a) to maximize cash income in an increasingly monetized environment; (b) to gradually accumulate enough cash to increase their irrigated landholdings. The objective of many small farmers (seen at the micro level) is to achieve economic independence from other farmers as well as non-farmers and to be in a position where they can operate independently of small-scale co-operative organizations. Yet, given the smallness of their individual plots, the fact that they often have to invest in electrical pumps *jointly*, and the fact that they all experience the most intense needs for cash, water and labour at approximately the same periods in the agricultural calendar, they are inevitably drawn into highly interdependent webs of debt, bullock-sharing and water-sharing. Especially for smaller farmers, this interdependence at the village level, which often creates bottlenecks which impede production, tends to diminish their commercial incomes and, in the long run, to reduce their chances of economic autonomy. Thus, the micro-motive—to achieve long-term independence by investing in commercial agriculture—often leads, at the macro-level, to bottlenecks and failures which assure continuing reliance of small farmers on each other and on bigger farmers.

This tension between micro motives and macro outcomes has important implications for the measurement of rural economic change. It means that we need to be sceptical about interpreting increases in certain aggregate measures, such as number of wells, number of electric pumps, acreage of irrigated land, or yields of commercial crops, as automatically an index of increase in well-being at the micro level. Nor is this only because such increases can disguise increases in the concentration of agricultural capital in the hands of a small rural elite. What it can also disguise, at least in certain parts of rural India, is an increasingly involuted agrarian landscape in which irrigated, commercial agriculture implies a large number of *small* commercial farmers eking out a precarious subsistence in a heavily monetized agrarian economy. To analyse this particular irony of aggregation properly it is important to look, at the village level, at the full *relational* implications of petty commercialization.[2]

Economists have long been aware that any macro perspective implies, methodologically, some understanding of the *aggregation process*. Neo-classical theory, both in its understanding of equilibrium and in its conceptualization of externalities, recognizes the complexity of the relationship between micro-behaviours and the context within which they occur. But most economists would concede that it is illegitimate to postulate algebraic homologies between micro variables and their macro counterparts and that it is difficult to work out the aggregate implications of specific micro relationships. One solution, essentially based on a number-crunching approach, would be through computer simulation of the aggregation process based on the numerical specification of the values involved in micro relationships. In addition to the massive magnitude of computations involved, I believe this approach rests on an approach to measurement which seeks to quantify essentially qualitative social facts. But I would like to suggest that another way to illuminate the aggregation process would rely on relatively standard analytic/sampling techniques but build them on an alternative approach to observation and measurement. This alternative approach, discussed more fully in a subsequent section of this essay, would be built on the assumption that social life is constituted by a series of small-scale interactions in which large-scale factors are embedded, rather than by large-scale factors as such.

This aspect of social life is precisely what is unlikely to be captured in the current methodologies of large-scale survey research, not simply because of problems of method but because no persuasive theory of this feature of large-scale social phenomena currently exists. It is worth paying particular attention to this dimension of the relationship between small- and large-scale phenomena, for here is a problem to which conventional survey approaches *as well as* conventional anthropological approaches have no obvious solution. It is thus a

[2] For a fuller treatment of the micro-sociology of irrigation in rural Maharashtra, see Appadurai 1984c.

prime justification for co-operation. The question, of course, is: how is it to be operationalized in the study of rural economic change? But before this question can be addressed, it is necessary to turn the critical spotlight on to how anthropologists have generally fared in their study of rural economic life.

LIMITATIONS OF VILLAGE STUDIES

By and large, village studies in India have been undertaken by anthropologists and sociologists, although the study of villages by economists and agronomists has a fairly long history (see, for example, Mann 1967 and Slater 1918). The bulk of these studies, conducted largely after World War II, paid cursory attention, if any, to rural economic life, apart from certain aspects of it, such as the so-called 'jajmani' system. The problem in regard to the *systematic* study of change is doubly vexed. Longitudinal research is still in its infancy in social anthropology at large (see, for example, Foster *et al.* 1979) and in India, with a few notable exceptions, such as Scarlett Epstein and, more recently, Murray Leaf (1984), there have been few 're-studies' of particular villages. So far, therefore, anthropologists working at the village level have not had much to say about rural economic change.

But even at the impressionistic level, there is an emerging consensus among some anthropologists that 'things have improved' over the last few decades. It is worth asking why this impression should exist, especially in the face of a fair amount of data to the opposite effect.

Let me suggest the following reasons for this tendency on the part of some anthropologists to assess rural economic change in India in a positive manner. The *first* is the tendency (following a variety of official and semi-official cues) for anthropologists to end up in villages that are in largely prosperous regions, or in highly developed pockets in poorer regions. The *second* is the tendency to miss serious economic downturns in the seasonal cycles of the places they study (Chambers 1981). The *third* is the tendency to become restricted to the world of the powerful and the prosperous unless, as in the case of Gough (1981), a major effort is made in the reverse direction. The *fourth* reason is that since they are trained to use their eyes as well as their ears (and perhaps because of an unconscious interest in what used to be called 'material culture'), anthropologists tend to be excessively impressed by the presence of new commodities and increased amounts of them: watches, bicycles and radios are particularly damaging in this regard, for anthropologists are usually ill-equipped to measure the net costs of aggregate increases in such commodities, costs reflected in the gradual immiserization of some families, the hidden toll of migration and monetization on family life, etc. This fourth factor is exacerbated by a version of factor three, which is that people who are temporarily or permanently suffering an economic downturn sometimes vanish from just those casual, public interactional arenas in which anthropologists conduct their 'participant-observation'. They may retreat to their homes or they may leave the village suddenly and surreptitiously. Such small social demographic shifts in a single village are often the surface symptoms of rural stress. A *fifth* problem is more subtle: the random observations and free-floating dyadic exchanges in which anthropologists gather most of their 'data' are likely to encourage optimistic assessments of their situation by many respondents/informants. This can be a function of pride in the village (which can be a surprisingly important ideological factor) or of embarrassment about discussing bad fortune in the presence of friends and neighbours who are often present at such exchanges. Finally, the short time-frame in which much anthropological fieldwork is conducted means that it is difficult for the analysts as well as the actors to assess 'trends' correctly. The fifth factor should not be overemphasized, for Indian villagers can also, for a variety of reasons (ranging from fear of the evil eye, the tax-collector or the motives of the anthropologist) exaggerate their poverty or ill-fortune. But anthropologists (for some reason) tend to reserve their scepticism for exaggerations of the latter rather than the former sort!

These are some general (and easily recognized) reasons that anthropologists might tend to assess rural economic change in a positive manner, however impressionistic their methods. But even if they were to resolve to guard against these dangers, and revise their priorities to pay more focused attention to rural economic life, there are serious methodological problems with the systematic study of agricultural economy at the village level.

I shall draw upon my own experience in Maharashtra in 1981–2 to highlight a few of these.

A CASE STUDY OF VILLAGE–LEVEL ECONOMIC RESEARCH

In 1981–2 I spent ten months doing intensive research on agricultural decision-making in a village (with the pseudonym Vadi) in Purandhar Taluq, Pune district, Maharashtra state. Approximately three of these months were spent in doing research that must be described as preliminary. Another three months were spent in designing and supervising the administration of a fairly elaborate survey of all 193 households in the village. The remaining four months were spent in *intensive* interviewing and observation, both formal and informal, of the standard anthropological variety. I was assisted in these activities by no more than two research assistants at any time, so this was a small-scale research enterprise in every sense of the term. This study is still one of a relatively small number of efforts in India (1) to attempt the anthropological study of a localized agrarian social order, and (2) to attempt a reasonably intensive combination of survey research with ethnographic research. Thus I believe there is some justification in using some of my experiences as springboards for general discussion. I will not detail some of the standard problems I encountered in designing and implementing my research plans, which have been discussed by many others. I will stress that, like most researchers, I had to learn to be flexible and adjust my goals and interests continuously, as some doors opened and others closed. What I shall discuss below are four sets of problems which are less commonly discussed. They are as follows: (1) problems of agricultural terminology; (2) problems involving measurement; (3) problems involving the boundedness of the village as an agrarian social order; and (4) problems involving the timing and duration of qualitatively-oriented survey work. These are discussed serially in what follows.

(1) *Agricultural terminology.* All intensive local-level work, whether its focus is qualitative or quantitative, involves the solution of linguistic problems, even when native speakers are involved in the research. The linguistic problems faced by survey researchers in Third World countries are only beginning

to be discussed, and it has been noted in the Nepali context that there are inevitable gaps between the literate varieties of languages used in questionnaires and the local spoken varieties (Shrestha 1979) and that there are also more subtle problems of how specific words or turns of phrase may be reinterpreted by informants, leading to unintended misinformation (Stone and Campbell 1984). Nor is this simply a 'Third-World' problem (Schuman and Presser 1981; Fienberg, Loftus and Tanur 1984).

In the study of local agrarian systems, there are problems that represent special forms of the linguistic problems involved in all rural research. In a different context, it has been found convenient to label these as problems of 'agricultural terminology'.[3] I shall mention here only two terminological problems that seem especially relevant to the linkage of village-level studies with studies conducted at a larger scale.

Perhaps the least discussed aspect of agricultural terminology is the variable geographical spread of key agricultural terms. While certain Marathi terms used by farmers appear to be extremely wide in their geographical spread, others appear to be localized to one district or parts of a few districts. Thus, the term *ardholi* (or some recognizable cognate of this term) seems to refer to a crop-sharing arrangement in which the partners have 50/50 shares throughout the Marathi-speaking region. But the term *varangula* is used where I worked for certain forms of agricultural partnership, involving the pooling of bullocks and ploughing equipment, whereas in Satara district the term *payra* is used for a substantially similar arrangement (Schlesinger 1981). Furthermore, these terms are apparently not even recognized outside their respective area of use. Such examples of varying terminological micro–regions can probably be multiplied, but in the absence of a systematic survey of terminological variation we can only guess at its nature and extent. This terminological variation, even *within* linguistic regions, has a series of implications relevant to this discussion. First, it means that even questionnaires designed with the help of persons who

[3] The Social Science Research Council (USA) has hosted a series of conferences on 'Agricultural Terminology', where this topic has been explored in greater detail, and where results will soon appear in an edited volume.

have prior rural experience in the broad linguistic region are likely to use inappropriate agricultural terms. Second, it means that the problem of quantifying (or even comparing) the incidences of certain kinds of agrarian arrangements is compounded by such terminological variation. The inverse form of this problem is the existence of a common term to describe what are in fact divergent practices. Third, it means that intensive agricultural research in any given village or locality must involve a careful preliminary period of observation and interviewing simply to establish a basic and accurate lexicon of key local agricultural terms. I shall return to this last issue when I discuss the problem of the timing and duration of survey work on rural economies.

(2) *Measurement.* I have discussed elsewhere, at some length, the practical and epistemological problems raised in the analysis of rural agricultural discourse involving measurement (Appadurai 1984b). I shall mention here only a few points which are particularly relevant to this discussion. I am not concerned here with the problem of deliberate misrepresentation of magnitudes (of land, income, property, debt, etc.) by respondents, nor about errors in measurement (in the standard sense) by investigators. I am concerned with intercultural gaps in usage and interpretation. In my fieldwork, I found that there was an almost invariable tendency to represent magnitudes qualitatively and comparatively ('enough'; 'more than last year'; 'as much as I had hoped for', etc.) rather than quantitatively. Further, when quantities were described, there was a strong tendency to use what I have called 'hyphenated measures', (seven-eight; ten-twelve; twenty-thirty etc.) especially in regard to plot sizes and crop yields, but also in regard to other matters. When precise numerical replies are given, they frequently reflect 'official' or 'standardized' numbers rather than individual assessments: this is especially true of demographic inquiries. Finally, discussions of measure, which are frequently public and collective (especially in formal interview contexts) involve social consensus about magnitudes and not reference to context-free tools of measurement. In all these regards, the relatively technical, quantitative, and context-free assumptions of most interviewers regarding measurements are directly opposed to the more relational, qualitative, approximate and context-tied discourse of rural

respondents. In most rural survey work this contradiction is 'cleaned-up' in the interest of yielding usable (but often simply inaccurate) numerical data. The problem of designing surveys which can accommodate fuzzy and approximate quantitative responses (especially in regard to production and consumption data) has hardly been addressed anywhere. Of course, there are other contexts, typically involving demographic and marketing issues, where careful questioning (and cross-checks) can *legitimately* and usefully eliminate much ambiguity. Thus, the central challenge in this area is how to commensurate the structure of farmers' discourse involving measure with the very different requirements (at least at present) of large-scale surveys.

(3) *The boundedness of the rural economy.* The problem of the sense in which the local agrarian economy is a bounded entity involves difficult decisions about the local 'unit of analysis' which in turn affects problems of aggregation and of large-scale analysis. I have already mentioned some recent reactions to the overemphasis on the non-boundedness of the village, and a revival of interest in the village as a coherent and significant locus of agrarian organization. In general I am sympathetic with the recent arguments that the village should not be too easily dissolved into a larger interactional framework (Harriss 1983; Rudra 1985; Schlesinger 1981).

Based on my own fieldwork, the major preliminary challenge is how to develop some typology (however rough) of villages which classifies them according to the degree that they are relatively autonomous economic entities. In making this assessment, it would be essential to distinguish the village as a *polity* from the village as an *economy*. In the latter regard, the critical dimensions of linkage with the larger economy would have to do with (a) extent of outmigration of males or females, which affects local labour patterns as well as local monetization levels and (b) extent of commercialization of agriculture, which also ties local to regional economies. Of course, such a typology can be based on criteria and measures of varying degrees of sophistication, but some such typology would be essential in the sampling that underlies any large-scale survey work on the rural economy, in addition to regional variations of the sort that can already be disaggregated from the data of the large-scale surveys. My own very impressionistic hypothesis is that, over the last few decades, dramatic increases in the ranges of income are likely to have occurred in villages more closely tied to the regional and national economy, whereas the picture of changes would be flatter in villages which are less affected by the labour and commodity-needs of regional systems. Put another way, 'satellite' villages are more likely to show misleading signs of prosperity but be subject to deeper disparities in income than more (economically speaking) remote villages. From the point of view of integrating village-level analysis with large-scale surveys, the first methodological step would be to develop a model of village independence through intensive village-level research which could be used in subsequent sampling for the purpose of providing more sensitive information on rural economic change.

It is especially difficult for anthropologists to follow those processes and individuals that lead outside the village. My own experience in the village I studied was that it was very difficult to follow through *anthropologically* the two key links between the village I studied and the larger regional economy. The first involved the study of the economic and social structure of the domestic economies (especially in Bombay) of those families that maintained dual budgetary loci. This would have entailed an extended stay in Bombay which was practically unfeasible. But, in the future, it will be essential that at least some 'village' studies focus specifically on the 'dual-loci' households that increasingly characterize 'satellite' villages all over India. Except for migration studies (which have a very different thrust) there exists now virtually no method for the micro-sociology of such spatially bifurcated social units. Similarly, a full study of the impact of the commercialization of agriculture would have required understanding and following in detail the ties of farmers in Vadi to specific wholesalers in the vegetable and fruit markets of Bombay and Pune, ties which affect credit, volume of production, acreage under commercial cropping, and reliability of profit. This too is something, due to limitations of time and resources, I was unable to do. But it should be noted that the *anthropological* study of such *trans-local* social and economic processes is also in its conceptual infancy.

(4) *Timing and duration of survey work.* At least among anthropologists, there is rarely much public discussion of

research design and method. But a customary set of practices does exist, and this set requires rethinking, if anthropologists are to make any serious contribution to the study of rural economic change. Most anthropologists engaged in village-level work tend to conduct survey work (usually involving a simple census of households along with some preliminary genealogical work) at the *outset* of their research period, which is rarely more than a year. The result is that such surveys, even when they do concern matters of rural economics, are conducted during the period when the anthropologist is an *outsider*, in every sense. This is the phase when he might be weakest in the local language, most uneasy about his links to the community, shaky in his relations with his own research assistants, and when his own assistants are in the delicate process of building their own relations with the community. In regard to rural economies, specifically, this means that the survey is designed and implemented when the investigator's knowledge of the *specific* local structure, rhythm and terminology of the economy is most shaky.

My own approach in Vadi was to spend the first two months in informal interviewing and observation, with an eye to identifying the critical *local* dimensions of the agricultural system and in discovering the appropriate *local* way to phrase questions concerning them. I then spent one month designing and translating into Marathi a lengthy questionnaire (which had both numerical as well as qualitative dimensions). Each questionnaire took about two hours to administer and though I had two full-time assistants (who did about 3–4 households each per working day), it took almost two months for all 193 households to be covered. It then took another month to deal with ambiguities, errors and gaps. Thus, the administration of the survey took almost three out of the total of ten months of my research. However, in the last five months my focused ethnographic interviewing, with a purposive sampling of households, was greatly facilitated by what I had learnt (and failed to learn) in the course of administering the survey, though the analysis had to wait until after the completion of the field research. This procedure is one that I would recommend as superior to the traditional anthropological practice of having survey work precede intensive ethnographic work. The essential features of this approach are: (1) to do the survey work in the *middle* months of the allotted research time, to assure that the questionnaire is as culturally sensitive as possible and that the lessons learnt during its administration can be applied in the final months of the research period, which are for anthropologists traditionally the most profitable. I should, of course, point out that this procedure is not intended to solve all the problems of combining quantitative and qualitative work on village economies, but is only intended to address the problems of timing and duration, and these too in only one regard.

The purpose of these reflections on my own problems (and solutions) in the course of doing village-level anthropological research on agriculture was to suggest some areas for future discussion on how anthropological contributions to such studies might be improved. But the question of the link between small- and large-scale studies can now be addressed more directly.

LINKAGE BETWEEN LEVELS: A METHODOLOGICAL PROPOSAL

The reader should by now be aware that I feel a great deal remains to be done at *both* levels in order for work at the village level to be fruitfully integrated with work at larger scales. What I wish to do in this concluding section is to make a specific proposal for a research strategy which might be one among several formats for co-operation. Since this is an idea which I have only recently begun to consider, I warn the reader not to expect it to be completely clear or fully worked out. It is presented as an idea-in-progress.

But first a word about the context. Although contrasting and integrating research conducted at different levels and scales is a central problem of the social sciences, surprisingly little methodological attention has been paid to it, and what little has been written is scattered.[4] Speaking schematically, there seem to

[4] Two landmark collections of essays which address the problem are: (1) *Scale and Social Organization*, edited by Fredrik Barth (1978), which consists largely of essays by anthropologists and thus is concerned largely with problems of scale as they affect the analysis of 'simpler' and more 'complex' societies and (2) *Advances in social theory and methodology: Towards an integration of micro- and macro-sociologies*, edited by K. Knorr-Cetina and A.V. Cicourel (1981), which is written from a sociological and philo-

be three interesting approaches to the problem of closing the gap between micro and macro approaches.

The *first*, which I have touched on already, sees the transition from micro to macro phenomena as involving not just problems of aggregation, but also of unintended consequences, and of analysing the emergent properties of collective social forms which cannot be predicted from their micro-constituents. In addition to scholars like Elster, Hirsch and Schelling, whom I have mentioned already in relation to the issue of the 'ironies of aggregation', this approach is favoured by methodologists such as Rom Harre and Anthony Giddens (Cicourel 1981). The problem with this approach is that it has not so far yielded any clear operational lessons, though its theoretical position is hard to challenge. In my earlier example of the ironies of aggregation involved in the commercialization of agriculture in Maharashtra, I did suggest one implication of this problem: namely that micro-facts have to be looked at *relationally*, rather than only distributionally, even at the micro-level, in order to avoid false inferences at the macro level.

The *second* approach, which is narrow but very promising, comes out of A. Cicourel's important *Method and Measurement in Sociology* (1964) which set the grounds for a thoroughgoing micro-sociological critique of macro-sociology, in which Cicourel has himself played an important role. Cicourel's work criticized, firstly, existing methods of measurement in sociology, which relied on mathematical measurement requirements such as properties of scales that are hardly ever fulfilled with variables of the type used in traditional sociology. Second, Cicourel criticized methods which assumed that data, for example, collected in interviews, could be taken at face value (except for measurement error and bias, which however could be either statistically remedied or estimated). His own 'micro-sociological perspective' sees such data as 'unspecified collaborative products created during the interview in accordance with the practical procedures and background assumptions of participating actors' (Knorr-Cetina 1981: 13).

sophical perspective. These two collections give a fairly good sampling of the range of approaches that the micro-macro problems has generated, in anthropology and sociology.

In his own recent work, Cicourel has suggested that an important way to identify those processes and inferences that transform micro-events into macro-structures, is by looking at how certain routine problem-solving activities, in complex micro-settings, lead to the creation of macro-structures (Cicourel 1981: 67).[5]

The *third* approach, which underlies my own proposal, is very closely linked to Cicourel's micro-critique of macro-sociology, but takes an even more radical stance. It has been laid out by one of the more radical of the new 'micro-sociologists', Randall Collins, in a series of papers (Collins 1981a; 1981b; 1983). Since my own suggestion is influenced in part by Collins, it is worth stating his proposal in some detail, and noting those features of it that I find especially congenial.

Collins is one of a group of 'radical' micro-sociologists who is committed to some version of the idea that aggregate, collective, macro-phenomena are in large part artifacts of analysis and that 'empirical' reality is invariably composed of large numbers of events that are small-scale, in terms of duration, spatial extension and number of participants. With the exception of time, space and number, which are the only genuine macro variables admitted by Collins, the rest (examples would be 'class', 'state', 'distribution of wealth', 'mobility rate', etc.) are in fact simply concepts (used both by social scientists and actors)

[5] The following lengthy quotation gives the flavour of Cicourel's strategy: Bureaucratic organizations typically produce reports of routine and special board-meetings, or meetings in which a group decides whether to give someone a loan, a grant or a fellowship. In medicine and law, patients and clients are interviewed and a medical history or legal statement or brief is prepared that summarizes an interview and the assessment of tests and documents. In all of these cases, and many more that can be easily identified as routine practices within bureaucratic organizations, there are fairly explicit procedures that have been adopted or that have emerged. . . This 'rationalization' process has increased over the past 100 years and shows no signs of diminishing. Everyday settings, therefore, abound with highly organized ways of dealing with and producing macro-evaluations, reports and summarizations of relentless micro-events. . . In each case the activities are routine aspects of some organization and are independent of the way social scientists design and carry out their research.' (Cicourel 1981: 66)

to gloss what are in fact complex chains of micro-events. In this view, a genuinely empirical sociology would not be a matter of using quantitative data, but of careful analysis of micro-events. For reasons that fall outside the scope of this discussion, the micro-events that most interest Collins are 'conversations' in ordinary life situations, and his main methodological proposal for how to proceed with this radical micro-sociology involves the analysis of what he calls (following Goffman) 'interaction rituals', in which individuals transact and exchange certain forms of emotional energy, conversational or cultural 'capital' and their social reputation. Complex chains of such encounters 'distribute and redistribute various microresources among the aggregate of individuals in a society' (Collins 1983: 192).

The systematic analysis of such micro-events is what Collins calls 'micro-translation' (i.e., the translation of apparently macro-structures into their micro-constituents). He recognizes that, given the very large number of such micro-events that combine to form larger-scale phenomena, the central methodological issue is how to 'sample' such micro-events, and in his most recent discussion of this approach he advocates 'systematic sampling of certain microsituations' (Collins 1983: 195). However, he notes that there are serious challenges in sampling 'situations', especially if our purposes are descriptive, since we know very little about the distribution of various kinds of micro-events, there is no 'census' of them from which a random sample can be drawn, etc. But more purposive sampling can illuminate the relationships among certain variables, even if the representativeness problem remains.

There are several problems with Collins' proposal for micro-sampling of interaction-rituals (micro-events) as a way to create a genuinely empirical bridge between micro- and macro-sociology. These include: (a) a theoretical blindness to the sorts of 'unintended consequences' that have been repeatedly shown to emerge in the course of aggregation and which sampling alone cannot capture; (b) an extremely positivist conception of social reality; (c) lack of cross-cultural sensitivity in his specific proposals about authority, property etc.; and (d) a poorly developed statistical approach to carry out his methodological programme.

These shortcomings severely limit the viability of Collins'

proposals for the purposes for which he intended them, namely as the basis for a radical reconstruction of sociology from the bottom up. But it is possible that his proposal *may* be applicable (with suitable refinements) to the problem with which we are most concerned at present: namely, how can micro and macro perspectives be better integrated in the study of rural economic change in India and of the changes in standards of living?

For our purposes, the critical feature of Collins' scheme is the emphasis on *sampling*, the shift from *distributions* to *interactions*, and the move from *interviews* to *observation and recording* of small pieces of naturally occurring behaviour. The critical questions then become: (1) What micro-events or transactions are likely to be sensitive indices of rural standards of living? (2) What are the practical problems of observing and recording their structure without seriously interfering with them? and (3) What statistical methods can be employed both in the selection of such micro-events and in their subsequent aggregation? I am aware that each of these questions covers a host of more specific problems and puzzles, but at this stage they can only be discussed in very preliminary terms.

Question (1), about what micro-events or transactions are likely to be good indices of rural standards of living, can be rephrased as follows: is there a class of events that is a sensitive micro-indicator of (in Sen's terms) 'entitlement-maps' (Sen 1981)? The areas of transaction and interaction that come to mind are: (a) *actual* labour contracts (i.e. the real transaction in which a specific contract is set); (b) in situations where rationing of essential commodities is in force, *observed* transactions in these commodities; (c) *efforts* to obtain credit from banks and co-operatives; (d) specific acts of rural out-migration. The challenge is how to evolve a method for *observing* transactions of these types, since some of them happen outside official record-keeping contexts. This would require some hard thinking, and possibly the elimination of some possibilities.

What is the point of looking at such entitlement-events close up rather than taking the usual approach of trying to capture the outcomes of such events through interviews involving formal survey instruments or through census-style inquiries? There would be at least three payoffs in examining the events themselves: (1) it might permit some insight into the *nature* of such events (i.e. a qualitative or *relational* insight) rather than only an insight into the *distributional results* of such events; (2) it might give a better understanding of *failures* in the entitlement arena, i.e. why certain persons or groups, in real situations, *fail* to get some good, service or benefit, since the reasons may in part be based on very specific features (linguistic or otherwise) of the micro-situation itself; (3) in looking at actual negotiations or interactions involving livelihood, we may illuminate *aspirations* and *expectations* as well as *post facto* outcomes. In all these regards, this type of micro-scrutiny might add several important dimensions to the current forms of interview or census-generated material.

Further, even after a type (or several types) of entitlement-event' is identified as being relevant, observationally feasible and in some way statistically manageable, the concrete question remains: what exactly will be recorded and how can personnel be trained to record relevant linguistic and micro-sociological details of these transactions? There, the trade-off is between the qualitative and unpredictable structure of these events, and the standardization of technique required for reasonable success. Here too, I have no simple solutions but dialogue between specialists with different disciplinary strengths may be fruitful.

In addition to the construction of flexible but well-designed micro-protocols for the observation and recording of these small units of entitlement-related interactions, there remains the problem of the selection of a sample and of subsequent processing (for aggregate purposes) of the results. Though the statistical aspect may pose serious problems, the organizational aspect may be solved by having a few, limited 'pilot' projects of this sort attached to the ongoing, well-established activities of the National Sample Survey.

Nevertheless, in my judgement, the critical potential contribution of the analysis of 'entitlement-events' to improving the relationship between micro and macro analysis is not through (a) some miraculous resolution of the challenge of achieving a representative sample or (b) through some new angle on the thorny problem of unintended consequences. What it is likely to do is to contribute to the refinement of the macro theory which underlies analyses at the large-scale level. That is, by looking at entitlement-events in addition to entitlement outcomes, we are likely to discover aspects of the relational logic of rural life which will improve our sense of what to measure at the aggregate level. This does not mean that the analysis of entitlement-events will be free of statistical, observational or interpretive challenges. But it does not mean that *any* yield at this level might create a better theoretical basis for aggregative enquiries.

Finally, even if several of these very specific problems can be solved, there remains the challenge of how to use this method in some reasonably rigorous *longitudinal* manner, so that change can systematically be addressed. But this is a second-order challenge which is barely worth worrying about before establishing the viability of this strategy at a lower level of refinement. At the least, this sort of proposal has the virtue of not being just a diplomatic gesture towards better relations between village-level analysts and those working at larger scales.

FROM DISTRIBUTIONS TO RELATIONS

I wish now to draw together several strands of the argument and suggestions I have made so far. Specifically, I wish to clarify the link between problems of scale, terminology, relationality and the measurement of rural economic change.

My central claim is that current large-scale approaches to the problem of measuring rural economic change in South Asia need to move from *distributional* to *relational* analyses. That is, they need to cast light not only on net *outcomes* of social processes, seen largely in measurable bundles of goods and services possessed by households (and individuals) at given points in time. What is systematically not captured in current approaches is the *relational* dimension of the processes which lead to these outcomes. These relational processes, as I have already suggested, involve the on-going traffic in goods, services and information between individuals, households, larger corporate groups and classes. Many aggregate distributive profiles are complex outcomes of ongoing relational processes.

In order to create a better methodological interaction between small-scale relational processes of rural India and large-scale *distributional* profiles, I suggested a strategy (based on the work of Randall Collins), focused on the analysis of 'entitlement-events'. The problems of sampling, observer-effect and aggregation associated with such events are considerable, but may not be insuperable. But the great potential of such an effort would be to illuminate relational processes in a manner which enriches the theoretical basis of aggregate analysis.

My anthropological experience, discussed earlier in this essay, suggests that in order to properly grasp entitlement processes in rural South Asia, we need to be especially sensitive to terminological problems, especially those associated with measurement. In analysing entitlement-events at the small-scale, rural level, efforts at aggregation will fail unless we evolve an honest resolution of the disparity between the linguistic practices associated with the measurement activities of South Asian farmers and those associated with the practice of social science. Central among these is the fact that a good deal of rural talk involves approximation and comparison, whereas our standard social science techniques call for numerical precision and absolute measures. Since farmers often use *comparative* measures while our surveys demand *absolute* measures, our instruments create images of rural economy which are both meaninglessly precise as well as lacking in the comparative approach to magnitude which farmers realize is essential. Of course, these drawbacks in our instruments and approaches are directly based on our larger incapacity to rethink our theoretical bases for aggregate data collection.

Finally, the problem of rural economic change, from the viewpoint of *measurement*, cannot statisfactorily be solved until the prior question of *aggregation* is satisfactorily resolved. My own proposal is addressed principally to the theoretical basis of aggregation without reference to questions of change over time. But it should by now be clear that, in my view, it will neither suffice to (a) keep refining existing statistical techniques for longitudinal analysis or (b) encourage anthropologists to do 're-studies' at the village level. While these are laudable goals in themselves, they do not cut through the current methodological gap between large- and small-scale analyses. Until we develop ways of looking at relational processes at the micro level, and do so in a way that refines aggregation by improving the framework of macro-sociological theory, efforts to measure rural economic change will remain either trivial (because of their non-representativeness) or sterile (because they do not illuminate relationships between actors/social units).

ECUMENISM AND EPISTEMOLOGY

Since this volume does attempt to create a dialogue between anthropologists and economists working on problems of measurement involved in the study of rural change in India, it seems worthwhile to conclude with some thoughts on the nature of the dialogue itself.

From my perspective, there are two sorts of essays in this volume. The first sort, which is 'ecumenical' in spirit (and would include the papers by Breman, Harriss, Jodha, Tendulkar, Wadley and Derr, and Vaidyanathan) does not see any fundamental obstacles to a sustained dialogue between the two disciplines, in spite of important differences in methods, assumptions and goals. These essays see a difference in method as being largely *technical*, and therefore as soluble largely by *technical* innovations and self-criticism on both sides. The second sort, represented by the essays of Bhattacharya and Chattopadhyay, Rudra, Srinivasan and myself, though written with varying degrees of explicit combativeness, do raise problems that cannot easily be classified as simply technical and thus, as soluble simply by technical means. Juxtaposing this second set of essays raises a set of issues that I would call *epistemological* rather than *technical*.

In the remainder of my remarks, I shall not deal with the 'ecumenical' essays (nor the ecumenical component of the second set of essays) but rather with the essays that raise 'epistemological' issues, though some of the authors may vigorously resist this labelling of the problems they raise, as resistance is itself part of the problem. The problems I have in mind are reflected in the various positions taken on matters of 'conceptual subjectivity' *versus* investigator bias (Srinivasan), quantitative *versus* qualitative approaches (Srinivasan), sampling *versus* complete enumeration (Rudra), response errors *versus* non-sampling bias (Bhattacharya and Chattopadhyay), and the issue of relational *versus* distributional dimensions in the study of rural change (Appadurai). As most of the essays in this volume show, especially the group that I have called 'ecumenical', but also most of the essays in the second set, there is a point upto which these issues, also can be resolved once they have been recognized, and appropriate methodological steps are taken. But there remains an irreducible component of disagreement, most explicit perhaps in the essays by Srinivasan and myself, but certainly reflected to some degree in all the papers.

This residue of disagreement needs to be brought explicitly, if briefly, into public view in a volume such as this one, so that the debate between methods in the study of rural change in India (or elsewhere) does not become prematurely friendly. At bottom, in my opinion, are not issues about sampling size, respondent error, investigator bias, purposive sampling, etc., though these are important issues about which we all need to be clearer, and in regard to which this volume represents much valuable thought. The deeper issue is *epistemological*, and involves debates about the social scientist (and the effects of his or her methods on the objects of study), a problem which should not appear trivial to anyone familiar with the Heisenberg problem of observer-effect on experiments. Both in the social sciences as well as the natural sciences, those persons concerned with thinking *about* science, and not just practising it in the mode of business as usual, are conducting serious debates about what constitutes certainty in science, about the deep problems involved in separating epistemological *conventions* from ontological certainities, and about the relationship between numerical precision and the analysis of living forms, whether these are human or non-human.

It would be inappropriate to review this debate. But suffice it to say that we would all be well-advised not to pretend that there is some unshakeable and timeless edifice regarding measurement, objectivity, and the status of 'facts' and factual error. For those among us who wish to continue the practice of a statistically based social science, where all significant problems of measurement are regarded as either already solved or potentially soluble, I think there might be something to be said for reflecting more carefully about current debates among scientists and philosophers of science before concluding, as Srinivasan provocatively does, that the problem of the relationship between quantitative and qualitative factors is 'a phony one'. One might mix metaphors here and suggest that the larger desert is a phony problem to the ostrich with his head in the sand. Anthropologists, likewise, will have to worry a lot more about their long-standing fetish concerning 'holism', a fetish I have criticised elsewhere (Appadurai 1986: 1988). Here, my position converges with Rudra's, though the paths taken to our positions may not be identical.

The major questions are: whether problems of social life (and standard of living) can be reduced largely to their quantitative dimensions (and still remain significant); whether the difficulties of grasping even these quantitative dimensions can be further reduced to the technical issues of 'bias', 'error' and 'sampling', as defined and perceived through the lens of statistics; and whether the problems of how rural people talk and think can be divorced from the fact that serious differences of world-view and terminology separate them from the social scientists who study them. I doubt that these differences can be solved simply by more sensitive training of local-level survey administrators, or by more sophisticated use of stratified samples, and better statistical methods for aggregation, although I am all for such improvements. The problems of translation involved here, especially if they are as fundamental as I have argued, raise epistemological questions. Particularly, they raise the question of the degree to which what we want to 'know' is 'knowable' within the terms of our current apparatus (both of assumptions and of techniques).

To take the route, articulated most forcefully by Srinivasan, that problems (or dimensions of problems) that are not tractable to existing statistical techniques are irrelevant to measurement, and that measurement is the *sine qua non* of social science, is to commence a circular argument. In this argument, a certain idea of 'measurement' (itself employed without adequate attention to its epistemological assumptions) is made not merely a technique, but a criterion of what is a 'scientific' problem, and then anything which is intractable to this *specific* ideology of measurement is consigned to some non-scientific hell (or heaven). This not only amounts to putting the cart before the horse, it also amounts to making the cart pull the horse, and, if it fails, killing the horse or changing its shape by chopping off a few of its limbs, rather than redesigning the cart. I believe some version of this circular position is quite prevalent, and neither reducing the problem to its technical dimensions nor pretending that goodwill will solve everything is adequate. This volume opens a dialogue which, in my judgement, is most important because it exposes our differences at the level of our ideologies of measurement, of epistemology, and, dare I say it, of 'science' itself. Without admitting and addressing this problem, all talk of solutions, including my own, is probably over-optimistic.

REFERENCES

Appadurai, A., 'How moral is South Asia's economy—A review essay', *Journal of Asian Studies* XLIII (3): 481–97, 1984a.

————, 'The Terminology of measurement in rural Maharashtra.' Mimeo, 1984b.

————, 'Wells in Western India: Irrigation and co-operation in an agricultural society, *Expedition* 26(3): 3–14, 1984c.

————, 'Is Homo Hierarchicus?' *American Ethnologist.*, 13 (4): 745–61, 1986.

————, 'Putting Hierarchy in its Place', *Cultural Anthropology*, 3(1): 36–49, 1988.

Barth, F. (ed.), *Scale and Social Organization*, Oslo: Universitetsforlaget, 1978.

Bayliss-Smith, T. and S. Wanmali, (eds.), *Understanding Green Revolutions: Agrarian Change and Development Planning in South Asia*, Cambridge: Cambridge University Press, 1984.

Beteille, A., *Studies in Agrarian Social Structure*, New Delhi: Oxford University Press, 1974.

Binswanger, H. P. and N. S. Jodha., *Manual of Instructions for Economic Investigators in ICRISAT's Village Level Studies*, Hyderabad: ICRISAT, 1978.

Bliss, C. J. and N. H. Stern, *Palanpur: The Economy of an Indian Village*, New York: Oxford University Press, 1982.

Breman, J. *Patronage and Exploitation: Changing Agrarian Relations in South Gujarat, India*, Berkeley: University of California Press, 1974.

Chambers, R., R. Longhurst and A. Pacey (eds.), *Seasonal Dimensions to Rural Poverty*, London: Frances Pinter, 1981.

Chambers, R., *Rural Development: Putting the Last First*, London and New York: Longman, 1983.

Cicourel, A. V., *Method and Measurement in Sociology*, New York: Free Press, 1964.

———, 'Notes on the integration of micro- and macro-levels of analysis', *In* Knorr-Cetina and Cicourel (1981): 51–80, 1981.

Collins, R., 'Micromethods as a basis for macrosociology', *Urban Life* 12(2), July 1983:184–202, 1983.

———, 'On the microfoundations of macrosociology', *American Journal of Sociology* 86: 984–1014, 1981b.

———, 'Microtranslation as a theory-building strategy', *In* Knorr-Cetina and Cicourel (1981): 81–108, 1981a.

Dandekar, V. M., 'On measurement of Poverty', *Economic and Political Weekly* 16 (25 July, 1981): 1241–50, 1981.

Das, V. and R. Nicholas (eds.), *Welfare and Well-being in Rural South Asia*, In press.

Desai, M., S. H. Rudolph and A. Rudra, eds, *Agrarian Power and Agricultural Productivity in South Asia*, Berkeley, University of California Press, 1984.

Elster, J., *Ulysses and the Sirens: Studies in Rationality and Irrationality*, Cambridge: Cambridge University Press, 1979.

Epstein, T. S., *Economic Development and Social Change in South India*, Manchester: Manchester University Press, 1962.

———, *South India: Yesterday, Today and Tomorrow*, London: Macmillan, 1973.

Etienne, G., *India's Changing Rural Scene*, New Delhi: Oxford University Press, 1982.

Farmer, B. H., *Green Revolution? Technology and Change in New Rice-Growing Areas of Tamil Nadu and Sri Lanka*, London: Macmillan, 1977.

Fienberg, S., E. Loftus and J. M. Tanur, 'Cognitive Aspects of Health Surveys for Public Information and Policy'. Unpublished manuscript. 1984.

Foster, G. M., T. Scudder, E. Colson and R. V. Kemper (eds.), *Long-Term Field Research in Social Anthropology*, New York: Academic Press, 1979.

Gibson, F. K. and B. W. Hawkins, 'Research notes: Interviews versus questionnaires', *American Behavioral Scientist*, 12:NS–9–NS-11, 1968.

Giddens, A., 'Agency, institution and time-space analysis', *In* Knorr-Cetina and Cicourel (1981): 161–74, 1981.

Gough, K., *Rural Society in Southeast India*, Cambridge: Cambridge University Press, 1981.

Hannerz, U., 'Complex societies and anthropology: A perspective from 1979', *Ethnos* 3–4:217–41, 1979.

Harre, R., 'Philosophical aspects of the micro-macro problems', *In* Knorr-Cetina and Cicourel (1981):139–60, 1981.

Harriss, J., *Capitalism and Peasant Farming: Agrarian Structure and Ideology in Northern Tamil Nadu*, Bombay: Oxford University Press, 1982.

——, 'Making out on limited resources: Or what happened to semi-feudalism in a Bengal district, In: *Papers on the Political Economy of Agriculture in West Bengal*, (J. Harriss and B. Harriss), Reprint No. 170, School of Development Studies, University of East Anglia. (Reprinted from CRESSIDA Transactions), 1983.

Hill, P., *Dry Grain Farming Families*, Cambridge: Cambridge University Press, 1982.

Hursh-Cesar and P. Roy, (eds.), *Third World Surveys: Survey Research in Developing Nations*, Delhi: Macmillan, 1976.

Hirsch, F., *Social Limits to Growth*, Cambridge, Mass: Harvard University Press 1976.

Knorr-Cetina, K. and A. V. Cicourel, *Advances in Social Theory and Methodology*, Boston and London: Routledge and Kegan Paul, 1981.

Knorr-Cetina, K., 'The micro-sociological challenge of macro-sociology: Towards a reconstruction of social theory and methodology', *In* Knorr-Cetina and Cicourel (1981): 1–47.

Leach, E., 'An Anthropologist's Reflections on a Social Survey'. In *Anthropologists in the Field*, D. G. Jogmans and P. C. W. Gutkind, eds., pp. 75–88. New York: Humanities Press, 1967.

Leaf, M., *Song of Hope: The Green Revolution in a Punjab*

Village, New Brunswick, New Jersey: Rutgers University Press, 1984.

Mann, H. H., *The Social Framework of Agriculture*, Daniel Thorner (ed.), Bombay: Vora and Co, 1967.

Mencher, J. P., *Agriculture and Social Structure in Tamil Nadu: Past Origins, Present Transformations, and Future Prospects*, Durham, N. C.: Carolina Academic Press, 1978.

Mitchell, R., 'Survey materials collected in developing countries: Sampling, measurement and interviewing obstacles in intra- and international comparisons', *International Social Science Journal*, 17:665–85, 1965.

Rudra, A., 'Local power and farm-level decision-making *In* M. Desai, S. H. Rudolph and A. Rudra (eds.), *Agrarian Power and Agricultural Productivity in South Asia*, pp. 250–80. Berkeley: University of California Press, 1984.

Rudra, A. and P. Bardhan, *Agrarian Relations in West Bengal: Results of Two Surveys*, Bombay: Somaiya, 1983.

Schelling, T. C., *Micromotives and Macrobehavior*, New York: W. W. Norton, 1978.

Schlesinger, L. I., 'Agriculture and Community in Maharashtra, India', In *Research in Economic Anthropology*, George Dalton, ed., 233–74. Greenwich, Conn: JAI Press, 1981.

Schuman, H. and S. Presser, *Questions and Answers in Attitude Surveys: Experiments on Question Form, Wording and Context*, New York: Academic Press, 1981.

Sen, A., *Poverty and Famines: An Essay on Entitlement and Deprivation*, Oxford: Clarendon Press, 1981.

Shrestha, R., 'A socio-linguistic appraisal of survey questionnaires'. In *The Use and Misuse of Social Research in Nepal*, (J. G. Campbell, R. Shrestha and L. Stone), pp. 71–92. Kathmandu: His Majesty's Government Press, 1979.

Slater, G., *Some South Indian Villages*, London & New York: Oxford University Press, 1918.

Srinivas, M. N., 'Village studies, participant observation and social science research in India', *Economic and Political Weekly*, Special no., August 1979.

Srinivasan, T. N. and Bardhan, P. K., *Poverty and Income*

282   *Small-Scale Techniques and Large-Scale Objectives*

Distribution in India, Calcutta: Statistical Publishing House, 1974.

Stone, L. and J. G. Campbell, 'The use and misuse of surveys in international development: An experiment from Nepal', *Human Organization*, 43 (1): 27–37, 1984.

Sukhatme, P. V., 'On measurement of poverty', *Economic and Political Weekly* 16 (August 8, 1981):1318–24, 1981.

Zeller, R. A. and E. G. Carmines, *Measurement in the Social Sciences: The Link Between Theory and Data*, New York: Cambridge University Press, 1980.

Author Index

Subject Index

Aggregation, 256, 268, 274
Agro-Economic Research Centres, 7, 245, 251–3
Anthropology
  fiction of local system, 132
  longitudinal studies, 259
  relational perspective, 138, 242, 245
  situational analysis, 169
  structural-functionalism, 169

Bias
  investigator, 240
  response, 53–6, 86, 225, 228, 242
Bonded labourers, 106
Borrowing, 186
Brahman, 107, 110
  tenancy rights, 77, 102
Bride-price, 101

Calorie intake, 41
Capital formation, 181
Caste (jati), 87–120
  as analytic category, 115
  correlated with economic, 95, 117–20
  correlated with land ownership, 93–4
  correlated with occupation, 93
  ethic, 99
  interaction with class, 29
  sex ratios, 101
Cognitive dissonance, 8
Common property resources, 182, 187, 195
Consumption, 35–41, 64–7
  of cereals, 41
  durables, 57, 63–4, 182
  expenditure, 58

social consumption, 47, 207
Contractual arrangements, 25
Cultivation
  area, 147
  household dependence on, 151
Cultural Materialists, 8

Death rate, 49–51
Debt, 114
Decentralization, 129
Differentiation, 162, 164
Disease, 201
Diversification, of rural economy, 163, 166
Dowry, 96. 101
Dynamic processes, 6

Education, 207–17
Employment, 159, 161, 165
Entitlements, 169, 255, 274
Epistemology, 11, 275–8

Feminist anthropology, 85
Fertility, 99, 163
Fieldwork, 127, 130–35

Game theory, 244
Green revolution, 59, 78, 111, 113

Household
  budget data, 35–6
  intra-household allocation, 167
  life cycle, 183
  splits, 86, 180, 59–60
Housing, 41–5, 63, 191
  katcha, 42, 45, 63, 191
  pucca, 42, 45, 63, 190
Hunger, 98, 111
HYV, adoption, 104